LIFE'S INDELIBLE MOMENTS

LIFE'S INDELIBLE MOMENTS

Forks in the road of life...unexpected adventures

DR. NORMAN FERGUSON

XULON PRESS

Xulon Press
2301 Lucien Way #415
Maitland, FL 32751
407.339.4217
www.xulonpress.com

Printed in the United States of America

Paperback ISBN-13: 978-1-6628-0785-5
Ebook ISBN-13: 978-1-6628-0786-2

DEDICATION TRIBUTE

A large part of this book focuses on my love for Jennifer (Jenny), my wonderful wife. Therefore, I am not going to use this opportunity to write more about her virtues. I have a special place in my heart for Lori Lynette, my first child, who should be awarded for the struggles and hardships that she has faced as a single mother, raising Darci, my beautiful granddaughter. Darci just presented me with my first and only great-granddaughter, Harley Sky. Bradley Wayne, the son we adopted when he was a day old, has had some really hard knocks in life, part of them deserved, but he has been such a joy with his many letters and daily phone calls in recent years. Encouraging signs of an inward experience with the Lord in his life at this time gives us great hope for his future. We had the privilege of having our son Nathan Riley in our home on various short stints. He now lives close by in Flint, with his lovely wife, Melinda, and their two great kids: granddaughter, Jordyn, and grandson River, plus Melinda's two talented girls, Seana and Marissa. Nathan is consumed with his own business, called "Lawn Rescue," so we do not get to visit very often. Our daughter, Heather Jill, is so talented! She makes us all look like amateur painters in kindergarten with her artistic, scholastic, and athletic abilities. She is a hardworking single mother who serves as a dental hygienist, plays co-ed soccer, and excels in marathon runs. She is also a certified Cross Fit Trainer, and best of all, she is the mother of our delightful grandson, Austin.

I have really reserved this space for my daughter, Summer Joy! Despite a prediction by the medical experts, at age 4, that she only had a 25% chance to reach the age of twelve because of the genetic disease, cystic fibrosis, she has kept an optimistic spirit. She never complains. She excels at everything that she attempts to accomplish. Her achievements are monumental! A few of those are recorded in this book. Against all odds, she became a doctor of optometry and works full-time to support her family. She went through in vitro fertilization, a grueling process to have a baby without cystic fibrosis. That baby, my granddaughter, Bridget, only weighed one pound and four ounces at birth and is now a precocious eight-year-old. Summer has had an open port in her chest forever, which provides immediate access to her medications and any IVs that may be required. She may not have invented networking, but she has taken it to a whole new level, which includes thousands of admiring friends and co-workers. Her breathing capacity with the scarring of her lungs due to CF had dropped into the forty-percent range. The doctors in California were able to help secure a new drug that enables much of the mucous to come loose from her lungs. This allows her to cough up tons of phlegm and rid her body of it. She has now felt well enough to ride her bike and lead her husband, Adam, and daughter, Bridget, on exhausting hikes. This has increased her lung capacity back to the low sixtieth, seventieth, and even eightieth percentile a couple of times recently. During this COVID-19 virus epidemic, she lost her job! She is interviewing now, and with a positive outlook on life, remains happy and steadfast. With the end of summer and beginning of school, it became necessary for the family to move back to Boston, Massachusetts.

I noticed as she grew up, she never shied away from people or leadership roles. As our children's choir director, Jenny would assign her the long lead role in the Christmas musicals. Her first grade teacher required pages of memory work every week. Summer Joy won the "Miss Congeniality" award in the Miss Tyler Teen Beauty Pageant. She campaigned for class officer president in middle school. She decided that she wanted to be a cheerleader in high school and got herself elected! She swam for four years on the Robert E. Lee High School swim team, which required practicing every morning from 5:30 a.m. to 8:00 a.m. She then went to school and took the hardest courses available. Her senior year, she was captain of the swim team! She worked for Dr. Gene Bennett and Dr. Ron Smith before and in between her college years. With nearly an all "A" average and lots of scholarships, she was accepted into Baylor University and Chi Omega. That was not her ultimate goal. She went on to optometry school in California to become a doctor. I am sure that I could make a fascinating book on the life of Summer Joy Ferguson McGeever. Suffice it to say that this book was written with her constant urging and bugging me to write down all of the stories that she had heard from me, and about my life. I have written this book and dedicate it to her...my little HERO!

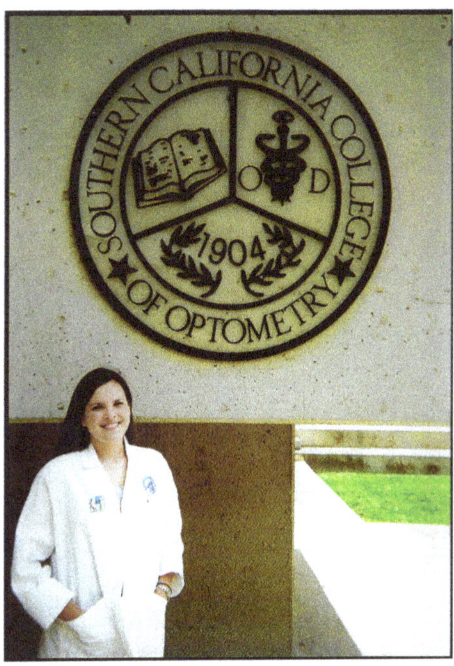

Dr. Summer Joy (Ferguson) McGeever

TABLE OF CONTENTS

Life's Indelible Moments

LIST OF ILLUSTRATIONS AND PICTURES

(FAMILY PICTURES)

(STORIES OF OUR TRIPS TO AFRICA, LONDON, GREECE, YELLOWSTONE, ALASKA)

ACKNOWLEDGEMENTS

Two roads diverged in a yellow wood,
And sorry I could not travel both
And be one traveler, long I stood
And looked down one as far as I could
To where it bent in the undergrowth;

Then took the other, as just as fair,
And having perhaps the better claim,
Because it was grassy and wanted wear;
Though as for that the passing there
Had worn them really about the same,

And both that morning equally lay
In leaves no step had trodden black.
Oh, I kept the first for another day!
Yet knowing how way leads on to way,
I doubted if I should ever come back.

I shall be telling this with a sigh
Somewhere ages and ages hence:
Two roads diverged in a wood, and I—
I took the one less traveled by,
And that has made all the difference.

"The Road Not Taken"

Prologue

LIFE'S INDELIBLE MOMENTS

By Norman Ferguson

Robert Frost's words, *The Road Not Taken*, came to mind as I contemplated a review of my life. I sat for quite some time cogitating on why I have taken some roads and unconsciously veered to another. There have been moments when a fork in the road often caught me with little forethought as to which one would be the best to take. WARNING: The forks in the road of life offer vast experiences and consequences. Some are surprisingly good, and others pose disaster. Both roads have potholes and pitfalls. Smooth sailing is, oftentimes a deceitful mirage. The temptation to take the scenic, smooth sailing, and exciting one is usually the most enticing. It is only as you look back down the road you have traveled that you become aware of the significance of a thoughtless decision to take a certain fork in the road. You say to yourself, "Wow! That instant and thoughtless decision changed my life!" As a twelve-year-old in a church service during the invitation, I faced one of those forks in the road: heaven or hell, Jesus or the devil, abundant life or self-inflicted pain. I walked the aisle that night and accepted Jesus into my heart and my life. To quote Robert Frost: "I took the one less traveled...and that has made all the difference."

Jesus spoke of two roads in life: the broad road, where most people travel, but it ends in destruction...the narrow and difficult road (the Christian life) that leads to life everlasting.

Have you ever been in the far left lane of a six-lane highway, traveling at seventy miles per hour, only to have your wife or your GPS tell you, "Exit...now?" This usually requires you to either risk suicide by darting across multiple lanes of traffic, or travel ten miles out of your way to get back to this particular exit. Many of the forks in the road of life come up in the same manner. Some come when the mix master of roads offers several choices, but not enough information or time to make the wise or best decision. This, too, happens in life. Many of these decisions take us years to realize and correct (like bad habits, alcohol, drugs, etc.). Thankfully, God has promised to help us correct these mistakes and get us back on the right road (Romans 8:28).

I experienced many forks in the road, just like you. I have been bruised and battered as a consequence of choosing the wrong road at times. Thankfully, on many occasions, God endowed me with enough wisdom to choose the best road, or one of His angels pushed me in the right direction. I confess that many times I was not even aware that I was choosing the wise and good road!

In one of Fredrick Speakman's book of monologues, he gives a dialogue of Luke, years after Jesus' birth, interviewing the innkeeper of Bethlehem, entitled, "Yes, I Remember Bethlehem!" Many times, I have dressed up as the innkeeper and given this dramatic monologue to congregations. About thirty years after the birth of Jesus, disciple physician Luke pays the innkeeper a visit. He queries the innkeeper about his memory of that night that happened long ago in Bethlehem. With some remorse in his voice, the innkeeper responds with, "Oh yes, I remember that night! I have never forgotten! But how are you ever going to know life's great moments when they come, Luke? They come walking up, looking like any other other. I think that has gnawed me the rawest–that I would have sent the couple away...Oh, kindly enough, but thankfully, my wife Leah saved me...she suggested the stable out back! I laughed...that was my contribution, I laughed!" The climax comes when Luke reveals that the baby he relegated to be born in a manger was a mind-blowing revelation. He shouts for his wife: "Leah! Leah! THAT BABY WAS THE SON OF GOD!"

Norm dressed as the innkeeper

During my years as pastor of the Northside Baptist Church in Corsicana, TX, my fellow minister of the First Baptist Church, Rev. Robert Woody and I developed a close relationship. We spent many afternoons on the golf course together. He was married to the daughter of Dr. Kyle Yates, a professor at Baylor University. He recalled the story of his father-in-law driving on a country road when, all of a sudden, a reckless and speeding car passed him. A short distance ahead, he came upon the same car, crashed into a tree in the middle of a fork in the road. Dr. Yates jumped out to try and rescue the man from the wreckage. He found him a bit shook up, but conscious. He asked him the obvious question, "Did you lose control of the car?" The man replied, "No, I just couldn't decide which road to take!"

So, how was I to know at the age of 43 that a visit to my dentist's office would cause me to face a fork in the road, the choice of which would change the direction of my life? This book is about that fork in the road.

WHICH
WAY?

LIFE'S INDELIBLE MOMENTS

Norman Wayne Ferguson

PART I: 1933 TO 1976

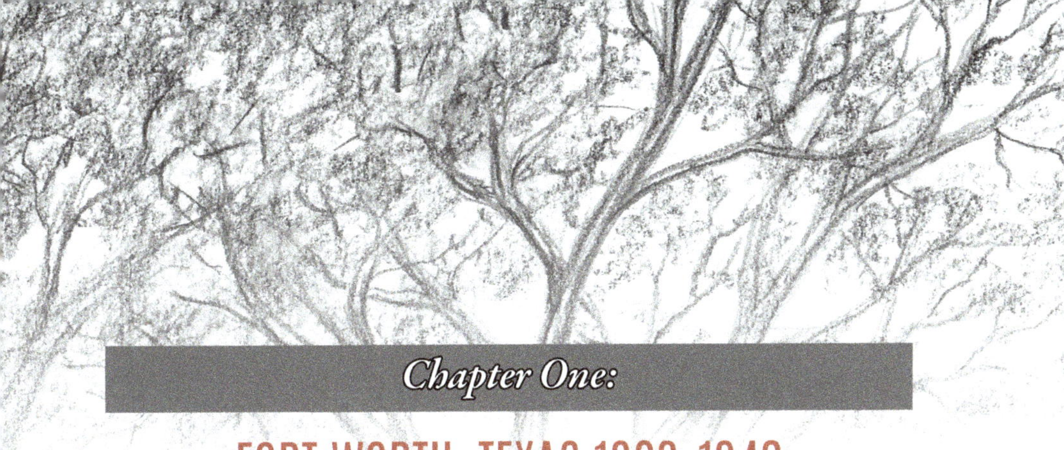

Chapter One:

FORT WORTH, TEXAS 1933-1940

Mom's parents, Mr. Van and Ms. Smith, and Mom's 80th birthday

Granny Smith, Van, Burns, London with family: Mom, brothers, Hubert, and Doyle, and sister Pauline

Allie and sister Irene with stepfather, Nathaniel Neville, and biological mother, Jennie McWherter

Granny Smith, Van, Burns, and last husband, Clark London

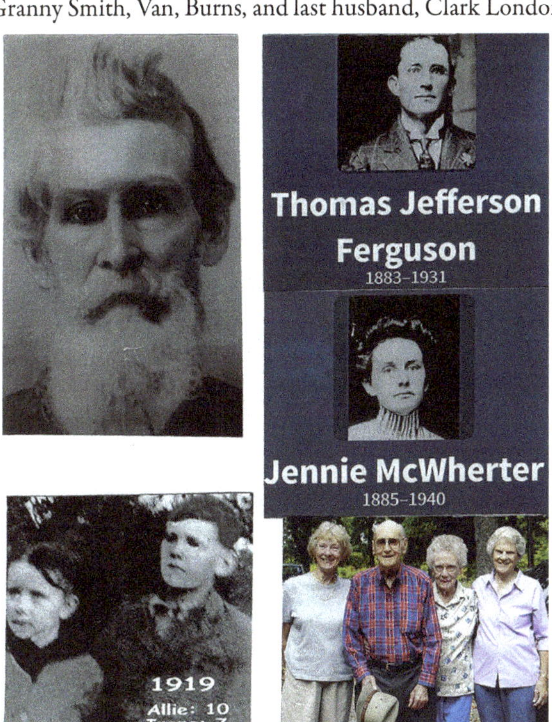

Allie's grandfather, Jim Ferguson and father, Thomas Jefferson Ferguson with maternal mother, Jennie McWherter with Allie's 3 sisters

Not that I can remember, but my birth certificate says that I came into this world on May 12, 1933 at the Harris Hospital in Fort Worth, Texas. My parents were Allie Fennel Record Ferguson, born in Tennessee, and Jessie Zeona Van Ferguson, born in the back of a covered wagon in West Texas. The attending doctor or midwife did not think she was alive and tossed her aside. A neighboring lady picked baby Mom up and detected pulse and breath. Thank the Lord, for I would not be here! Grandparents on both sides of the family had difficult lives working as sharecroppers in Arkansas, Oklahoma, and Texas.

My earliest memory was one of sitting in our driveway on Devit Street in Fort Worth, putting gravel in my mouth and then spitting it out. The taste of the gravel was so satisfying! I remember walking down the alley behind our house to one of the family friend's house and being instructed before going in: "Sit there and be still...you do not have to talk!" We were only a half-block from a railroad track, and hobos often got off of the freight trains and stopped at our house, asking for food. Mom usually obliged with a little yard work in exchange for a baloney or mayonnaise and tomato sandwich. The other memory at this location was chasing a ball into the hedges and getting stung by many wasps! The preferred medications for wasp and bee stings varied from Dad's Cotton Boll Twist tobacco or Granny Burn's Garret's Snuff, or Mom's *bluing*. Bluing was a blue liquid that she mixed in the rinse water tub when washing clothes with an old ringer washing machine that required two tubs.

We moved to Rosen Street on the north side of Fort Worth in 1938 when I was five years old. We shared the house with widowed Grandmother Ferguson, Uncle Thomas, Aunt Viola, and Aunt Sylvia. They occupied the other side of the duplex home. I remember Aunt Sylvia babysitting with me. She would make a pallet on the floor every afternoon by a breezy window and we would take a nap. I woke up one afternoon screaming...a scorpion had stung me on the neck while I was sleeping. Uncle Thomas would let me ride around on his shoulders. He joined the Army. I really missed him during World War II. Aunt Viola married Robert Stone, a mechanic for the Fort Worth Police Department's patrol cars. Grandmother Kennedy had an old Victrola that played 78-speed plastic records (the pictures of people receiving gold or platinum status still feature this type of record). To produce sound, it required inserting a steel needle into the head of the player so the needle would stay in the grooves of the record. There was a handle on the side of the machine that required winding often, or the songs would slow down in speed. Our favorite record was *Barney Google with the Goo-Goo-Googly Eyes*.

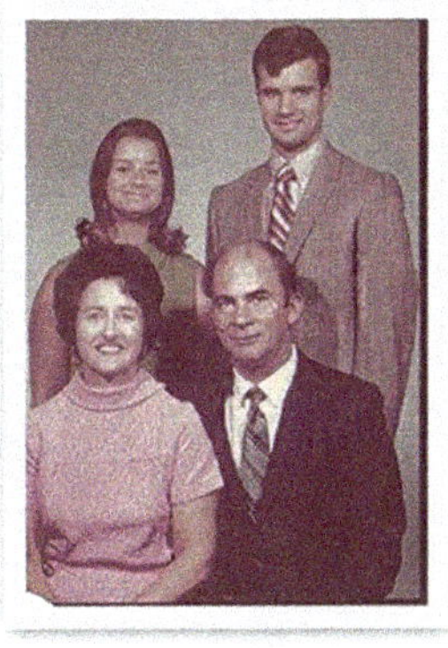

Uncle Thomas Ferguson, World War II, Air Force

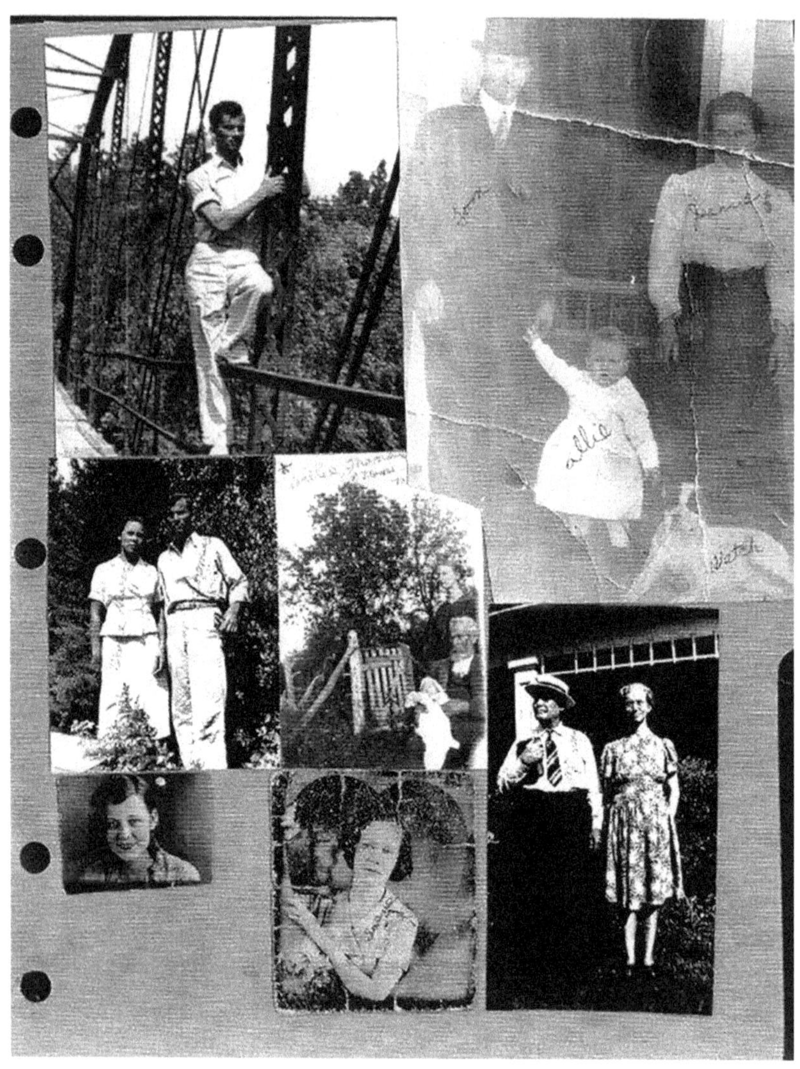

Jim Ferguson, Allie and Thomas's grandfather

Fourth of July celebration, 1956

Pictures of Norm and Glenna...preschool

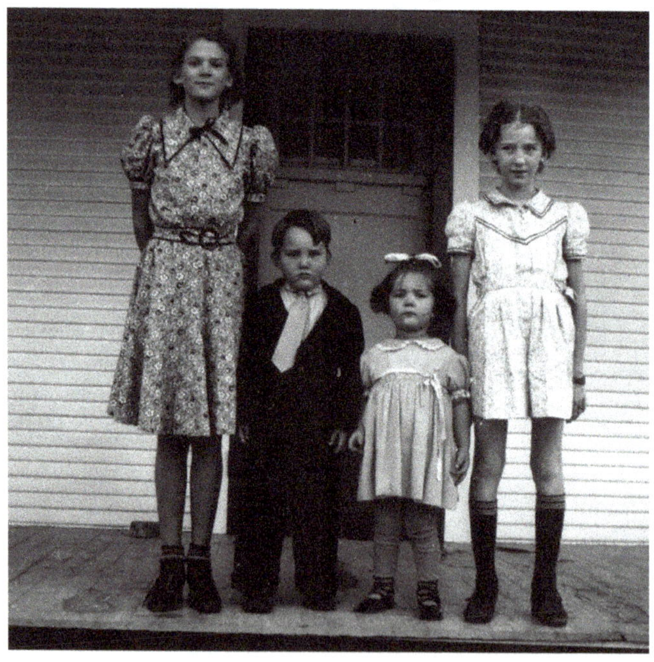

Aunt Viola, Norman, and Glenna, Aunt Sylvia

Grandmother Ferguson (Kennedy) with family

On our side of the duplex, my sister Glenna and I played and experienced the Depression before World War II. I remember my Dad would bring day-old bread home in a large gunny sack. Mrs. Beard's bread and Tastee bread companies would take the bread off of the grocery store shelves when it began to mold. It was our normal routine to inspect the bread and scrape the mold off before we toasted it or made a sandwich. Dad always took his lunch to Justin Boot Factory, where he was a shipping clerk for about 25 years. His starting salary was $25.00 a week. He and another young preacher, Bill McPhail, felt so compelled to preach that they rented a lot, got a few folding chairs, and preached to a half-dozen people. They appealed to the Church of Christ neighbor next door to allow them to plug into his electricity outlets in order to have lights. Most of the time, there were only two or three couples in attendance. Then came an opportunity for Dad to preach at a country church that had just about died near Weatherford. Following that, he petitioned Justin Boot Company for permission to have off one of the summer months for an extended vacation. This was for the purpose of spending the summer at the rural church in Dot, near Waco, Texas. Receiving a call from a church in Dallas, the family drove back and forth each weekend for about seven months. This ended when a carload of drunk Black people ran into the passenger side of our Model A Ford. Before the wreck, Glenna was in the bassinet in the backseat of the car, and I was lying on the seat. After the wreck, I was in the bassinet and Glenna was on the floor. Mom got the worst end of the deal with over 70 stitches taken in her broken knee. She was in the hospital for six weeks and had trouble with that knee all of her 80 years.

Beginning around 1938, Dad began to preach for a circuit of churches, which included Gartman's View in Comanche, Dot, a community near Waco, and Woodlawn. After this, he became pastor of a mission church on Commerce Street in Downtown Dallas. This eventually became The First Freewill Baptist Church of Dallas, where Rev. H.Z. Cox has spent his life as the pastor. Our home church was the Trinity Free Will Baptist Church on Azle Avenue in Fort Worth. Rev. M.L. Sutton was the pastor. Brother Hodges was an old retired Free Will Baptist preacher. I remember his 90th year birthday celebration! They showered him with 90 real silver dollars. My mother was impressed when I started saying "Amen" during my dad's sermons. She thought I was listening and agreeing with Dad's statements. I finally confided in her, "When I say 'Amen,' Daddy is supposed to quit...like in dominoes!" Most of the Free Will Baptist churches in the Texas area where I was growing up were located in the country. Dad preached at many of these. On one occasion, I remember after the long sermon, the ladies were busy putting their covered dishes of food on the make-shift tables made from boards laid on sawhorses. The small pin oak trees provided a little shade, and they tried to set the makeshift tables up under these. There was so much food on those boards that they seemed to put a strain and make the legs of the tables bow-legged! There were tons of fried chicken, potato salads, fruit salads, and fresh vegetables out of their gardens, plus every imaginable kind of desserts: banana pudding, cake, pies, cookies, etc. This was where I preferred to start or go back to for seconds! One particular mother of a preschool boy was busy getting her food on the table and did not notice that her boy had climbed into the family pickup. It was situated on a small hill. The kid started playing with the long stick shift, which protruded from the floorboard of the truck. Suddenly, the truck started rolling downhill. It ran through a fence and nosed down into a steep ravine with a creek full of water. There was screaming as people were running everywhere amid the panic! Thankfully, the boy was rescued and rushed to a local hospital. All kinds of chains, tractors, and trucks were attached to the pickup to try and pull it out of the creek. This effort consumed the rest of the day! During all of the excitement experienced while watching this, I do not remember anyone getting back to that beautiful "dinner on the grounds!"

Members of Gartman's View Freewill Baptist Church
in the West Fork Association, Comanche, Texas

While I am remembering, I think I should insert a couple of memories of the Gartman's View Church near Comanche, Texas. Dad drove down once a month to preach on Saturday nights and both services on Sundays. He almost always went for a two or three-week revival held outside the main church building in a brush arbor. August was chosen because the peanut farmers had wrapped up their thrashing of the peanut harvest by then, and it was a quiet time for them. Most of the men would bring the family and park their pickups around the arbor. The men would sit on the hood or in the back of their pickups. The women and children would come inside the arbor. Often, the kids would run up and down the dirt aisle and stir up a cloud of dust! I can hear Dad saying, "Mothers, will you please get your kids and keep them still...I cannot preach while choking on all this dust!" I remember observing my dad pausing in the middle of one of his sermons, "Excuse me, folks," and behind the pulpit, he dropped his pants and killed a big red ant that had invaded and stung him. He took a lot of teasing about this event. Once in a while, one of the men sitting on the hood of a pickup would get under conviction and make their way down the dusty aisle to profess Jesus as their Lord and Savior while the choir sang and the invitation was extended. We always spent Saturday nights with one of the church members. One family lived right on a creek and had a water well pump right on their screened-in back porch. Once, Dad was asked, "Do you want to wash your hands before we eat?" Dad answered, "Yes, I better! I've been shaking hands with all of those Baptists!" I remember seeing fish in that little creek. I would pester one lady that I needed a fishhook and some bait so I could catch a fish. The lady of the house found a large diaper safety pin and put it on a piece of string. They could not believe it when I came in with a flopping perch!

These country folk in Comanche lived down a long dirt road, and they would often let several of us kids ride in the back of the pickup. We would sit on the tailgate and drag our feet in the sand. If we could get the driver to go slow enough, we would jump off and run along in one of the ruts, then jump back on.

There were several barns and buildings on the farm, and I really enjoyed crawling under each to see what treasure I could find. I found nests of chicken eggs...some with fifteen or twenty eggs. Of course, most of them were rotten. I crawled under and through a lot of spider webs. I scared a few snakes out from under those barns but never did get bitten or have a wasp sting. I really have a good guardian angel!

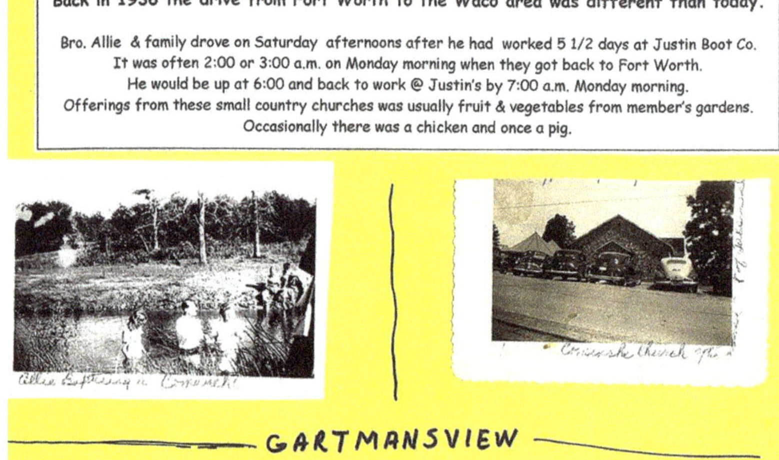

Back in 1936 the drive from Fort Worth to the Waco area was different than today.
Bro. Allie & family drove on Saturday afternoons after he had worked 5 1/2 days at Justin Boot Co.
It was often 2:00 or 3:00 a.m. on Monday morning when they got back to Fort Worth.
He would be up at 6:00 and back to work @ Justin's by 7:00 a.m. Monday morning.
Offerings from these small country churches was usually fruit & vegetables from member's gardens.
Occasionally there was a chicken and once a pig.
GARTMANSVIEW

Gartman's View Church and baptisms

A big custom back then was to "pound the preacher." Getting in the car to head back to Fort Worth, the trunk of our '38 Plymouth would normally have a toe sack with a couple of chickens or a squealing pig to take home, fatten up, and make ham & bacon in the future. The back-seat and floorboard was always full of fresh ears of corn, black-eyed peas, butter beans, green beans, tomatoes, okra, onions, and sometimes eggs and butter. On one of these trips home, I remember Mom being in great pain with appendicitis. I was so afraid that she was going to die before we could get her home and to the hospital the next day.

Pleasant Mound Church near Waco, TX

I do not remember my mom or dad doing a lot of sports, but while we were living in the duplex, I do remember going to the North Side High School tennis court just down the street to play tennis. My job was to retrieve the tennis balls. Dad did have two other sports that he enjoyed: playing softball for the Justin Boot softball team, and pitching horseshoes for the same. One of the Justin Boot owners lived only a couple of blocks back from Rosen Street, and Dad would take me with him quite often to the man's backyard where horseshoe pits rang with the clang of horseshoes under their outdoor lights. We preschoolers enjoyed playing together while they pitched horseshoes. One evening, the neighbor next to us on Rosen Street brought a HUGE catfish home and hung it up from a limb in a tree in his backyard. The catfish was bigger than I was!!! About that same time, Glenna was sitting on the big steps that went all the way across both duplexes and connected us to grandmother's side. Mother was working in the yard. Glenna could see inside the kitchen door and very calmly said, "Mother, the house is on fire." Mom ran up the steps where she found a dishtowel had caught fire and the fire was climbing up the wall and cabinets. A pitcher of ice water was setting on the cabinet, but in her haste, she dumped the ice water out, then turned on the faucet to fill pitcher again. She finally threw the water on the fire. Someone had called the fire department and they arrived to make sure Mom had extinguished it completely.

While living on Rosen Street, I turned six years old and Mother took me to my first day of school at Sam Rosen Grade School. I felt so big! I was wearing my cowboy boots! By noon, I was not feeling so big, and the teacher said, "Those of you going home for lunch may leave now." That was my cue! I split and got lost trying to find my way home from the school. By the grace of God, a friendly policeman found me crying and took me back to school.

One event really stuck in my mind. Uncle Thomas was home on furlough, and one of his friends had really gotten his car stuck in the mud during heavy rainfall. About five or six guys got behind the old car and started pushing. Uncle Thomas slipped and fell face down against the bumper. It broke all of his front teeth. From that time on, my Uncle Thomas, who was a very jovial and happy person, displayed a mouthful of gold-crowned teeth as he smiled!

Chapter Two:

LAKE WORTH, TEXAS AND INDIAN OAKS COMMUNITY 1940-1945

Growing up during the Great Depression, I never really was aware that we were poor. We did not seem any different from anyone else. Everyone was about like we were, but there always seemed to be a lot of laughing! Mom & Dad were really strict and presented life as a matter of fact. We were not given a lot of choices and were never allowed to talk back to adults! It was, "Shut up whining! Eat what's on your plate or go to bed hungry!" "Eat all of those vegetables...a lot of starving kids in Africa would love to have that much to eat!" Although I did not say it aloud, I wanted to retort with, "They can have mine." My only memory of going to a big grocery store was when Dad took me to Leonard Brothers Grocery in Downtown Fort Worth. As we approached the entrance, the doors opened and Dad threw his arm across my chest. We jumped back as he said, "Hold on a minute, son." The people behind us came up and the doors opened again automatically. They walked right on in. Dad was so shocked at the new fangled contraption that would make doors open automatically when walking up to them!

The Depression blended into World War II, which produced a lot more hardships.

Everything was scarce and rationed. Each family was given a book of coupons. If you had both money and a coupon, you could get a pound of sugar, a bag of flour, shoes, gas, tires, etc. No new cars were available during the war. Gas for the car was rationed, so we saved our mileage for Dad's weekend trips to his preaching appointments. In special cases, you could get new tires once a year. I remember tires were really hard to come by. It was common to see cars upon blocks because tires were not available. A car on the side of the road with a flat tire or a blowout was a common sight. One of our tires lasted the entire duration of WW II. Service stations had an attendant who would come to the car, fill the gas tank, wash the windows, check the oil, and check the air pressure in your tires. A person never had to get out of the car. All that service was free. These stations specialized in patching tires and selling good used tires.

As kids, we collected and compared the big balls of aluminum that we saved from gum wrappers and cigarette packages. This was our way of contributing to the war effort to build airplanes, tanks, guns, and ammunition. Mom insisted on shopping at stores that gave Green Stamps when she wanted to buy something. With a cash payment, the store would gift you with a green stamp for each ten cents spent. We licked these stamps and placed them in a book until the book was full of stamps. Upon the accumulation of several books of Green Stamps, it was possible to trade these in for all kinds of prizes. I also remember the gold star symbols placed in the window of a home where the family had lost a son, father, or husband in the war.

Our folks bought a four-room house and a "path" (to the outhouse) in the Indian Oaks division on the north side of Lake Worth, now part of Fort Worth. In addition, there was a dirt floor garage and a smokehouse. The purchase included enough acreage to have a cow, pigs, chickens, and over an acre of garden. We toiled day and night to grow our own vegetables. Mom canned hundreds of Mason jars filled with vegetables each summer. On one of those summers, she canned more than 1500 jars of vegetables and fruits. This was "on the halves" with John Justin, Dad's boss. We took the seed from watermelons, cantaloupes, tomatoes, okra, etc. and dried them on the tin roof of the chicken shed so we would have planting seed for the next season. We saved the old shriveled up Irish potatoes so we could cut them up with an "eye" of the potato in each "seed cuttin'." We used these for planting the new potato crop. When the potatoes would come up (as well as the tomatoes), they would be attacked by big green-horned worms and beetles eating the foliage. My job was to take a can of kerosene or gas and pick the critters off. I would drown them in the can of gas. I was also given the task of planting the black-eyed peas, "Poke holes in the freshly plowed dirt and plant two peas in each hole about a foot apart." After one row, and four more rows to go, I wanted to finish and go play, so I dug a hole at the end of the row and poured all of the peas into the hole. A week or ten days later, a wad of sprouted peas came up out of that hole. I found out what Numbers 32:23 says is true: "And be sure your sins will find you out." This revealed to me that the punishment for a sin is painful!

Mr. Swift lived next door with our acre of crops in between. He came to the house one day and wanted to borrow our lawnmower. Dad went to the garage and rolled out the old rotary push mower. "No, no. I want your automatic mower back there," pointing to our cow. So, Daisy mowed his grass and enjoyed a fine meal. Mr. Swift was the one to whom Dad asked, "How did your potatoes turn out?" and he answered, "They didn't turn out, I had to dig 'em out!" When the explosion of a fertilizer plant blew up way down in Texas City near Galveston, both he and Dad ran out into the backyard. Dad yelled to him, "Is that you stomping around, making the ground shake?" He was a rather portly man. His stomach was so large that he had to move the seat so far back he could barely reach the steering wheel. His head was visible from the side window in the backseat. Later, he moved to one street back of that property, and owned our source of public water–a large water tower. We often traded milk, butter, & eggs to pay our water bill. Moving in to occupy his old house came the Faircloth family. They had adopted two kids from one of their relatives, Terry Don and Delores Waters. These two became our good buddies and playmates. Terry Don and I were trying to ride our calf one day, and my sister, Glenna, came out sporting a brand new dress that Mom had just made for her. We helped Glenna onto the calf and told her to hang on. We hit the calf on the rump. It ran up against the fence and scratched her leg, plus it tore her new dress to shreds. That episode did not end well for me either!

Other neighborhood friends were Dorothy and Nadine Palmer. These two lived catty-corner from us on the other side of the road across from the little neighborhood grocery store. The iceman delivered ice every other day and knew how much ice we wanted by the rotating sign in the window: 12.5 lbs., 25 lbs., 50 lbs., or 100 lbs. The little storeowner was our source of income. We had a route that we ran door to door every few days to collect soda pop bottles. Once we had a sizeable number, we would make a trip to the little grocery store and market them for two cents each. My first gold mine!

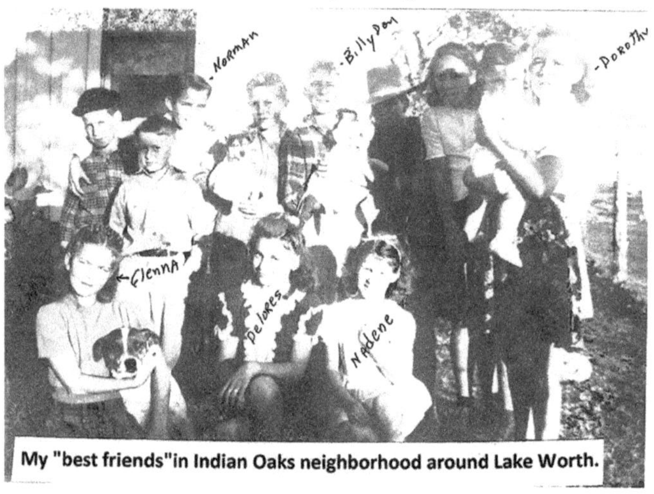

My friends, Indian Oaks: Delores and Billy Don Faircloth, Dorothy, and Nadine Palmer, Glenna (sis holding our dog, Skipper) and me

The six of us would ride our bikes, play Monopoly, Pollyanna, Dominoes, and yes, at times our parents conscripted us to help hoe, cultivate, pick, and shell each crop of vegetables. Black-eyed peas were picked every other day, as was okra, tomatoes, squash, cucumbers, polk (for salads), etc. At times, there would be 6 or more #3 washtubs and/or bushel baskets full of black-eyed peas waiting for us to shell and prepare for canning in the pressure cooker. The three families of kids: Norman, Glenna, Terry Don, Delores, Dorothy, and Nadine were then challenged to see who could shell the most peas! The big incentive was a big freezer of homemade ice cream if we finished a certain amount of the shelling. Dad and the other dads would busy themselves with the ice cream preparation by crushing the ice, pouring in the salt, and turning the freezer. We just shelled peas! One night, one of the other families brought a freezer of ice cream too. This gave us two flavors: vanilla and peach. We could not eat all of the ice cream, and since we had no way of keeping it (this was before refrigerators & freezers), we fed it to Skipper, our dog. He greedily gulped it down. The poor dog immediately began howling and crawling on the grass. His insides were frozen and cramping. Dad and the men heated towels and wrapped them around the poor dog to try to comfort him in his misery.

One of the advantages of growing up during this time was the fact that during the summer, school was closed from Memorial Day until after Labor Day. As soon as we finished working in the garden, feeding the chickens, slopping the hogs, and milking the cow, we were allowed a lot of freedom to ride our bikes all over the Indian Oaks and Lake Worth area. With no televisions, computers, cellphones, or video games, we opted for the great outdoors. During these summers, I developed several friends around the lake where I learned to swim and fish. The cardinal rule of instruction: "Be home before dark." This kind of freedom did not mean we were being neglected. It was a special kind of freedom we earned by being good and doing our chores. Dad, being a preacher, firmly believed in the biblical admonition of the Scriptures: "Spare the rod and spoil the child!" Suffice it to say I was not spoiled! But neither can I say that I did not deserve every spanking and whipping that I received. I was probably deserving of all of those and more!

Taking a bath was an every Saturday night ritual in a big # 3 galvanized washtub. Mom would set the tub next to the old woodstove, heat water on the kerosene stove in the kitchen, and also place more water to heat on the wood stove until she had about 6 inches of water in the tub. The water was not poured out or changed between family members' baths. Sometimes more hot water was added between baths and all four finished bathing in the same water. This was how we looked prim and proper for Sunday church. On the other days of the week, we sponge washed our bodies with a washcloth.

Mom churned our butter and sold some to the neighbors to have a few coins to buy incidental requests that my sister and I would request, such as one cent Kool-Aid packs or penny candy. Glenna and I were the cheap labor that Mom used to churn the butter. We had to bounce the paddle up and down with a long pole extending into the churn (a churn is a large crockpot with a hole in the lid for the pole to fit through). We continued the up and down bashing of the cream in the churn until it turned to butter and buttermilk. Once we milked the cows, the big crock of whole milk was placed into the "ice box" (later we had a real electric refrigerator). The cream would rise to the top of the crock of milk, and Mom would skim the cream off into another bowl. When she had a gallon or more, she would pour it into the churn. At this point, she would turn the chore over to me and/or Glenna. That is when the argument as to whose turn it was to do the churning would begin. What a great new day it was when Dad came home with a new fangled contraption called a "Daisy Churn." This only required us to turn the handle (for an eternity) and the butter would appear. Mom then had to work the buttermilk out of the butter and place the butter in a wooden mold to form a pound of butter. The mold had an extra wood piece attached to a handle so you could push the pound of butter out onto wax paper and place it in the ice box to get cold & firm. We drank some of the buttermilk, but most of it was allowed to set out and sour. This produced "clabber," a pre-curser to yogurt. The clabber was given to the chickens, who devoured it like it was a "June bug" desert (something chickens would fight over)!

Living during the Depression and World War II, at least in my kid's view, was the normal way of life. "This is how life is supposed to be... no questions asked." The most difficult part was trying to get through a night with my asthma attacks. With no air conditioners, the Texas heat was suffocating and made it hard for me to catch a breath. Many nights, I had to sit in a sofa chair and try to sleep because I could not breathe while lying down. Gasping for the next breath prevented me from participating in any physical activity until the asthma attack was over. This limited my sports activity until I became a teen. My parents took me to a chiropractor when I was about eleven or twelve. He could relax me and almost immediately chase the asthma away. He had a philosophy that he shared with me. "I think you need a large chest capacity to combat an asthma attack. Go home and build yourself a 'chining bar' and do pull-ups every day." Within a year, I began to look like Mighty Mouse.

During the growing-up years, Granny Burns, Mom's mother, introduced me to several hobbies and domestic past times. She showed me how to take an old light bulb and insert it into a sock, thread the needle, and mend the holes in my socks. Later, I graduated to the fine art of embroidery. I watched with amazement as she knitted and crocheted and "tatted." I never did attempt any of those! The most fun was quilting. The quilting frame was hung from the ceiling in the back bedroom. The quilting frame was then lowered from the ceiling and would occupy most of the room with only enough space around it for a dozen workers to quilt on it at the same time. Prior to the actual quilting, a lot of preparation had to be completed. This entailed weeks and months of cutting out quilting pieces made from all colors and designs of cloth. A pattern or design for a block had to be selected, and the pieces had to be sewn together (by hand or later by sewing machine). These blocks made up the quilt cover that would cover the entire bed with some draping over. A lining material was attached to the quilting frame first. Cotton was rolled out to make a soft layer between the lining and the quilting top. The quilting top was comprised of the blocks sewn together and was added on top of the cotton layer. Now the quilting process could begin. Each person would choose a block and proceed to sew around each piece of cloth that had been stitched together. As the quilting progressed, we would roll the wooden frame toward the center, reducing its size. I finished my personal quilt when I was in the fifth grade.

As World War II raged on, there were so many activities that reminded even kids like me, who were ages 8 through 13 during that time, that a war was going on somewhere. We were taught to respect our country, our flag, and our soldiers. As a kid, I read a lot of comic books. In one of those, I saw an ad of an Air Force uniform that could be ordered by mail. Somehow, I persuaded Mom to order one for me. I rushed home from school every day for a month to see if the mailman had delivered my suit. It took forever! I was so proud of it when it came. I had my picture made fully dressed, thinking I would someday become an airplane pilot!

Norm's proud moment to wear his Air Force uniform!

I bought detailed plans to build model airplanes made of balsam wood. I spent days in the construction of these model airplanes. During the war, our news came by radio every day featuring Walter Cronkite, Gabriel Heater, or Paul Harvey. On Friday nights, the community of Indian Oaks sponsored an outdoor movie on a vacant lot. This was just up the road a quarter of a mile from where we lived. The feature was a 16-millimeter newsreel as families sat on quilts or the grass to view all of the gruesome results of war. We viewed airplane "dog fights" of our USA planes versus the Japanese and German planes. We saw tanks and close-up pictures made in the trenches, and foxholes showing our soldiers fighting. Some were encouraging, and some were depressing. There was usually at least one Road Runner cartoon, or a Bugs Bunny, or maybe an Elmer Fudd cartoon. This, plus the daily radio and week old newspapers, gave us the only avenues of keeping abreast of the fights against our aggressors. Some were graphic movies of real Spitfire fighter "dog fights," B-19, B-24, & B-29 bombers targeting various fronts of the war. These planes were assembled just across the lake from our house at the Chance Voigt Factory and Army air base. The runway had been extended out into Lake Worth to allow the necessary distance needed for the bombers to take off and land. They came over our house every three minutes! The planes flew so low I could see the rivets in the wings, and sometimes the gunner soldier sitting in the rear gun and nose turrets would wave to us. The trees in our backyard swayed from the breeze they created. I remember vivid pictures on some of the newsreels depicting our soldiers in trenches and foxholes. Bombs and shells were exploding all around them. Bodies went flying through the air. I especially remember pictures of the pontoon boats used in the Normandy invasion, where thousands of soldiers landed. Our boys jumped into the water, running ashore. They were being gunned down by the thousands as they fought to stop the aggression and defeat Hitler and the Germans, as well as the Japanese.

General Eisenhower, General Patton, General MacArthur, and the English General "Monte" Montgomery were prominent in the news, as was the German Chancellor Adolf Hitler, the dictator of Italy, Benito Mussolini, and the Emperor of Japan Hirohito. Our own leader, President Roosevelt, as well as president of our English ally, Winston Churchill, always gave a close-up interview with an urgent need to buy war bonds. Those who did not fight found jobs as factory workers, making airplanes, tanks, guns and artillery. President Roosevelt died a few months before the end of the war. This was a great shock to the nation.

Harry Truman, the vice president became president. He was a no-nonsense leader, but many did not agree with his firing of General Douglas MacArthur. Reviewing history, in my humble opinion, one of several mistakes was made when General Patton was prevented from going in and liberating Berlin, Germany. He got to Berlin first and had the opportunity. His troops broke through the German lines, but he was told to stand down until the Russian army could catch up with Patton on their side of Berlin. Their argument was that it would allow everyone to put the squeeze on taking Berlin from all sides. But the result was the division of Berlin into sections. Russia's section imprisoned the German people in their section by the construction of the Berlin Wall. This separated East from West Berlin and enslaved so many German people to a brutal communist dictatorship.

Another event that our family engaged in was a home Bible study one night a week. About four or five families would meet at a house for a Bible study. We were given a list of the daily Bible readings accompanied with a set of questions to answer and bring back the next week.

This was one of my first experiences of really enjoying searching and reading the Bible. Sometimes my parents read these passages aloud. I listened and read carefully myself to see if I could answer the questions correctly. The winners usually received some award like a Bible marker. I remember the joy I experienced by winning a ribbon marker.

The Lake Worth school sat just off of the Jacksboro Highway on the main road of Indian Oaks. I attended grades second through seventh, but do not remember much time spent learning inside the brick school building. I do remember the one-room unattached building that we met in because the school was overcrowded and needed more space. I remember the poor girl who got lice in her hair and had to shave her head. She always wore a toboggan. Recess activity of playing softball on the makeshift diamond was the best part of the day. This necessitated being the fastest person to jump when the recess bell rang and race to the playground to claim a position of pitcher's mound, catcher, or one of the bases. The slow ones were relegated to play anywhere in the field. There were two possible options to get to become batter: rotate from field to third, then to second, to first, to pitcher, to catcher, and then to batter. The quickest way to get to bat was to catch a fly ball! This allowed you to immediately take the batter's place. It made my day to catch a fly ball and get to bat. I even hit a few home runs!

Someone torched our school and it burned to the ground while I was in the fifth grade. In such an emergency, our neighboring school, Castleberry Elementary, offered to let us use their classrooms while ours was being rebuilt. Castleberry students went to school in the morning, and we traveled by school bus to attend afternoon classes. I do not remember learning much, but I did not like riding the bus or getting home late in the evening. I even persuaded Glenna to walk slow to the place where we had to catch the bus to Castleberry. This resulted in our missing the bus. Mom did not accept our tardy excuse. We had left in plenty of time to catch the bus, so we were punished! Another bad learning experience!

As I got older, learned a number of things from my step grandfather, "Toots" (Granny Burns' husband, who was an alcoholic hobo and rode the rails on freight trains from place to place). He taught me how to mow lawns and work in flowerbeds. I secured a couple of jobs taking care of neighbors' lawns. The first lawn was the Seaberry's yard across the road from us. I also mowed the enormous lawn across another adjoining road, which had a septic line running through the middle of it. The grass on the septic line would get to be knee deep before the owner would come and ask me to cut their lawn. I had to use a Yo-Yo to get the grass low enough to use the lawnmower on it. The Yo-Yo is an instrument with a double-edged blade on the bottom of the instrument. To get an effective cut in the grass, it was necessary to swing the Yo-Yo back and forth with all of your strength, just above ground level. Most of the time, the grass was so thick it would only cut a few inches at a time. This was a grueling amount of work for fifty cents! This same family had a paraplegic son, who had become an invalid because of polio. He was over 40 years old and could not sit or speak. They would bring him out in his wheelchair to watch me work.

More about Toots, we never knew when he was going to show up. He would come smelling awful due to his lifestyle of drinking and bumming rides on freight trains. Mom would make him take off several layers of shirts and pants. She would wash them in our old wringer washing machine. Often times, he was still inebriated when he arrived unannounced. It usually required a day or two for him to sober up. One time, he arrived when it was cold and snowing. With Dad's preaching and scolding, he staggered out into the backyard in his underwear and knelt in the snow, begging God to forgive him. I decided at that moment that I would never take a drink of wine, beer, or alcohol, and I did not until I was 38 years old. This first taste occurred during the 1968 summer while we were on a tour of France, Spain, Italy, Germany, etc., for a total of 15 countries. The taste was awful.

But for all of his faults, Toots was a very hard worker! He loved to sit and play games with Glenna and me. He always won at Dominoes until I figured out he was cheating. He would match anything on the domino board that would tally up to a 10, 15, or 20 count. He was really good at math. He loved to play jokes on us. Once he asked if I wanted to see him make an earthquake. I said, "Yes!" He instructed me to get one of Mom's canning jars. He held it to his ear while rubbing his finger around the mouth of the jar. He then had me do the same, and in the midst of doing that, he asked me, "Do you feel the JAR?" He then asked if I would like to see him pin the jar of water to the wall. Gullible me! I responded with a "Yes!" I retrieved a straight pin and put some water in the jar. He had a bad palsy of the hands and his hands shook. Holding the pin with one hand and the jar of water in the other, he proceeded to pin the jar of water to the wall, but with the shaking of the hand, he would drop the pin. I would hurriedly pick up the pin and hand it back to him. About the third time while I was bending over to pick up the pin, he poured the water down my back!

Glenna and I were the "milk maids" of the neighborhood. Mom would bottle the fresh milk, place cardboard stoppers in the top, and tell us where to deliver the milk. We were to pick up empty bottles and bring them back. Such a mundane task was tiring. To break the monotony of the walk and delivery, with a quart of milk in each hand, we would gently clink the bottles together. This made a little musical rhythm. As we discovered, too hard of a clink resulted in two broken bottles of milk! This brought the wrath of Mom and Dad upon us; another lesson in dos and don'ts.

When I was about 12 years old, I spent the summer for my asthma with Mom in the Miller Sanatorium in Mineral Wells, Texas. This was not the famous Crazy Crystal waters, for which people traveled to the city for healing by bathing in the warm waters. This was a holistic approach to treating all kinds of ailments. I was treated for asthma, and Mom was being treated for cancer. Between treatments, I observed the dietician making salads. When we got home from the clinic, Mom had to return to the hospital. I decided to surprise Dad with dinner when he came home from his job at the Justin Boot Company. I created a nice-looking salad with lettuce, peaches, and pears. Since we did not have any mayonnaise, I topped it off with mustard. When Dad came home, he was really surprised! Instead of criticizing me for my blunder, he said, "Wow, that was so nice, but I was thinking of taking you kids to the restaurant tonight." This was the first time that I had ever been inside of a real restaurant. My first order from a menu was chicken fried steak. What a treat!

A country feed store next to our house provided a convenient place to buy grain to feed our chickens, pigs, and cow. When one of the colorful feeds' sacks was emptied, Mom would sew and make curtains, dish towels, shirts, and underwear. I was the only boy in school who had matching shirts and underwear shorts! The feed store always had a mountain made of many rectangular bales of hay. Most of our neighbors had cows, horses, pigs, and chickens. One Halloween, we found ourselves drawn to an exciting gathering of about fifty local kids sitting on the mountain of hay. A few had fireworks. Some of the older teens decided it would be fun to block the road at the crossing where the feed store, grocery store, the Palmer house residence, and a vacant lot all came together. Strong guys carried dozens of bales of hay and blocked the roads in all directions. The traffic built up as far as we could see in each direction. Finally, the sheriff arrived. He drove into the ditch and through the vacant lot and came to shine his spotlight on all of us sitting on the mountain of hay. I guess there were too many of us to arrest. With his good sense of humor, he said, “Okay, you’ve had your fun! Now, these folks need to get home. Let’s see how fast you can get these bales back where they belong.” What an indelible night to remember!

It was also an exciting time when Uncle Thomas came home for a furlough with his new bride, Jeannie. She was a beautiful girl, with long black hair, from Rhode Island. She spoke with a heavy Yankee accent. She had never seen a cow! As Dad was milking, she asked, “Which spigot do you get the chocolate milk from?” She was aghast when the cow started to urinate and screamed, “What’s wrong with her?” Uncle Thomas and Aunt Jeannie found the Promised Land during his enlistment while he was stationed in California. We never got to spend any time with them after that.

We had a very mean old rooster. He was sneaky! Upon entering the chicken yard or cow lot to perform a chore, or go to the outhouse, that old rooster would wait until your back was turned. Then he would charge and flog or spur the victim with long claws, causing scratches and bleeding wounds. As a precaution, I usually took a chunk of wood into the yard with me for protection. When I spotted him from the corner of my eye, charging full speed to attack me, I turned and threw the chunk of wood and hit him in the neck. It was partially effective. From that good shot, he could barely crow! Later, while Aunt Sylvia was spending the summer with us, Mom said, “If you guys will catch that mean old rooster and kill it, we will have it for dinner.” After some serious chasing, we cornered the old bird and Aunt Sylvia said, “You stretch his neck out on the chopping block and I will cut his head off with the axe.” As I was holding his neck down, I happened to glance up at Aunt Sylvia. She was poised to bring the axe to execute the mean old rooster by cutting his head off WITH HER EYES CLOSED! I yelled, "Wait!" and let go of the rooster while jumping back. Mom finally wrung the rooster's neck!

I did experience a bit of my Mom's fury one day while drying the dishes. I made some smart talkback to her and she immediately slapped me! "Don't you ever sass me!" Another time when I got to be a big teenager, she was going to give me a spanking. I ran. I taunted her that she was not fast enough to catch me. Big mistake! The next morning, I woke up rolled in my sheets. She proceeded to beat the daylights out of me with a broom. There was a peach tree growing on the back corner of our house. I was told too often to go get Mom a switch off of the peach tree for my whipping on my legs. I don't think that peach tree ever grew enough branches to bear peaches! On another occasion, Dad was repairing the porch. Glenna and I had to hoe out the grass burrs in the yard. We kept arguing over who had to hoe which part. After several warnings to quit the arguing, Dad grabbed his saw and made music with it on our behinds! Years later, I had an evangelist who would play hymns on the same type of carpenter's saw with a violin bow. Mom was always so quiet and meek that any outburst or anger was a shock to me. While drying the dishes, she told me that when she was a teenager and washing the dishes, her cousin kept taking the clean dishes and setting them back down on a dirty dish. This was very irritating because it caused Mom to have to wash the dish again. After warning her several times, the cousin defiantly set a clean bowl on a dirty one. Mom scrapped her nose with a fork. She got into trouble for that, but she had the satisfaction of knowing the cousin never crossed her again.

Chapter 3:

WEATHERFORD, TEXAS

About the beginning of my first year in the eighth grade, we moved to Weatherford, about 30 miles west of Fort Worth. That year, I spent most of the days skipping school to help Dad build our house on Pythian Road. The teacher and principal told my parents at the end of the year that I had not been in school enough days to pass on to the ninth grade. Their response was, "He skipped the third grade and is now the youngest in his class, so go ahead and let him repeat the grade."

The First Free Will Baptist Church on Line Street had extended the call for Dad to become their full-time preacher and paid $20.00 per week for three weeks. In order to be a full-time church, Dad said he would do the whole month for $60.00. Our first winter was spent in a couple of rooms with the Doak Bennett family west of town near the Greenwood community. I remember riding the bus and getting acquainted with two beautiful girls, Dorothy and Frances Frysinger. They lived across the road from the Bennett family. I met them at the Greenwood Community Center. A couple of years after I had moved into our new home on the Pythian home road, I rode my bicycle on a Saturday night across town and out to the Greenville Community Center (about twelve miles) to see them again. After a Saturday evening of fun and games at the community center, I headed home on my bicycle, which did not have any lights. An approaching car blinded me so that I did not see the one-way bridge ahead. At the last minute, I saw the bridge and made a sharp turn to the right, where I dove headfirst into the creek running under the bridge. I finally arrived back home wet, muddy, and tired.

Doak Bennett, with his wife, Rose, and the kids, David, Elaine, and Doug, were also building a home next to ours on the Pythian home road. Their house was ready to move into before we finished our house, so we moved in with them near the Greenwood community west of Weatherford. Their house was finished before hours so we left the Greenwood area and moved in with the Faulk family and their son, David. We became good friends. The Faulk family lived on an old dairy farm place nine miles north of Weatherford on a creek with a large old barn across the road where their job was to milk a herd of cows. The house was pretty big, and both families seemed to get along well while we shared the space and lived with them. There was no electricity and no running water. The "bathroom" was situated down a path over a creek about 40 yards away from the house. The pump in the yard required a priming most of the time. This involved picking up the bucket of water saved and set aside for this task. While pumping the handle, water was poured down the shaft until a seal of water allowed the pump to begin the sucking process of producing water. We filled several buckets and tubs to have water on hand. The house was heated with a couple of fireplaces and a woodstove in the kitchen. Among my responsibilities was the chore of cutting the kindling and sawing the logs into stove and fireplace size. Next, I had to bring it in and fill the wood box. Every morning, I had to clean out the fireplace and kitchen stove and haul the ashes to the creek. We did not stay up long after dark because we had to read by kerosene lamps or candles. We always got a long night's rest by going to bed when the sun went down and getting up as the sun came up. A chamber pot was used during the night for going to the "restroom." The disposal of the contents of the potty was not my favorite job. The creek, again, was the designated disposal site. This potty jug was sometimes referred to as the "Thunder Jar." I admired the brilliance of the man who lived there before us and had the forethought to build the outhouse over the creek. This eliminated the stinking chore of cleaning out the toilet as the rain would come and wash the waste away. Once a flood came and washed our potty, the outhouse, downstream, we had to build another! This time, we made it "a two holler toilet," one large hole for adults and a smaller hole for kids.

David and I roamed the woods with our slingshots and BB guns. We came across a HUGE wasp nest (about a foot across) swarming with yellow jackets. Without so much of a thought of the danger, we searched for objects to throw and knock that nest down. We found some large chunks of dead wood and crept slowly toward the nest. We threw the two ballistics of wood together! Bull's eye! We hit! We immediately regretted our actions! This was a very dumb idea! Screaming and running as fast as we could to outrun the yellow jackets, we arrived back at the house covered with wasp stings. Ugh! We were doused with more stinkin' tobacco medication.

The result of our move to Weatherford negated the income from Justin Boot Company. Dad made extra income by working on small carpentry jobs. We applied the money from the sale of our home in Lake Worth to buy lumber for the building of our new house. We drove to Mineral Wells, Texas, on a couple of occasions to tear down two old military Quonset hut buildings and salvage the lumber to build our house. Another source of income was to thrash and pick up pecans "on the halves" during the late fall. Dad always took several bushel baskets and some toe sacks or gunnysacks along with some very long fishing poles strapped to the top of our '38 Plymouth. While thrashing pecan trees down on the river bottom with the long fishing poles for one of our customers, Dad was about forty feet up. He climbed out as far as he dared with one of the fishing poles, and hit the ends of the limbs with the pole, causing the pecans to fall. My job was to pick up the pecans and fill the buckets and sacks. I heard Dad scream, "Look out!" I looked up to see him falling forty feet and landing on his back! For a long minute, he did not move and I thought that the fall had killed him. I suppose the soft dirt from recent rains helped cushion the blow. Shortly, he moaned and sat up. This was a really scary moment for me! I do not remember Dad ever telling anyone about it. I still relish picking up pecans in the fall and have always dreamed of retiring with a large orchard of pecan trees to sustain me.

The land we bought in Weatherford had formerly been a nursery. Many old fruit trees still existed on it, and Dad assigned me the task of digging the dirt around these trees and cutting the roots out completely. This would allow our old horse, Tony, to pull the plow and till the sandy soil to grow corn, sweet potatoes, cantaloupes, and best of all, watermelons! I learned to plow behind Tony, the horse, with a "Georgia stock plow." I experienced the pain of the plow hitting a big root that I failed to dig out and the plow handle would hit me in the groin and take my breath away! The gentleman who sold us our five acres retained about the same amount of land, and he supplied the First National Bank their window display watermelon each year. It always exceeded 100 pounds. The Bennett family had purchased about two acres between us. David Bennett and I decided to "borrow" one of our neighbor's nice, big watermelons. We got caught. My mother took me by the ear and marched me up to his front door. When he answered, I had to tell him what we had done, apologize for it, and offer to make restitution (pay for the damages). He accepted my apology and assured me that if I ever wanted a watermelon, all I needed to do was come and ask, and he would be happy to help me pick one out.

My first jobs were with neighbors:

Our rural mail carrier, Mr. Miller, told me that his wife needed someone to help mow the lawn, wax the floors, clean out the chicken coop, sun and turn the mattresses, etc. She nicknamed me "Bugsy" vs. my sister calling me "Bubba." Ms. Vestal owned several acres about one-fourth of a mile from our home. On it were ten on- room cabins, the forerunner of the motel. I had to keep these repaired and painted, plus mow around each one. These cabins were old and creepy! Jay Mock was the leather saddle maker. Another neighbor across the road was Junior, a bricklayer. The Patterson family owned a drugstore located on the square. The Becks owned an Esso (Exxon) service station. Keeping all of these neighbors' lawns and doing odd jobs for each kept me occupied and provided me with some income.

Although I mowed lawns for all of my steady clients, Jay Mock was my favorite customer. He had a saddle shop. When I got too hot mowing, I would retreat into his cool shop and watch him tool leather. He made beautiful wallets, belts, bridles, and saddles. He observed that I had an interest, so he handmade four leather tools fashioned from large nails in his workshop. He gave me scraps of leather on which to practice my carving and tooling. Soon, I was making extra money tooling wallets, belts, school notebooks, moccasins, etc. I continued to earn my spending money through high school by tooling leather. Periodically, I still bring out my tools and make something for one of my grandkids or friends!

Ms. Childress, my music teacher in the eighth grade, was very good. She taught us to detect and recognize the sound of each instrument of an orchestra. She also led assemblies using chorus books of old popular folk songs like, "K-K-K-Katy, beautiful Katy, you are the only g-g-g-girl that I adore." Or, "I came from Alabama with my banjo on my knee," and "She'll be coming around the mountain," etc. When we got noisy and were not paying attention, she would say, "Empty cans make lots of noise." Singing became fun for me. I sang in the school choir. Dad drafted me into the radio quartet to sing alto since my voice had not yet changed. In fact, I sang high tenor and alto until I was in college. Even while answering the phone during my first year as a pastor, people who called thought I was a girl by the sound of my voice. They would say, "Ma'am, is your father there?" Singing gospel music was such fun. I made a request of my parents to allow me to stay with Grandmother Kennedy in Dallas to attend the Stamps Baxter Music School. Grandmother Kennedy had a job at the first Frito plant, which was in walking distance from her large house! Streetcars were still running in the streets of Dallas at that time. This was my means of traveling part way to the school in Oak Cliff. I was privileged to take voice and piano lessons and sang in two quartets. We performed on the radio during the program that aired all night after the concluding session. During this time, Mr. Stamps and Mr. Baxter split up their partnership. I remember Mr. Stamps getting up and admonishing us not to make a lot over their spat and split. His advice, "Never burn bridges over a disagreement because you never know when you might want to come back and use that bridge again."

Several of my buddies had BB guns, and we enjoyed hunting. One night, I received permission to go "coon hunting." We had a couple of dogs, and one seemed to pick up the trail of what we assumed to be a raccoon. The dogs stopped at a hole under a stump. The dogs were trying to dig into the hole. We started poking in the hole to persuade the coon to come out. The varmint that exited was a very mad skunk. He sprayed us good! Mom tried ketchup, lemon juice, and everything under the kitchen sink to get rid of the awful odor. Nothing worked. She sent me on to school the next day anyway. Before long, my teacher, Ms. Childress, came to my desk and said, "Mr. Ferguson, we are going to allow you to go home for a day or two. Please come back when you get rid of that smell."

On another trip to the creek across the road from our house, I shot a squirrel, brought it home, skinned it, and had my mother cook it for me. The next day, I was back on the creek in the same area as the day before. I could hear a lot of chatter and crying from up in the tree where I had shot my squirrel. I climbed up the tree to the squirrel's nest, where I found a baby squirrel that did not have its eyes open yet. I carefully removed the baby and took it home. We had plenty of milk, so I took an eyedropper and held it full of milk to the baby squirrel's mouth. I thought he was going to swallow the whole dropper! It was a struggle to take it out of his mouth to refill with milk. In a few days, his eyes opened and he began running around. We found a lot of things to feed him, and laughed at his antics. His favorite was peanuts in the shell. I talked a lot about my pet squirrel at school, and along with some of my classmates, we received permission from the teacher to bring my squirrel to school. I wore my bib overhauls and the squirrel nestled in my chest bib pocket. My two-side pockets were filled with peanuts. We spent most of the day watching my pet shell peanuts and entertain with his antics. My popularity grew that day! As time passed, I left the squirrel in his cage a lot and ceased to pay a lot of attention to him. He evolved back to his wild nature, and one day as I took him out of the cage, he bit me! I pulled my shirt over him and held him tight against my stomach before releasing him back into his cage. I am not sure whether my blood poisoned him or my squeeze was too hard, but the results: we had a burial service the next day!

My first big job was during the summer at the ripe old age of 14. Raymond Jackson and I both got a job holding the grain sacks for Virgil Watkins' thrashing machine crew in Aledo, Texas. First, we followed the mower and shocked the bundles of oats or barley. Barley really caused me to itch while working with it. After the grain bundles dried out under the sun, we came back to the field and used pitchforks to throw the bundles into hay wagons. Tractors would pull the trailers up to the thrashing machine. At this point, a person would climb on the top of the oat bundles and pitch them into the thrasher. Large claws chewed the bundles and this thrashing of the bundles of grain would separate the grain and blow away the hay chaff to create a huge haystack. The grain was blown through the pipes and came down out of a spout into the toe sacks held by Raymond and me. He and I took turns holding one of these sacks and sewing it shut. We had to be quick in taking turns, or else the grain would dump in the bed of the truck. This was not the way to keep Virgil Watkins happy. Virgil did have a bit of compassion for the crew. Twice a day, his beautiful teenage daughter, Virjean, would bring hot coffee and iced water to cool us down in the 100 to 110 degree weather. Upon finishing the thrashing in several fields, we would return at a later date to bale the straw.

At times, when Raymond and I would be pitching the bundles of hay, we would be surprised what critters had made their home under the shock of oats. Once, Raymond hit me across the chest with the blunt edge of his pitchfork. At first, it made me mad. Then I saw the reason: he had used his pitchfork, after pushing me back, to nail a very big rattle snake's head to the ground. Snakes came in great varieties where I grew up. The worst were the rattlesnake, the water moccasin, and the copperhead. Virgil's straw boss, Slim, was driving the old spike-wheeled tractor while we pitched the bundles into the wagon to take to the thrasher. After being on the tractor all day, he told me to get up here and trade places so I can stretch my legs. It was chugging uphill at a crawl pace until we turned at the top of the hill and started down. We began to pick up steam...fast! Slim was running alongside, yelling at me to down gear! I was grinding gears with all the energy that I could muster, but we were going too fast. As we approached the fence and a creek beyond, he began to yell for me to JUMP! I was petrified at the sight of the huge spiked legs churning on both sides of me. I finally stood up and dove over one of the large metal spike wheels. I stood up in time to watch the tractor go through the fence and end upside down in the creek! Virgil was a very unhappy man. I think he must have enlisted every neighbor in Aledo, Texas to bring their tractors, bull dozers, and trucks with every device imaginable to try to extricate the old tractor from the creek. I was relegated back to my original job of holding sacks."

Type of Virgil Watkins tractor in Aledo, Texas, that I abandoned with no brakes, and it crashed into the creek.

The next summer, I secured a job with a neighbor, Junior, who lived across the road from us. He was a bricklayer. My job was to mix the cement, sand, and water into mud for him to lay the bricks. I also had to keep him supplied in brick. To this day, I have dreams of him yelling, "MORE MUD! MORE BRICK!"

When I turned 16, my summer job was with a roofer. I thought the previous two summers had been hot, but roofing is a real deterrent to avoid HELL! Nothing is fun or comfortable with roofing! Hauling heavy bundles of asphalt shingles up a ladder to the roof is about as pleasant as it gets. As the sun hits the roof, it can become hot enough to fry eggs! Wearing gloves and knee pads help very little. Thankfully, I lived through each summer job and made a little spending money.

These jobs also gave me a winnowing experience to sort out and avoid certain occupations.

It was during my SECOND eighth grade year that I seemed to have a great awakening. I began to notice other people. A verse in Proverbs caught my attention: "He that is to have friends must show himself to be friendly." I began to speak to everyone first without waiting for them to speak to me. I spoke to everyone. I began to be more sociable and friendly. Earning my own spending money was expected because my parents did not have any extra money. Before learning to do leather tooling, I earned money by mowing lawns, cleaning out chicken houses, mopping and waxing floors, turning mattresses, etc. I was able to forego taking my lunch to school when Mom said I could spend as much as a quarter a day of my earned money for lunch. I went to the little hamburger cafe next to the theater and bought a nickel hamburger consisting of bread, meat, relish, and mustard. Next, I walked around the square to the pharmacy where I ordered a ten-cent milk shake (no ice cream–just milk, flavoring, and ice blended together). This left me with ten cents. I saved this dime and used it to go to a movie and view a Western on Saturday. Favorites were "The Lone Ranger," with his silver bullet plus his Indian sidekick Tonto, "Hop Along Cassidy," or "Roy & Dale Rogers," with his horse, Trigger. At the end, there was always a continued movie trailer. It ended with a suspenseful and dangerous situation designed to leave the audience hanging with suspense. It was supposed to motivate you to come back next Saturday to find out how the hero escaped.

As our small church began to grow, we were pressed into the necessity of building a new sanctuary and remodeling the old one into Sunday School classrooms. Dad and some of the laymen were hanging the roof joists. On a missed nail with the hammer, Dad bashed his thumb. He yelled and started down the ladder in great pain. All the men stopped working and were trying to sympathize with him. Dad looked around and said, "Well, can't one of you laymen say something appropriate?"

Behind our church was a Pentecostal church and a grade school. The holiness church services always lasted much longer than ours (although I thought Dad could cut about thirty minutes off of each sermon and it would improve his preaching dramatically). With nothing else to do while our parents were visiting with church members following the evening service, a number of us would walk over to the Pentecostal church and watch through the open windows. None of the churches had air conditioning at that time. Their rituals were quite a bit different than ours. They usually had a band with several musical instruments, such as guitars, tambourines, drums, and horns. This was often accompanied with a lot of shouting and raising their hands in praise (I think Baptists have been a little shy about expressing as much emotion as they did). The preaching and music was often punctuated with shouting, "Hallelujah!" The real odd part was when the altar call was made, people would come forward, and the minister would touch them on the forehead, and they would pass out or, as they put it, "they were slain in the Spirit." Loud expressions were expressed with an "Amen" or two. We did have an occasional shout from brother Brandon, and it would scare "the dickens" out of me. My eyes would nearly come out of my head! Dad was not one to put up with disruptions during his preaching, and a couple of times when he would see me on the back bench talking with my buddies, he would stop preaching. The silence from the pulpit caused me to stop and look up to see why he had stopped and found my dad glaring at me. Before the entire congregation, he would say, "Norman Wayne, if you cannot behave, come up here and sit by your mother!" What a way to embarrass a teenager!

Mom was the best Sunday School teacher that I ever had during those years growing up as a young Christian teenager. She spent all week cutting out flannel graph characters of the Bible and then telling the Bible stories with such vivid visual aids. It created attention and made the stories come alive. She involved the class with the construction of building a miniature model Tabernacle as described in detail in the Old Testament. We learned every Sunday of the adventures of the Israelites and their 40 years of travel in the wilderness. What a blessing! Years later, I benefited from all of this training as I taught the same material to my Tyler Junior College Bible classes.

Finally, I got to the ninth grade! It was another Easter Sunday, and, as usual, the church was sponsoring an Easter egg hunt. Some teens thought they were too big to participate in an Easter egg hunt, but I always looked forward to hunting for the eggs. The surprise that I found on this egg hunt awakened something that I had never experienced in life, the emotion of love for a girl! There was a new young lady named Virginia Peoples and her sister Margie at this event. Virginia was in the 7th grade and was the prettiest thing I had ever seen in her cute little Easter dress. I was dumbstruck and could hardly contain my admiration for her. She and Margie were the daughters of the construction supervisor for what was known as Conaway Town. This was a large development of small lower-rent type homes. The Peoples lived next to the lumberyard in a very nice home. Not long after we met, I asked her if I could walk her home from church. This was about a four-block walk. I informed Mom as to where we were going while they fellowshipped after church. She agreed that they would drive down and pick me up when they locked up the church buildings. This became our pattern of getting to know one another. She told me one night that her mom and dad wanted to meet me. For some reason, we went around to the back door, and as I walked into the den, this BIG guy came out from behind the door with a shotgun in his hand, demanding to know who gave me permission to date his daughter. Virginia came to my rescue with, "Oh, Daddy, that's not funny! Quit playing games!" I was relieved to know he was quite the tease. She had an older brother, but he was already married and gone. I loved her mother and we later named our old Model T Ford after her. We painted "Lillian" on the front of the old car. At school, Virginia, whom I nicknamed Petunia (after her love of the flower called petunias), was in the white brick junior high building and I was in the red brick high school. Both of our school buildings were located directly across from the First Baptist Church. Across the highway was an "Old Fashioned Hires Root Beer" stand. Tommy Graves and I frequented the root beer place between every tennis game we played. Because of the extreme Texas heat, this would be about every 15 minutes. At lunch, Petunia and I met between the buildings and hung out together. She was such a fun loving individual and laughed easily. Her laugh was infectious!

In the tenth grade, a well-known evangelist by the name of Rev. Jack Schuler came for a city-wide revival. Services were held in the old North Side Baptism Brush Arbor, or as some called it, The Tabernacle. Les Barnett was the organist. Over 300 of my high school classmates made a decision for Jesus during these Spirit-filled services. Many of us were concerned as to how we could keep the momentum of the revival going among our youth. Les Barnett met with us and suggested that we organize a "Youth for Christ." We would meet every Saturday night. He suggested contacting Southwestern Baptist Theological Seminary in Fort Worth to see if one of the students there would be interested in coming to be our sponsor (most of the pastors were too busy to make such a commitment). We found Jack Patterson, and he met with us and helped us organize and secure the community center for a meeting place. The city did not charge us, but we had to set up chairs, clean up after any refreshments, put away all folding tables and chairs, and sweep after each meeting. Tommy Graves became our first president of the Weatherford Youth for Christ. A year later, I was selected to be the president. Tommy dated Jody McKinney, and I dated Virginia. The four of us became inseparable. Tommy's dad was the editor of The Democrat, a weekly newspaper. Guy was one of the few Democrats with whom I ever had a close relationship. He had a quiet and subtle humor, and he was always so helpful to any needs that Tommy and I had. It was with his assistance that we acquired the Model T Ford. This became our source of travel to football games and Sunday afternoon jaunts to the Brazos River to swim and play. It was on one of these Sundays that I made a remark to Tommy, "Hey, I'm not sure you were baptized properly in the Methodist church because you were only sprinkled with water. I tried to explain: Jesus was baptized in the Jordan River and Baptists believe that the word *baptize* means to dip or plunge beneath the water, and is a symbol of our death to sin and hope of our resurrection to a new life, in both the here and hereafter. He listened, and said, "OK then, baptize me!" So, in great solemnity, I plunged him beneath the Brazos River water. Jody and Virginia were witnesses.

Norm's sweetheart, Virginia Peoples, wins a beauty contest.

Jack Patterson got more involved in local church life around Weatherford and Parker County. He accepted a little Baptist church at Tin Top. They wanted to build a new church, so Tommy and I got a dozen of our Youth for Christ together to go to the little church and help build. We made several trips out to raise the walls and put the decking on the roof. The ladies fed us dinner on the grounds! Later, Jack became the pastor of the mission church of First Baptist on South Main. He was a very popular young Seminary preacher.

Back to school! I finally got over my asthma enough to play football and basketball. I enjoyed football on the "B" team during my ninth grade year and was on the scrimmage team my sophomore year. I remember how dumb I was when I tried to put on my first football equipment! I placed the thigh pads in the wrong legs of my football pants, which resulted in a lot of pain when someone tackled me. It really put my manhood on painful alert!!! On the scrimmage team, I was introduced to Herman Stroud, the fullback on the varsity team. I played the position of safety. During a scrimmage, he came through the line of defenders, and neither a guard nor tackle touched him. Wearing one of the old hand-me-down leather helmets, I ducked my head to tackle Herman. I was going to impress coach Emmons. Herman did not go left or right. He ran straight over me like a freight train! Coach Emmons ran out to see if I was ok. At first, I thought maybe I had lost my eyesight, but discovered the old leather helmet had slipped around on my head and I was peeping out through the ear hole. Coach said, "Norm, you have to tackle harder and with more speed than the person you are trying to tackle! Do you understand?" I had three coaches. Redheaded Coach Emmons, who loved to whack us with his paddle on a naked butt when we came out of the shower. Coach Ranspot delighted in making us duck walk or leap frog the entire PE period if the weather would not allow us to go exercise on the football field. Coach Whiteside was the other coach. Each of his eyes was a different color.

"A" TEAM

Front Row Ernie Tullis, Tommy Copeland, Charles Harper, Herman Stroud, Tommy Hedspeth
Second Row—Norman Ferguson, James Simms, Mike McDaniel.
Third Row—Ernest Williams, Bill Puryear.

Norm's high school basketball team, Weatherford, Texas

About this time, we had new neighbors move in to the natural rock house next to the east of us. They had two boys, and we became good buddies. This particularly beautiful day, they were at my house, and we were playing on the hay in the barn. One of them noticed our detached fence charger. We had used this to prevent old Tony, our horse used for plowing, from pawing down the neighbor's fence and getting out. One of the brothers asked what it was, and I told him it had an electric current that gave a shock to the horse. Not all of the ideas that come into kids' heads were good rational ideas! Their mom was washing clothes. The end of their clothesline came close to our barn. We hooked the fence charger up to the clothesline. Their mom came out to hang up the clothes. She touched the wire with wet hands and screamed! Running back to the house, she was screaming and thought that she was having a stroke! The fun was short-lived as none of us thought we would live through this idiotic episode!

Future note about Coach Ranspot: while teaching Bible at Tyler Junior College several years later, a young lady came into one of my Bible classes after the school year to enroll late. She handed me her class permit to enroll. The name was Carolyn Ranspot! I said: "Carolyn, I have tried to forget that name. I had a coach named Ranspot in Weatherford, Texas. He was the meanest coach that I ever had! She said, "Yeah, I hear that a lot. He's my dad." Is there anything more embarrassing than sticking your foot in your mouth?

Norm's self-decorated high school bedroom (black and yellow!)

Well, my Dad had tried to convince me that I was foolhardy to play football. But if I insisted, then no matter how tired I was after workouts and walking the three miles home, there would be two cows waiting on me to be milked. One of those evenings when I had experienced a hard workout and then walked the three miles home, I found two old cows, Daisy and Babe, bawling to be milked. I went to the barn and put the first cow in the milking stall. In the dark, I could not locate the feed bucket. I remembered that I had flipped the bucket over the corral fence into the feed area that morning. There was a barrel of cottonseed hulls and a box of bran with a lid on it. I reached over behind the box of bran, thinking the bucket may have fallen over behind it. The hair on the back of my neck stood up as I froze. I was touching something cold, soft, and slimy. I ran to the house and got a flashlight and my .22 rifle. What I found was a huge copperhead snake! I shot it and went to school the next day, telling Mr. Skiles, my agriculture teacher, that I had a new FFA project. I wanted to run electricity to our barn and light it up. It took about 175 feet of wiring and a lot of work, but eventually, we had a lighted barn!

Driving our old 38 Plymouth was a privilege given to me on Saturday nights to go to pick up Virginia, go to Youth for Christ, and "drag Broadway Street," which consisted of driving back and forth on Broadway going south, turning around and going north, and waving at all of the other cars full of teens in the opposite side of the road. Sometimes we were diverted to excursions down "Ghost Hollow" near Holland's Lake. This is the lake where I enjoyed swimming in the summer time with friends. It was also the destination on April first when many of us played hooky and played at the lake all day instead of going to school. Needless to say, somehow my parents and the school always figured this out, and I ended up getting punished at school and home for skipping school.

I guess it was about this time that I decided maybe I would be better at basketball than football. That is what I did the next two years. However, I did make the football travel team a couple of times for some of the out-of-town trips. This was really exciting. My motivation was not that I expected to get to play in the game, but on a trip, the coach always stopped either going to the game or coming home to treat everyone to a chicken fried steak dinner! This was a real incentive for me!

Norm's 3 years of FFA, projects, president, bi-district president, winner of state-wide poultry-judging contest, and winner of the Texas "Lone Star Famer's Degree"

The thought of studying during my high school years never crossed my mind. I do not ever remember bringing a book home to study. This did not hold true with Sis as she was valedictorian! I did enjoy algebra and was pretty adept at understanding it. Maybe it was because my teacher was young and beautiful, and I really wanted to please her. My interests were: sports, football, basketball, and Petunia. She always came first! In church, I was Saturday night custodian, folder of bulletins, and the Sunday School superintendent. I enjoyed singing in the church's radio quartet. Promoting the Saturday night Youth for Christ was a fun responsibility. The FFA (Future Farmers of America) consumed much of my time and energy. I enjoyed the projects and field trips. Study was way down the list! I think that I viewed myself as becoming a BIG farmer one day since so much of my life's experiences had been with cows, pigs, and chickens. Note: I did earn the degree and medal of a "Lone Star Future Farmer of America" during my three years. Sammy Skiles was my "Ag" teacher. He probably did not weigh a hundred pounds, but really challenged us in class and on field trips. We learned all about crop rotation, soil composition, and terracing used to "make water walk off of the field" versus flooding and eroding the soil. We learned about the value of planting legumes that replaced the nitrogen in the soil. On field trips, we rode across terraces in the back of his pickup at break-neck speed and had to hang on or get bumped out! We dehorned cattle, castrated roosters, and learned how to cull non-laying hens. Then we learned how to judge milk cows: Jerseys, Guernseys, and Holsteins. We learned how to judge beef: Angus, Brahma, Whiteface, and Longhorn. We learned all about shop techniques too. We operated saws, drill presses, welding machines, sanders, etc. I developed as a leader and was elected as president of the FFA chapter for two years, and was elected as district and bi-district president. I was given $100 to escort the FFA sweetheart, Laura King, to the Texas State Fair and was sent to Kansas City to the National FFA convention. Laura's steady boyfriend did not think that my escorting her to the state fair was a good idea, but we had a great time anyway!

On another memorable trip to Abilene for the state poultry-judging contest, we made the trip in an old school bus and spent the night in the bus because there was no money to stay in a hotel. Mr. Sammy Skiles allowed us to roam Abilene that evening. We boys all tried smoking cigars! This was a very new experience for me as the only thing I had ever tried to smoke was the cedar strips off of a cedar fence post! This one time made me sick enough to take away any desire to ever smoke again! The next morning, we started the judging contest of laying hens. This consisted of about thirty groups of laying hens of all breeds, and each group would consist of eight to ten hens. We made a selection list as to which one was a better hen. This consisted of picking up each one to check the beak, comb, feet, Eyes, and plumage. Then we had to hold the hen under one arm and gently lay four fingers across the rear end of the chicken to check the capacity for producing eggs. About three o'clock that afternoon, we met in the auditorium and were live, on the air radio for the prize presentation. To my astonishment, I won the state poultry-judging contest. The reward was a ribbon, a new chicken brooder, and one hundred baby chicks! I went home and converted my pig shed (which I had built as another FFA project of concrete & tile) into a chicken house. Raising and marketing chickens was one of those experiences where once is enough! After about eight weeks of buying expensive feed and changing the sawdust and litter made of wood shavings (a very stinky job), I had to find a market for about 95 broiler chickens. They weighed about two pounds each and would fetch a good fifty cents per pound when plucked of the feathers and gutted. I made the rounds to the grocery stores and restaurants and would get ten to twenty each weekend to market. This involved hanging three on a clothesline, taking a head with the neck of each between my three fingers of the left hand and a sharp knife in my right hand to decapitate them. It was a horrible and bloody experience, and almost every week, I would cut the knuckles of my left hand. If the first whack left one still alive, the flopping of the others did not allow an accurate kill. I still have scars from those Saturday massacres. Mom then dropped them into boiling water, which made it easier to pluck off the feathers. Then I would wrap them in wax paper & go to market, all for $1.00 each!

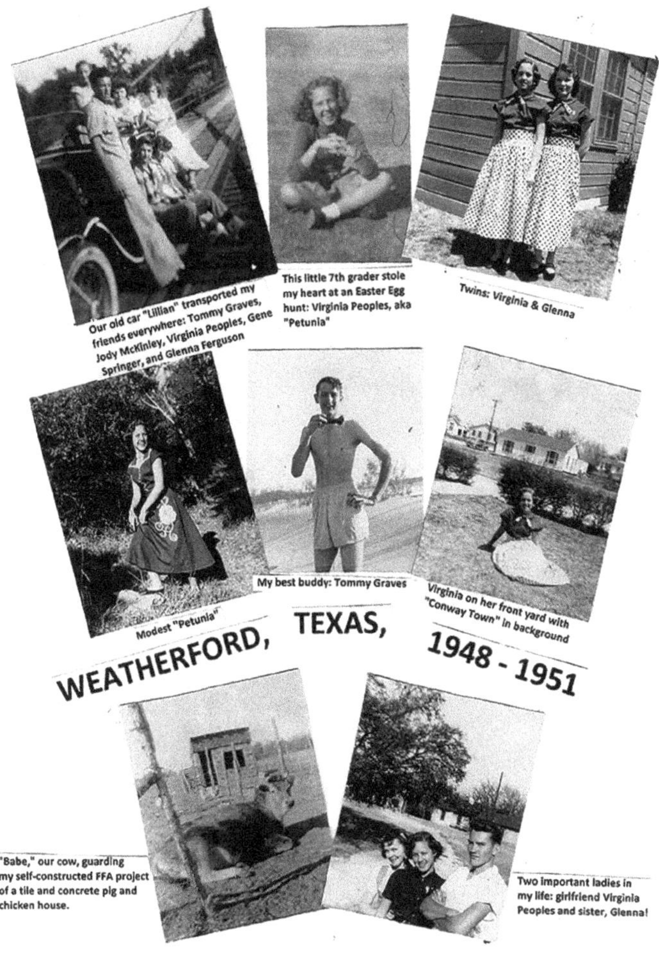

Virginia, Glenna, Tommy, Jody, Gene, with our old Model T car "Lillian" (named after Petunia's mom)

Tommy Graves became part of the family. We were inseparable. He was the greatest buddy that I have ever had! He liked to visit with my parents and called them, "Ma" and "Pa" Ferguson. I spent so many nights at his house. The first such night, I bounded down the stairs with a, "Good Morning" everyone! No one spoke.

His mom said, "Norman, around here, we have a rule: no one speaks until after our first cup of coffee!" Jody McKinney was Tommy's girlfriend, and along with my Petunia, we rode everywhere in "Lillian," our Model T Ford. Most of the time, we had to push it or let it roll downhill to get it started by popping the clutch. Petunia and I rode in the "rumble seat," which was an open trunk affair. As stated before, I never studied. After failing junior English under teacher Maybelle Whitsett (a neighbor who lived up on the hill behind our five acres), I had to repeat junior English while at the same time taking English Literature as a senior. Tommy insisted that I go to Bob Jones University with him. BJU was the university from which our Youth for Christ director, Jack Patterson, had graduated. Prospects for me making graduation did not look promising. Tommy took things into his own hands. He made flashcards for both English grammar and English literature, with authors, dates, and writings on each card. He grilled me nightly until midnight at his home until I had mastered the answers on each card. I passed both courses and became eligible for graduation!

Besides grades, there was the element and huge hurdle of a lack of finances. One of my last FFA projects was to raise a crop of sweet potatoes. Our backyard was stacked about three feet deep with sweet potatoes. Getting these out of the ground and into the backyard was via our horse, "Tony," and a sled. We could not use a tractor because the sand was too deep and a tractor would get stuck. Getting money for all of these sweet potatoes was another monumental marketing job. Along with this money, plus the money I had from the nine pigs that I had raised and sold, I still did not have much in my bank account at First National Bank. I was on a first name basis with Fred Measures, the president as well as the vice president, Charles Brinkley, who was a great Christian and a very popular singing layman. During the summer after high school graduation, I worked at the Chance/Voight airplane factory in Fort Worth, the same one that made bombers that flew over our house in Indian Oaks. I started bucking rivets on the oil and gas tanks of the wings of the B-19, B-24, and B-29 bombers. Sometimes I got to work in the sheet metal division and the "K" and "Y" parts division. This really helped get a few dollars saved to go to college in the fall of 1951.

Speaking of my pigs, let me tell you about the day my old sow delivered those nine pigs. It was on a Sunday afternoon, and I had converted the once pig house to a chicken house and now back to a pig's home. I had to install rails a foot out from the walls all the way around the building. This allowed the baby pigs an escape space when the very large momma, called a sow, decided to lie down and possibly smash the baby pig up against the wall. Well, this Sunday was also the set date for me to preach my first sermon at church. I somehow lost my sermon notes during the excitement of delivering new pigs in the afternoon. I was forced to preach without any notes. The sermon did not last very long! Afterward, my mom had a question, "Where did you get your illustration on tithing?" My answer: "Well, I see people who come to church and give their tithes and offerings every week UNTIL they go on vacation. Then, they conveniently forget to catch up on the tithes of the weeks missed. In my adolescent way of interpreting the Scriptures where Jesus said, "In my Father's house are many mansions," and in another, "I go to prepare a place for you!" I assumed that maybe this is the way we are to furnish our mansion. Since there is not any mention of the furnishings of the house prepared for us, and since the apostle James said, "Faith without works is dead," I put together the idea that maybe God is furnishing our mansions with the tithes and offerings that we give and the angels fashion our furniture with these "works." So imagine, again, these people getting to heaven and checking their beautiful mansion. They come to this nice-looking rocking chair, and the man decides to sit in it for a moment. Immediately, it flips over backward. He gets up and exclaims to the touring angel, "What happened? I thought everything was perfect in heaven?" The angel patiently replied, "Remember the vacation you went on and did not catch up with your tithes and offerings? Well, we were in the process of building the rocking chair during that time. When you did not finish sending your tithes, we could not finish the chair." Mom shook her head and said, "Son, you have a great imagination, but that is not in the Bible!"

Chapter Four:

1951-1953 BOB JONES UNIVERSITY

Bob Jones University, Greenville, SC

Tommy Graves was not one to give up his dream of our going to college together. He had me fill out the application papers, and I was greatly surprised that a letter came back saying that I was accepted. The only problem was matriculation fees and semester charges for living in the dorm. One evening, my Dad heard something at the front door. He found a mysterious envelope between the door and the screen door. The envelope had $500.00 cash inside! No other markings as to where it came from. I was pretty sure that my financial angel was Tommy and his folk. I made applications to get work/loan scholarships and received enough for me to make the trip and become a college freshman.

My best friend, Tommy Graves, who enabled me to advance to college!

Tommy's mom and dad decided to take the trip to Greenville, South Carolina in their car to deposit us in the dormitory. We went by way of Arkansas and visited their relatives in Pine Tree. That night, Tommy and I participated in catching lightning bugs with some of his cousins. We got into the Smoky Mountains, and his dad, Guy, would veer across the centerline, going around the curves, and Tommy's mom would yell, "Get over, Guy, here comes a big truck!" As soon as he veered back into the lane near the edge of the mountain, she would look down and see clouds drifting below us. She would then scream, "Get back over, Guy!" Finally, she said, "Guy, Stop the car! Stop the car right now!" He said, "Yes, ma'am!" We stopped, and she got out the maps. We had no idea where we were, so she said, "We have got to get out of these mountains! Now! So, I want you to take the next road off of this mountain. We will go south until we get out of these mountains." After another two hours of winding on very small roads, we came to a crossing road. Guy saw a girl sitting on the porch of a clapboard house. He pulled over and got out. As he got close, he told the young lady (probably in her early twenties), "Hello, ma'am! We are trying to get out of these mountains. Could you tell us what town each of these roads will take us to?" She, still in her rocking chair, said, "Mister, there are mountains everywhere!" He repeated the question a couple of times, and she always answered with, "Mister, there are mountains everywhere." Guy came back to the car and said, "The poor girl has never been out of the mountains!" We finally came into civilization on the north side of Atlanta, Georgia. This was 1951, and Atlanta did not yet have any freeways or interstates. It took us four solid hours to get through Atlanta on our way up to Greenville, SC. Arriving on campus, I had never seen such a beautiful campus. We were so excited to be freshmen in college!

We enrolled in Bible classes, a song leading class, and all of the required classes of English, history, etc. All freshmen had to take an English assessment test. I passed it, and Tommy had to take sub-freshman English. He was really upset! I guess it was a case where the student (me) did better than the teacher (Tommy).

We had Chapel every day in the beautiful Rodeheaver Auditorium. Dr. Bob Jones, Sr. usually spoke, or more accurately, PREACHED! He had a book of chapel sayings that he preached to us every day:

"Learn how to live, and you will always be able to make a living!"

"People who succeed make stepping stones out of their stumbling stones!"

"Do Right (it does not require a lot of brains to determine the right choice!)!"

"It is never right to do wrong in order to get a chance to do right."

"Finish the job!" Do not start projects and never finish them. This includes your education.

"Duties never conflict!"

"The door to success swings on the hinges of opposition."

"When gratitude dies on a man's heart, he is almost hopeless!"

"It is a sin to do less than your best!"

"The measure of your responsibility is measured by your opportunities."

"Simplicity is truth's most becoming garb."

"Beware of the person who bows to his superiors, or is rude to his inferiors."

"The greatest ability is dependability."

"Every dissipation of youth must be paid for with a draft on old age."

"God and one person make a majority in any community!"

"You can do anything that you ought to do."

"Go as far as you can on the right road."

"Back of each of God's commands, He puts His omnipotence!"

"Figure on the worst, but hope for the best."

"Two WRONGS (decisions) do not make a RIGHT! Example: when someone makes a mistake and tries to cover it up with a lie.

"Give God your heart, and He will comb the kinks out of your head!"

Two truth-type sayings I learned as a kid while growing up that stuck with me:

"God gave us two ends!
One to think with, and one to sit on.
It's a case of: Heads you win! Tails you lose!"

"Life is hard, yard by yard!
Inch by inch, it's a cinch!"

I also learned to observe people with a beware alert: "Some people are so heavenly-minded, that they are no earthly good!"

These bedrock truths have shaped my thinking and actions throughout my life. Chapel was a requirement. I spent the first two years listening to Dr. Bob Sr. preach for an hour every day on one of these truths. He told us that we could have different opinions and theological differences, but our focal point should be on serving Jesus in all we do. Dr. Bob had such a down to earth common sense approach! This has given me a solid footing to stand on. My dad, being a Free Will Baptist preacher, had many discussions with other ministers about the possibility of losing your salvation after you become a Christian. This is called Arminianism. Dr. Bob had been a Methodist preacher, with the same corresponding view, before founding Bob Jones University in Cleveland, Tennessee. In Chapel, he said, "We are not here to argue about whether you can lose your salvation or not. Our job is to make sure everyone has a salvation experience. We will leave that up to the theologians and each individual as to whether they can lose it after they get it." I solved this in my own mind with the definitions of the two words: RELATIONSHIP, which is permanent, as in family, and FELLOWSHIP, which is sometimes broken by bad behavior.

That first week, an announcement was made that anyone in music courses should take the "music qualifying" exam on Wednesday. Since Tommy and I were taking song leading and we were enrolled to take a class of voice lessons, we thought that included us too. So, we showed up. The monitors passed out music paper with the treble and bass clef bars printed for us to use to fill in the notes. The professor on the stage started to play notes. He asked us to listen and determine which note it was on the scale. We were then to pencil it in on the proper line. This could be on any line in either the treble or bass clef. We did not have a clue as to what he was talking about. The professor progressed to play chords, major and minor chords. Again we were to fill in several notes on the scales. Tommy and I jokingly filled in notes and laughed throughout the whole test. It was not until after we graduated from Bob Jones University where we viewed an "F" on our transcripts for the music-qualifying exam!

I settled into a routine of going to the library every evening to study because the dorm was pretty noisy. I had no idea that I would ever get an "A" in anything. Imagine my surprise when the dean's list came out and was posted on bulletin boards, and my name was on the all "A"s and "B's list! It is amazing what a little study and concentration with preparation can produce! I was adjusting to a new routine of "lights out" after room prayers. I set my alarm to get up and get to the dining common for one of my jobs serving three tables food for breakfast, lunch, and dinner. This did not last long. By the end of the first month, I owed over $30 in broken dishes! They moved me to serving food in the kitchen. This was great. Servers were not required to wear ties. We were allowed to eat all we wanted as we served ourselves and ate together in the basement. Tommy and I each weighed 135 pounds when we entered college. We had a contest to see who could get to 150 pounds first. I think I had the advantage by eating in the kitchen. We were not allowed to have any kind of stove in the dorm, so we improvised by heating cans of meat under the lavatory faucet running the hot water. We toasted the bread for a sandwich with our iron, which was supposed to iron out wrinkles.

D.D. Elway, my senior roommate from West Virginia, knew the funniest folk songs. I wish I could remember them. He persuaded Tommy and me into joining the Excalibur Literary Society during "Rush" week. He also involved us in playing soccer. I had never seen anyone play the game before this. Tommy became a "fullback" and I merited the job of "goalie." This was before the ruling that prohibited anyone of the opposing team to touch the goalie. That first day of scrimmage as a goalie, I bent over to pick up the soccer ball to throw or kick it back down the field and prevent our opposing team from scoring. Marcus Gacunni, from Greece (I will never forget the name), a 250-pound forward on the other team kicked the ball and me over the goal for a score. D.D ran up to explain, "Norm, you have to get rid of the ball quicker!" Now he tells me!

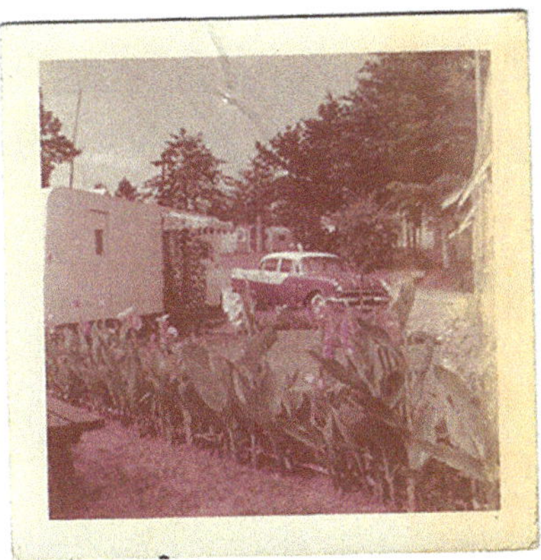

Literary Society's "Excalibur" soccer team with Fullback Tommy Graves and goalie, Norm Ferguson

One of our Excalibur players went on to become famous as a world-wide minister from Korea. I remember him for his dexterity with a soccer ball. We recently reconnected with Billy Kim when he came to Dallas for his children's choir to perform in the George W. Bush Library. Summer Joy and husband, Adam, met him while they were in California.

Another roommate, Mel Bitner, wanted to be an entertainer. In order to build a repertoire of instant retrievable stories, we would challenge each other with one word. Immediately, the other would have to respond with a story or joke related to that word. For example, I would mention a subject, "elephant," or "fisherman," or "wedding," etc. He would then respond with a related story to the subject. This became our mental filing cabinet. This discipline shaped my future ministry with illustrations or stories incorporated in my sermon preparation or even while preaching. Once in a while, in a serious situation like a funeral, a trigger word would cause my mind to dump tons of stories onto my consciousness while speaking! I would have to mentally push back and say, "Not now! Not here!" Those interrupted moments can cause serious loss to your train of thought!

After Chapel each morning, I made my way to the post office to see if I had a letter from Mom. She wrote once a week and always tried to find at least a dollar to include in my letter; sometimes even a five-dollar bill! I kept encountering a brown-eyed young lady each morning in the post office who smiled at me. I did not know her name. I pointed her out to Tommy, and he made inquiries to discover that her name was Mary Jane Riley. She lived in the Ann Margaret dorm. Tommy and I lived in the Graves dorm (not related to Tommy). The school had a mail system to communicate between dorms. Since boys were not allowed to go to a girl's dorm after dinnertime, the Panhellenic council sponsored a mail delivery system that allowed a male student to send a note or package to a young lady in her dorm. A drop box was available in the library and also a mailbox on each floor of the dorms. The council sorted and delivered the mail each evening before room prayer meetings at 10:00 and "lights out" at 11:00 p.m. This system allowed time to scribble a return note and drop it in the box for an early morning delivery also. Behold, the forerunner of texting today. Freshmen could only date in the "dating parlor" on Friday nights. Upper class members could date on more nights. Chaperones were posted in the dating parlor and along the route to the girl's dorms after dinner to make sure there would be no touching, hugging, or kissing during the walk of his girl back to the dorm after. We were also allowed to walk a girl to the dorm after an event, such as an opera or a Shakespearean play. On one occasion, my date stumbled and I grabbed her by the arm. The chaperone saw it and reported it! Both of us had to appear before the discipline committee to argue our case. If a student received 150 demerits within a year's time, that person had to pack up and go home! It was easy to get a demerit. Each room had 3 to 5 students, and each roommate had a cleanup responsibility. These chores rotated about every 3 weeks. The monitor checked each room during breakfast and would write up the person responsible for not cleaning the lavatory or mirror, or for not making his bed properly, or failure to sweep the floor, or empty the trash. One of our favorite jokes was to talk about the girl who got "shipped" home for a hole in her swimming suit...in the knee!

Mary Jane Riley became my date to ask for Shakespeare plays, operas, and Sunday afternoon vespers. Vespers were on a show level that I had never been exposed to in my life. It was a religious Hollywood-type production of music, drama, and inspirational events. The staging, lighting, and sound were on a professional production level. These were produced and directed by the music and drama/speech departments with the cooperation and supervision of the WMUU Radio and movie studios. The experience of working on the stage crew my second year there provided me with some fantastic insight in understanding the production of these events. Mary Jane became "Jane," and we dated on each other's literary outings. These were always fun because it was off campus (still heavily chaperoned), but we were privileged to explore places like Grandfather's Mountain and other such venues away from the campus. Tables at meal times were assigned on a 3-week rotation system. This rotation allowed you to meet different people and greatly expanded your "friends" list. Chapel also had assigned seats. Row captains checked attendance each day. A tie was required for most events like meals, chapel, and vespers. It was customary for a guy to have a clip-on bow tie tucked in his jacket pocket. Such preparation prevented demerits for forgetfulness. Thankfully, the tie did not have to match anything.

I was really homesick that first Thanksgiving. It seemed like 90% of the students left campus and went home. It was too far for us to think about a visit home. So, we really began to look forward to Christmas.

Tommy and I were privileged to go home and visit family during the Christmas holidays. I inquired of my high school sweetheart, Petunia, and was so very disappointed that she had married a guy by the name, Bobby King that fall. After that, being home was sort of boring. I thought about hitchhiking to Illinois to visit that other girl, Jane. Against good judgment and my parent's wishes, I started out on a wild trip to Illinois using my thumb to hitch a ride. My suitcase weighed a ton! Eight hours of hitchhiking placed me just on the north side of Dallas by dark. Finally, a guy in a car stopped and offered me a ride. He was going to Kansas City. I said: "Ok, I'll ride to where the road splits to St. Louis and get out there. About 2:00 a.m., we came to that split in the road. It had been snowing and it was a blizzard outside. I made a quick decision to go on to Kansas City. We arrived there a little after 7:00 a.m. He apologized and said he had to go directly to work. I got out with my heavy suitcase and began to walk across Kansas City. I arrived on the east side of Kansas City on the road toward St. Louis at about 4:00 p.m. I stopped at a service station and the worker informed me that a Greyhound bus was past due. He did not know if it was even running because of the heavy snow. Thankfully, the bus arrived. I got on. The only seat was by a very large man smoking a cigar. I was exhausted and fell asleep immediately. We arrived in St. Louis about 9:30 p.m., and I found the only transportation at that time of night to Jane's house in Cottage Hills, IL. was by taxi. It was past midnight when I arrived and knocked on the door. Thankfully, again, they took me in! The next day, Rev. Clarence Riley, Jane's dad, put me to work nailing insulation in a room he was building over the garage. I do not know whether he wanted to keep me away from his daughter or see if I was a good worker! A couple of days later, Jane's roommate drove up to her house. Five of us piled into the car with luggage everywhere and made our way back to school in Greenville, SC.

Some of my education at Bob Jones University did not happen in the classroom. Tommy and I responded to an invitation to learn how to perform "Gospel Magic" by Dave Hoy, whose father, a professional magician, had taught him slight of hand magic before he became a ministerial student. We had several weekly get-togethers with Dave as he demonstrated to us how to make some of the magic illustrations and where to order others. Another opportunity presented itself with the

WMUU (Worlds Most Unusual University) production of Dr. Bob Jones, Sr.'s new film, "Sin Will Find You Out!" Tommy and I signed up to buy a 16 mm projection system to show the film. We planned to convert our world during the fast-approaching summer by booking our *Movies and Magic* program in all the churches in our part of Texas. This was the summer of 1952. It was a hard sell trying to convince the pastor of a church that *Movies and Magic* had a strong evangelical appeal to win people to Christ. Many flatly refused to allow us to "desecrate" the sanctuary with movies or magic! Some would allow us to present our program if we would agree to do the show in the Fellowship Hall or outside.

At the end of that semester, we came home and I got a job working in the Armour Meat packing plant. Tommy and I booked *Movies & Magic* events at night and on weekends with churches. My job varied from loading freight trains with dog food, peanut butter, pickled pigs' feet, etc., or loading half a beef onto hooks in refrigerated boxcars. At about 150 pounds, I had to hug the beef side, lift it off the hook, and haul it out to the railroad car where I tried to throw it onto a hook hanging in the freight car. I missed more times than I made it. This required my helpers to come to my rescue. They probably requested that I be given another job, and I ended up in the peanut butter processing part. It smelled and tasted much better! The refrigeration pipes throughout the plant leaked poisonous chlorine gas. Some days, we were required to wear a gas mask while working because of the chlorine gas leaks. The summer came to an end, and I did not have enough money to go back to school. I had written home during the past spring semester to Mr. Fred Measures at the First National Bank for a loan to finish the semester. He was so nice and easy to work with. He sent me a one-page form and said, "Fill in the amount you need and we will deposit it into your account." My first few checks from the meat-packing job went to pay that $600 back. I continued to work until Christmas and felt that I had enough money to make it back to school for the spring semester. It turned out to be just in the nick of time! Mom sent me the draft board notice that I was to appear for duty and fight in the Korean War. I wrote to them and asked for a student deferment. They upgraded me to a 4-D student. This allowed me to finish school.

On May 8th, Jane got the shocking news that her 46-year-old father had passed away with a stroke. She drove home for the service. While home, I got a notice from the school switchboard to call her. She shared some sobering news on the phone. "The deacons here at Mt. Sterling First Baptist Church know you are a ministerial student and would like for you to come and be the pastor here for the summer." In the next sentence, she said, "My mother says if you come, we should get married since we will be in the same house together." I think her mother was trying to get rid of the responsibility of paying for one of her daughter's college education. Her older daughter, Martha, was married, and Gloria and Sharon were still in middle school. I do not remember much discussion about marriage prior to this! I had two sermons in my file of sermons! My first thoughts were, "The summer is 13 weeks long! This would require me to prepare three messages or sermons a week. Oh my gosh! That is nearly forty sermons! Where would I get that many sermons?" So many questions...and then she said, "We can get married on June 7th when we get out of school. I was not mature enough or experienced enough for such a decision. At that point, it did not dawn on me that I had a choice. Looking back, this was one of the forks in the road where I took the wrong road. Under pressure, I consented. Mom & Dad met us in Illinois, and Dad performed our wedding ceremony. I stayed with the Steinbecks until the wedding. We went on a honeymoon about four hours away on a lake. I have no idea of the location of that lake. We had to be back for the Wednesday night's service, and I had to prepare my first two sermons for Sunday. Then, Vacation Bible School was scheduled to begin on Monday! This rude awakening to reality made me grow up overnight!

Chapter Five:

MT. STERLING, ILLINOIS: 1953-1954

My first pastorate: First Baptist Church, Mt. Sterling, Illinois

The people in Mt. Sterling were such patient and wonderful people. They were supportive and encouraging. Our youth program mushroomed, and we won the attendance rally of our Baptist association in Quincy, IL. almost every month.

Not knowing what to teach on Wednesday nights, I asked the congregation what they wanted to study. Their response was "The Book of Revelation." Preparation for this study took most of my time reading, researching, and making a time chart on a roll of wallpaper. This visual timeline of the events of the last days of prophetic happenings in the Book of Revelation required more time than the preparation of both Sunday messages!

We booked some outstanding evangelists for revivals! Rev. O.W. Stuckey preached and provided special music every night by playing hymns on a carpenter's saw with a violin bow. He also helped teach the same choruses that I had learned in Youth for Christ to our congregation. In another revival, the evangelist was invited into the public school systems to speak to the high school students and also the grade school students. We were in a severe winter with lots of snow. He invited the grade school students to walk over to the church for an afternoon of Bible games and fun and assured the students riding the bus that "Pastor Norm will give you a ride home!" On two of those days, I ended up in the ditch from driving kids home on slick roads. Both times, a neighbor with a tractor would have mercy, come, and pull me out. The evening service was nearly over by the time I got back to the church! We really had some wonderful results of many people accepting the Lord as their Savior. At the request of a wife, I went to visit her husband, Harvey Butler. He usually drove an oil delivery truck, but the day I went to visit him, his eighth grade daughter, Beth, said he was up in the attic putting in insulation. I climbed up the ladder into the attic and started talking to him. It was hotter than Hades in that attic. Both of us were sweating profusely. Harvey said, "Preacher, you're going to melt up here; let's go down and get a glass of tea." We did, and to everyone's surprise, he came nearly every night of the revival. Toward the middle of the second week, he came forward and made his profession of faith. He was followed by his son and two daughters, his wife's mother and father, her brother, his wife, and their two kids. Another family, a dairy farmer, came with his family of seven kids. He told me his story. "I have been a Catholic, but the church keeps assessing and hounding me for money that I don't have. How much money am I required to give to be saved and become a Baptist?" It was a joy to help him understand the love and grace of God and that Jesus paid the price of his salvation. I told him that the Bible teaches ten percent of our income belongs to God, but in reality, all that we have comes from God and we give whatever we can because of a grateful heart.

Don McCoy was a most helpful deacon in the church. He was quite a tease! He missed a Sunday and I told him that we missed him. He said, "Well, the ox was in the ditch, so I had to get him out." My reply: "That's ok so long as you did not push him in the ditch in order for you to stay home and get him out."

Sharon Lane was a beautiful hardworking teen, whose single mother worked hard and raised wonderful kids. Three Reisch families were faithful supporters. I still have e-mails from Helen, whose mom, Lucille, was such an inspiring and faithful supporter of our ministry. We stayed in touch with Lucille until she passed away in her nineties. The eighth grade girl, Beth, and her husband, Don, have just passed away the past couple of years. They were so faithful in keeping up with us.

My first funerals, weddings, and baptisms took place in this little church! I think any historian recording these fifteen months would probably describe it under the heading of "how to persecute the saints."

MY WEDDINGS: Let me tell you of a couple of these fiascos. On the Monday morning after we got married, I was running around without a clue as to what I was doing, directing my first Vacation Bible School, when a young man walked into the church. I greeted him, "How can I help you?" He said, "I want to get married." So I said "When?" He emphatically said, "NOW! I am in the service and only have a 10-day leave." Thankfully, you cannot see my shock or consternation. I tried to act calm and told him to have a seat with his bride-to-be. I hurried to the parsonage and ran upstairs to the study that had been my father-in-law's. I began to frantically search for a wedding ceremony. I found a *Minister's Star* book with funeral and wedding services. I think I must have used the Episcopal ceremony on that first wedding, because it went on and on and on! I filled out their license and they went on their way. The next week, we were still in Vacation Bible School, and he showed up again. I greeted him with, "How is the married couple doing?" "Well, that's what we need to talk to you about. The clerk in Brown County where we bought our license said we were not legally married. You are in Schyler County, and the law says that we have to get married in the same county where we purchased our license." So, I got in the car, we drove across the county line, and I remarried the couple. This time, I used a shorter ceremony!

Then there was my first BIG church wedding. The couple wanted a church wedding in August. It was HOT! The church had no air conditioning. The Saturday night rehearsal went well. On Sunday afternoon, the church filled up. There were two aisles. The pastor and groomsmen came down one aisle, and the bride and bridesmaids went to the altar down the other. Waiting with the groomsmen in the foyer, I looked around and said, "Where is the groom?" "Oh, he forgot the license and went back to get it." I thought, "Oh no! He lives 10 miles out in the country!" Sure enough, he was twenty minutes late getting back. By then, everyone in the church was sweating and fanning. The small boy and girl candlestick lighters proceeded to the stage where they were to light the candles. They had taken a cigarette lighter with them to light the lighter. After flicking the lighter unsuccessfully, they came back down the aisle and got some matches. Finally, I started the procession. I proceeded to the front of the stage as the music played. I was followed by the best man and groomsmen. Then the bridesmaids came. As the beautiful bride came down on the arm of her father to the tune of the bridal march, they dutifully stopped just a step back from the groom. I spoke, "Who gives this woman to be wed to this man?" His nervous answer: "Her father and mother and me." The nervous groom did not wait for the father to place her arm in his, but turned and took her by the arm. The problem was they were now facing the audience. I waited for them to turn around for what seemed forever! Finally, I lowered my head and poked him in the back with my ceremony book and whispered, "Turn around." They turned, and in doing so without dropping arms, he swung her to the groom's side. He was with the bridesmaids. I left well enough alone and proceeded. I was relieved when I came to the conclusion, " You may kiss the bride!" During the kiss, Mrs. Steinbeck, playing the organ, began the strong and loud notes of the recessional music. The couple turned and started down the aisle. Relieved, I stepped back, kicking the organ plug on the floor behind me. The organ died with a great groan! The people broke out laughing and applauding!

BAPTISMS: The baptistry was located under the floor of the preaching platform. Part of the flooring was on a hinge that laid back and exposed the concrete baptistry. A white sheet was placed over the flooring door, and a spray of flowers garnished the middle with fake green grass around to give the appearance of an open grave. We had curtains on each side that were drawn and shut between individuals being baptized. One side was the dressing area for the women, and the other side was for the men. There was only one stair into the baptistry; on the ladies' side. My first candidate was a young man, Ivan, who walked with a limp. I motioned that he was next, and turned toward the stairs to wait for him to come down the steps. Suddenly, I was drenched! He had stepped off on the side with no steps. I think we did a Methodist-type baptizing of half the congregation that night with the splash he made. The next candidate was Elmer Steinbeck, president of our bank in town. He was a very distinguished bald-headed gentleman with a fringe of gray hair above the ears. He was also our men's Sunday School Bible teacher. One Sunday, he came down the aisle and I asked him what his decision was. He said, "I want to be baptized." Shocked, I said, "I thought you were already a member here. You teach our men's Bible class, your wife is the organist, and your boys have both grown up here." "Well, no, actually, I am a Presbyterian. I kept thinking my mom would be disappointed if I became a Baptist. She is in her 90's now, so I guess she has accepted the fact that I really am a Baptist. I have never met the requirement of being "buried in a watery grave." Now, Elmer made his way down the steps into the baptistry. As I laid him back in the water, his head hit the corner of one of the wooden steps in the baptistry. He came up dazed, shook his head, and sputtered. The next day in the bank, he had a Band-Aid on his bald-headed "baptism wound." People kept asking, "Elmer, what happened?" His answer, "Well, the young preacher told me baptism would really make an impression on me! Little did I know what kind of impression he was talking about!"

FUNERALS: This is a very important part of a minister's responsibility, and after hundreds of funerals, it is still my least favorite. A policeman knocked on the parsonage door about 2:30 a.m. I staggered sleepily to the door in my pajamas. He looked at me and said, "Is your dad here?" I said, "No, sir." Well, I need to speak to the pastor of the church." So I replied, "You're looking at all they have." He told me to get dressed. We had to deliver an accidental death message. There had been an accident where Mrs. Brooks' daughter had been killed in a car wreck. This left the 8-year-old daughter in the custody of the grandmother, Mrs. Brooks. I will never forget that night! Similar events happened. A teen, driving home, hit a horse on the road, and she was killed instantly. There were other funerals that were like "home goings." Mr. Givens was in his 80s and had a full head of white hair and a large mustache. He never missed a church service and was popular with the kids as he handed out candy and gum. We celebrated at his funeral too. I had the funeral of the oldest deacon of the church. I only met him once before he passed away. In that get-acquainted time, he played "In the Sweet Bye and Bye" on his violin for me.

While in Mt. Sterling, I learned a lot about corn because most of my members grew acres of it. I also inherited a great bed of asparagus that Rev. Riley had prepared. I found the joy of hunting for edible mushrooms in the woods and cooking them in such a way so as to make them taste as good as steak! Our brotherhood had squirrel stew a couple of times. They sold jars of it to raise money for projects.

Jane's mother moved out to an old house nearby, but it did not have a good kitchen. I had learned a bit from my carpenter dad and volunteered to build cabinets and make a kitchen out of one of the bedrooms. In this endeavor, the cabinets turned out well, and I gained a bit of plumbing experience. Glenda Riley, with her two young girls, Gloria and Sharon, stayed in Mt. Sterling when we returned to Bob Jones University. About a year later, she followed and bought a lot near Greenville, SC, where she built a new home. Jane got a job with the new school near her mother and had the opportunity to teach, organize, and direct a new band at the Blue Ridge High School. This is where Sharon met and fell in love with one of my favorite brother-in-laws, Bud Turner. The same kids in Jane's band were the football players. She and the coach made an agreement. That first year, a football player could stay out on the field in his pads and play an instrument in the marching band.

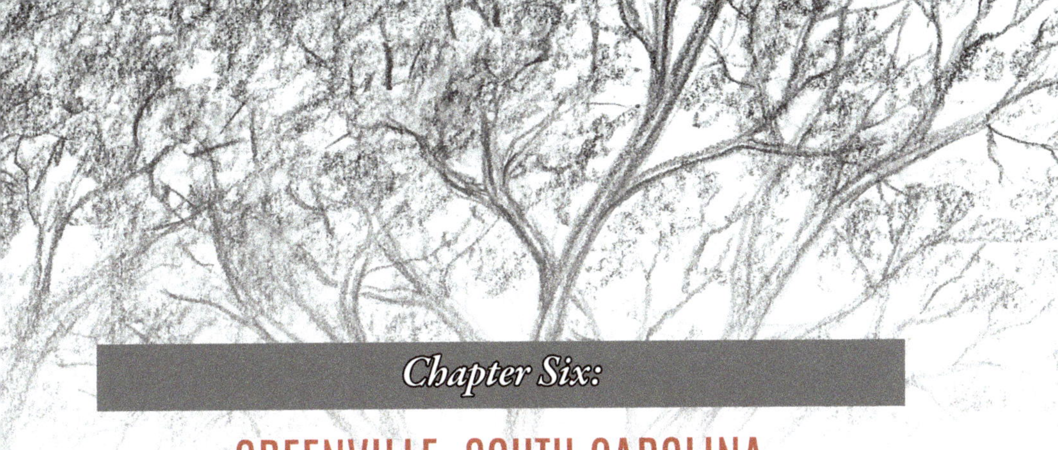

Chapter Six:

GREENVILLE, SOUTH CAROLINA, BJU 1954-1956

When Jane and I got back to school, we had saved money and were able to buy a brand new 1955 Pontiac and a mobile home across from the school. She acquired the band director's job for half a day of teaching. She then went to school the other half. I bought a bakery route. This required getting up at 2:00 a.m., loading donuts, pies, and goodies into my panel truck to run the first route to restaurants and textile mills. I came back to the bakery about 7:00 a.m. to reload and go on my second route. I tried to finish by 11:00 a.m. when my classes were scheduled until 4:30 p.m. We then ate, studied a bit, and went to bed. Repeat, repeat, repeat. Prior to the bakery route, I tried an early morning paper route. This did not produce the income we needed. My old delivery truck had poor tread on the tires. One rainy morning, I was driving around a mountain and my truck started skidding and spinning. It slammed into the rock mountainside near Honea Path. The truck spun some more, hitting the mountainside again and again. I kept on spinning and banging. On the first impact, my head hit the dash where the little clock was mounted. This blow cut around my eye, cheek, and nose. I thought, if this truck would only stop, I might live through this. Finally, the truck came to rest, and my foot hurt pretty badly where it had struck the brake pedal and broke it off. At first glance, my foot looked bloody. I panicked, thinking I may have cut my foot off. On closer examination, it was only strawberries from the pie tarts that had made a mess on my shoe. I got out. The road and the mountainside were splattered with pies and meringue. I hitched a ride into the next little town, and the service station attendant said, "You have some nasty cuts. There is a doctor who lives about three houses up that street. I knocked, and the doctor came to the door. He was not interested in being aroused at such an early hour and told me to go to the hospital. I hung around the station until almost noon. Finally, the attendant said that he had a car that needed to be delivered to Greenville. I took it and went to the hospital first. While getting stitches, a policeman came in and questioned me about the wreck. He threatened to give me a ticket for "leaving the scene of an accident."

When summer came, we had time to work on our mobile home a bit. I painted the outside using our vacuum cleaner and a fruit farm sprayer of paint. We took the cabinets out to move a piano into the back bedroom for Jane to practice her piano. She was preparing for her senior recital. One neighbor was an avid hunter with the bow and arrow. Barbara Bales and her friend, Lindsey, lived on the other side of us. Behind us lived some of our best lifelong friends, George "Alabama" and Barbara Henderson. While I was sitting in their mobile home with my back to the open door, except for the screen door, the old TV was on. Barbara was watching a live birth on their small TV. Someone bumped the "rabbit ears" on the table and her TV picture went askew. She jumped up across me to get the picture back and physically knocked me over backward and out the door into the yard!

While carrying an armload of meringue pies into a restaurant, I stepped on half a brick and turned my ankle. Pies went everywhere, and I ended up doing my route on crutches. Shortly after this, I was at Blue Ridge High School, waiting for Jane to finish band practice. I saw activity at the shop department of the school and hobbled over on my crutches to observe. Some of the boys were having difficulty getting the garage door to close. It seemed to hang about halfway down. I finally stepped forward and bragged, "Let me show you how to do it!" Leaning on my good foot, I threw the door up and then pulled down with all my strength. The door came down like a bolt of lightning and never hit any resistance! It crushed my good foot because I could not put weight on the other foot with the crutches. Now I was really crippled! This required someone to travel with me each day to deliver my bakery goods. I had also turned an ankle three years before while working in the kitchen and slipped on greasy steps going down into the basement to eat. I had also turned and sprained both ankles playing basketball.

I was on crutches a lot the second semester of my senior year. In my speech class, I had performed a five-person dialogue of the reading, "Justice and Little Boys." My speech teacher recommended that I enter the Declamation contest. I won first place in the contest. This award placed me under the coaching of the head of the speech department because the winner was scheduled to give the winning Declamation speech at commencement. My coach said, "Do you want a wheelchair to do your reading monologue at commencement?" I said, "No, I should be well by then." She was so excited and said, "You mean you can walk? I thought you were handicapped because I have never seen you when you were not on crutches."

Chapter Seven:

ALTON, ILLINOIS, COTTAGE HILLS COMMUNITY-SUMMER OF 1956

After graduation, Jane and I traveled to Illinois to live with her sister Martha and Uncle Charlie. He was another of my favorite brother-in-laws! Jane got a job working in the Owen Illinois Glass Works Company where nearly all of Uncle Charlie's family worked. I got a job with the Salle Brothers in Alton, Illinois, near St. Louis. They owned a lumber yard, a granary, and a large appliance store. We installed refrigerators, stoves, and a many GE air conditioners. Some days, I worked trying to unload lumber from a freight boxcar where the lumber had flown around due to a jolt when one car jammed into another. The lumber resembled a big box of fiddle sticks. It was like working a puzzle to find a piece of lumber that did not have a ton of other pieces on top of it. On another day, I would shovel wheat in a large elevator grain storage unit. The second day, I was transferred to a different storage unit and immediately had an asthma attack. I came out and asked what was different about that wheat than the other wheat bin that I had worked in the day before. The manifest showed this unit was "Wheat with wild garlic." The asthma attack necessitated me to take off work for a couple of days. Coming back to work, I was assigned to be Dwayne's helper. Dwayne was a companion of Uncle Charlie's brother, Raymond. Raymond also worked at Owen Illinois Glass and weighed about 450 pounds. He sat in a special chair and drank a full case of beer (24 cans) every night. When he got to 600 pounds, they did a gastric bypass of his stomach until he lost down to about 280. As soon as they reconnected his stomach, he went to that enormous weight again. Dwayne was something else! I learned not to get close if we were working in an electric fuse box. He would touch an open circuit and then reach over with his other hand and touch my ear, shocking me cross-eyed! We delivered appliances in an old blue Dodge truck. Every fender was dented from his driving. At a four-way stop, he almost dared anyone to venture out before their turn. He yelled and cursed at anyone in his way. On a rainy day, we had a delivery to make in St. Louis, located in a very nice neighborhood. We were to install a "thin line" GE air conditioner in a house, which had asbestos siding or shingles on the outside. Muddy and wet, we rang the doorbell. A timid lady came to the door. When we told her of our assignment, she delayed us long enough to spread papers on all of her carpeted areas so we would not get mud on her carpet. She escorted us into a bedroom. She could not decide which wall would be best for the location of the air conditioner. Dwayne was not paying her much attention. He was connecting the skill saw to an outlet, and started the saw with a loud roar. Then he swiped the saw across the wall, cutting a large gash! "How about right there, ma'am?" I thought she would faint! She hurried out of the room. It was an all-day job, especially with the outside asbestos shingles. The siding was almost impossible to cut without breaking. When we got back to Salle Brothers, we received an earful from the boss about how we had upset the poor lady.

A lot of our work was delivering appliances to apartment buildings. Many of these were up two or three flights of stairs. One such assignment required moving an old refrigerator with a large and heavy gas unit on top of the refrigerator. I was going down the steps at the bottom, and Dwayne had the top holding the dolly. He yelled, "I can't hold it! Look out!" I jumped onto the side of the old refrigerator as it crashed into the wall at the bottom of the stairs and caused serious damage!

This summer job offered the rare opportunity when the four brother-in-laws got together for a hunting trip. Jane's older sister's husband, Uncle Charlie, Gloria's husband, Uncle Ian, and Sharon's husband, Uncle Bud Turner, all embarked on a hunting trip. We explored the woods between the Mississippi and Missouri Rivers. We did not find a lot of game to shoot, but we enjoyed the camaraderie and fellowship of each other. About noon, we came upon the dilapidated ruins of an old log cabin. Hardly anything remained of the building, but steps to an old cellar produced an antique wine press. The feet of the press were rotted but otherwise intact. I expressed a desire to have this old relic. Uncle Charlie, a BIG guy, grabbed the largest piece. We each had a part to lug back over a mile to the car. This antique has now been in the family for over fifty years. Much later in time, Jenny surprised me one birthday when she had the feet of the instrument restored. As a minister, many eyebrows have been raised when they heard the preacher has a wine press!

Summer was coming to an end. I had to make a choice between Northern Seminary in Chicago and Southwestern Baptist Theological Seminary in Fort Worth. Another fork in the road! The choice of the road to Texas was a very good one! Lucky us, we found an upstairs apartment owned by one of my professors. Before we could start school, my dad and I had to make a trip back to Greenville, SC to pack our furniture and sell the mobile home. While we were away for the summer, the roof had developed a leak, and the flooring made of particleboard had come apart. The piano was about to fall through the floor. We put new flooring down, took the cabinets apart again to get the piano out, and finally sold the unit. Two days later, about ten miles out of Dallas, the trailer with our furniture blew a tire and ruined the rim. We had to spend the night in the car. We finally got another rim and tire and were back on the road before noon. I do not know how many times we drove around Dallas on Loop 12, but after about 4 hours, Dad said, "I think I have seen that particular business earlier today."

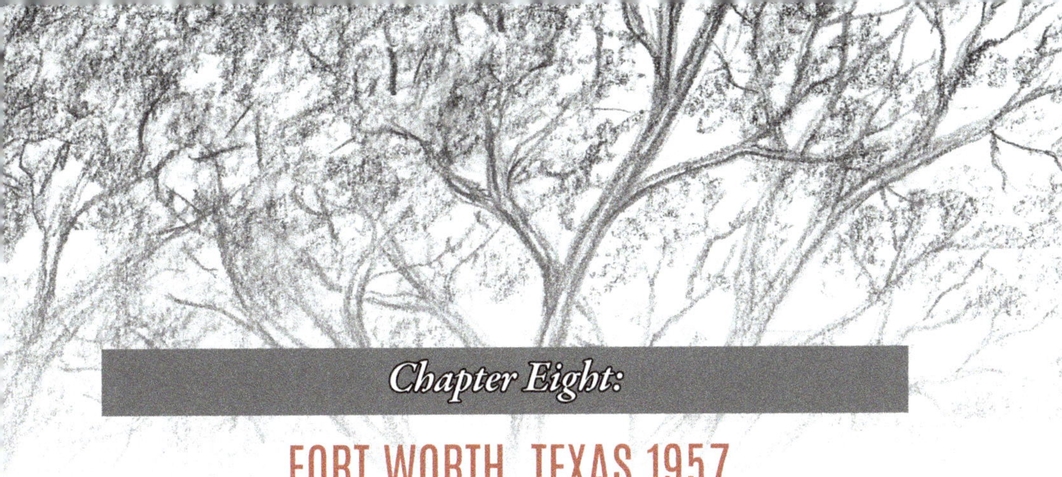

Chapter Eight:

FORT WORTH, TEXAS 1957

Move to Midlothian, Texas 1957–1959

We arrived at our apartment across the street from Southwestern Baptist Theological Seminary after dark. What a surprise to find the couple in the apartment below us were former Bob Jones University friends, Dan and Dottie McGinlay. Dan's father was the famous annual Bible week speaker from Scotland. When Dr. McGinlay came to BJU for a Bible conference, he would kid during his lectures that his boys were always "campused" (restricted to campus for bad behavior) and he could never take them anywhere off campus while he was there. Jane got a job teaching in the Fort Worth public school system. She got sick and missed several days of teaching. One day, Dottie came down to check on her and found her unconscious. We took her to the doctor twice. She found no relief, and he only gave her painkillers. Our landlord's doctor was recommended, so we changed doctors. He recognized the problem at once and ordered her to have emergency surgery. She had a tube pregnancy and it was apt to burst at any moment.

I thought that I had learned to study at BJU, and compared to high school, I suppose I did. Seminary shot me into a stratosphere of learning and hard work I never dreamed that I was capable of performing. Pop quizzes came almost daily, and term papers requiring over 100 pages each were common. On top of these came the learning of the Greek language plus some Hebrew. We had to roam through aisles of dusty books of antiquity doing research. This was before the days of the IBM Selectric typewriter. The computer had not been thought of yet! Imagine doing a research paper and not allowing enough space at the bottom of the page to do all of the footnotes. Some nights, the paper on the floor was more than the pages that I could keep! Often, I would finish the paper just in time to shower and hit the road for class.

We only had four days of classes, Tuesdays through Fridays. Saturdays and Mondays were travel days for ministerial students who had to travel on weekends to their churches. That fall, I was leading singing in a revival with Rev. T.D. Hall. A lady was visiting her daughter and came to one of the services. She came up afterward and wanted to know what church I was working in. I told her that I did not have any church home yet and was just a student attending SWBTS. She went back to First Baptist Church in Midlothian, Texas, and the next week, a committee was at our apartment inviting me to come and be their music and youth director. We had been attending the Birchman Avenue Baptist Church, but soon moved to a duplex in Midlothian. About a year later, we moved to a very large two-story house with covered porches on two sides and a nice greenhouse. While living there, I bought some used books from a little lady. Flipping through the pages of *The Works of Josephus*, I found twenty-dollar bills scattered among various pages, about 10 of them. I really got my money's worth out of that book. A tornado tore part of our garage roof off next to that old house. But we were far better off than one of our church members who lost their pickup truck and their house. They found the motor of the pickup about half a mile away. A sink in the barn ended up inside where the house once stood. A check lying on the breakfast table with nothing to hold it down was still in place. The telephone poles and fence posts had pieces of grass driven into them that resembled hair transplants. The wife in the family suffered a broken leg when a door fell on her. Tornados are phenomena that certainly deserve your undivided attention!

We did get a few breaks between classes at seminary, and I loved to challenge some of my buddies to a ping-pong game. There was Dan McGinlay, Al Laymon, "Hinney" Hinman from Flint, Michigan, and Frank Pollard, who later became famous as the pastor of the First Baptist Church in Jackson, MS. He also became the president of

Golden Gate Seminary. We met frequently in the local coffee shop, about a block off campus on McCart Street. Texas was in the midst of experiencing a severe drought when we got to the seminary campus. There was hardly any live grass or living shrub anywhere on the grounds. Walking through the rotunda of Scarborough Hall one day, a nice older gentleman stopped me and asked how I was adjusting to seminary life. I replied that the classes were challenging, but so far, I was really learning a lot and enjoying it. "Good, grab a root and hang on," he said as he walked away. I later found out that I had been talking to the president of the seminary.

My organist at First Baptist Church in Midlothian was James Goad. He worked at the Texas State Highway Department, which happened to be about 3 blocks from the seminary. His mom cooked dinner for about 30 people every Sunday after church. James had me come to the highway department to be interviewed for a job in his department. I became the head of the nighttime printing department. I ran the photocopier, Mylars, Sepias, and Ammonia prints of the right-of-way maps. I learned to operate the ABC Dick memo-graph machine, Thermo-Fax, and blue line machines. Entrusted with a key, I often worked until midnight to catch up on all the miles of maps that had to be printed for public hearings. I played cupid for James and Lila, the secretary of the department. James was an old bachelor of 40 years when they got engaged. It was a joy to perform their ceremony.

Pastor M.B. Baldwin had been a sergeant in the Army. He had three boys. I cut their hair every other week. One Sunday, as I was teaching a Sunday School class in the choir loft, Pastor Baldwin had gone into the attic for something. He fell through the choir ceiling above my startled class. One of the members wanted to know if he was practicing for the Rapture. The pastor wanted to relocate his office to a space above the church office. James and I volunteered to work on making the move. We did not think it necessary to call the phone company to move a telephone connection. It seemed easy enough to transfer a three-wire connection to another room. I was bending the third wire with my teeth (not recommended) when the phone rang! It lit up my eyeballs and rang bells in my head! The jolt sent electric shock waves through my body! This is how I made the discovery that the current necessary for the ring of a phone increases the voltage going through the wire exponentially!

Saturday nights were *Youth Nights* at the church. We reached a lot of the community youth through our organized games and competition. While I was there, the church wanted to ordain me to the ministry. Wayne and Betty West were two young people that married and came to my first pastorate in Corsicana. He was a pharmacist, and they helped organize our young married couples' class. For my ordination into the ministry, I asked Dr. T. Hollis Epton, pastor of the First Baptist Church in Waxahatchie, to give the charge. My former pastor of the Birchman Avenue Baptist Church in Fort Worth, Dr. Charles Osborn, was head of the council. After the questioning of my doctrinal beliefs, Dr. Epton got up to give the charge. I anticipated a long sermon. To my surprise, he said, "Norman, I only have one illustration to share with you. Listen closely and it could save you a lot of heartache and misery." He then proceeded to tell his story, "When I was a kid, I loved to go home with my grandparents after church on Sunday. My granddad owned some cattle, and while grandma prepared dinner, he said, 'Let's go check on the cows.' We walked across the fields and down into the creek. I loved to jump from rock to rock along the creek. Suddenly, I slipped and one foot hit the mud and splattered it all over the bottom of my Sunday pants. I knew Mom would be upset, so I started to try and brush it out. He grabbed my hand and said, 'Don't touch it!' We walked on and he counted all his cows. We finally got back to the house. I was really ready to eat now. Then he turned to me and said, 'Now brush your pants off!' To my amazement, the mud had dried and it dusted right out." Then Dr. Epton said, "There will be many times in life, perhaps in your marriage or in your church business, where things are going to be 'a mess!' You will be tempted to rush in and try to solve it immediately. Have the presence of mind to back off and let the situation dry out a bit before trying to correct it." This is some of the best advice that I was ever given.

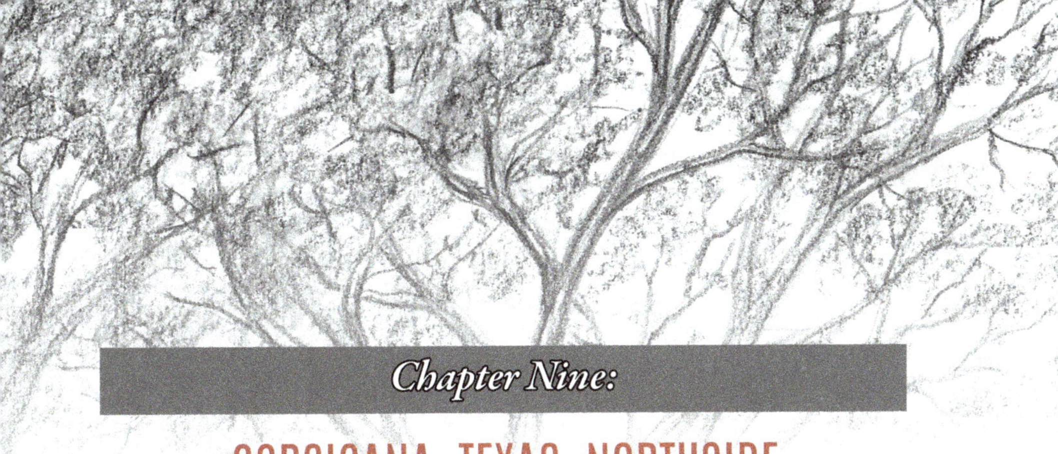

Chapter Nine:

CORSICANA, TEXAS, NORTHSIDE BAPTIST CHURCH 1959-1963

Upon graduation from SWBTS in 1959, I was notified that Dr. Charles Osborn had recommended me to the Northside Baptist Church in Corsicana, Texas. After the trial sermon, PaPa John and Lou Spencer took us out for lunch. He told me that he owned the Cattle Barn in town and ran an auction once a month selling cattle. The waitress came to our table and was taking our order. I did not want to appear too extravagant, so I said "I'll have the fried chicken." He interrupted, "No, you won't, not on my ticket. I'm a beef man; it's either steak or hamburger!" "Yes, sir, I understand. I'll have the steak." It was my good fortune to follow a very popular preacher at Northside Baptist by the name of Rev. Bob Cheek. He had moved on to the First Baptist Church in Baytown. I heard so much about him that I invited him back on two different occasions for revivals. He blended in with people like he was part of their family. I learned a great deal watching him relate to people. I was a member of the Kiwanis Club and took him to be a guest speaker at the club at noon. I gave him this introduction: "Last week, we had a doctor speak to us on birth control. This week, I invited a layman expert to give us his view on this subject (Bob had seven kids). With everyone laughing at my humor, he got up and said, "I'm not Catholic, just a very passionate Protestant!"

Jane became pregnant again and showed signs of a miscarriage (we had gone through five miscarriages already and were destined to lose another baby boy in Tyler). The doctor ordered her to bed. I took meals to her, gave her a bedpan because she was not even allowed to get up and go to the bathroom. It was a long 9 months! One night, she said, "I believe my water broke." I rushed her to the hospital and Dr. Hansford delivered our beautiful redheaded daughter, Lori Lynette. As she got older, and people asked, "Where did you get your red hair?" She would answer, "K-Mart!" Passing the cemetery, she exclaimed, "There's heaven!" When I questioned her, she said, "Well, that is where people go when they die!" Near Mother Frances Hospital, she saw a nun and priest in their religious garb and declared, "There's Mary and Joseph!"

Many of our elderly members entered the nursing home a couple of blocks from our church. Pauline Stubbs, owner of the nursing home, was a member of our church. She made several sizeable contributions to the church's special needs, such as curtains for the baptism opening behind the choir. She called me, day or night, when one of our members was in critical condition. I would go read a few verses of Scripture and have prayer with the patient. More times than I like to remember, while holding hands with my friend and fellow church member, the elderly patient would take their last breath. As hard as this was on me, it was even harder when I was the one who had to go to a family and break the news that their loved one had passed on to their eternal reward!

Brother Miley, our older custodian, was quite entertaining. I discovered water on the floor near the low brick flower wall hiding the organ from the congregation. I showed him water on the floor and asked if he thought we had a leak somewhere. He admitted that he had been watering the flowers in the flowerbed to keep them alive. The flowers were artificial! While hanging a picture of my art class lettering of John 3:16 where I had burned the edges and oil-treated it to give it an antique appearance and had it framed in wormwood, he remarked, "Preacher, this is hardly worth salvaging or hanging on the wall! It is nearly burned up, and something has eaten up the frame!"

Northside Baptist Church began to grow. We had an outstanding young couples' class that met at the parsonage every Sunday night following the evening service to play "42," Dominoes, cards, etc. We had so many kids running around while we were talking and playing mostly "42" that we hired about 4 of our youth to take the kids outside to play games. We reached some of the new leadership moving into Corsicana. Our nursery was overrun with babies. I took some of the deacons back to the nursery one Sunday morning to show them how crowded we were. The drawer on two chests of drawers had been pulled out to make beds, and a baby was in each drawer! Under the direction of Jerry Forderhase, our choir attracted many talented singers. His lovely wife, Mary Frances, had the most beautiful voice! When she performed a patriotic program for our Kiwanis Club featuring her beautiful voice, she received a standing ovation! We attracted the history professors at Navarro College, Dr. Ed Byrd and his wife, Marty. Both made great contributions to the choir. The Trammels moved from across town to become our dynamic Training Union directors. There were some really good, down-to-earth deacons. "PaPa" Spencer was chairman. Supporting deacons included Bill "Slim" Bolen and his wife, Beth. United States Postman, Joe Hambrick, and his wife, Faye Nell, were steady and dependable leaders. I really stood in awe of my retired pro golfer, Gilbert Stubbs. There were seven Stubbs brothers. Three were sign painters and four were house painters. They claimed that the family was like rabbits–they all took to the brush! Gilbert could draw or paint equally well with either hand! He really enhanced my golf game with his wise tutoring. About three times a week, he would come by the office at about 4:00 and take me to the country club. The club was only about five minutes from our church. Most afternoons, we only played a few holes of golf. With his help, I was able to score in the high 70s and low 80s. There was another golf course on the main highway, and it had nine holes of sand greens. This fit my pocketbook better, so this was the chosen location to play often with another one of my new deacons, Tom Boecking. We enjoyed each other's company and the bantering that goes on between golfers. After I hit a ball into a pond of water, he said, "Preacher, the reason you hit that ball in the water was because you hit an old ball. You should take out a new ball and that would show you have the confidence to hit it across the water." He talked me into taking out a new ball. Guess what? I hit my new ball into the water! He laughed. One day, Tom's ball rolled under a low hanging tree limb. Trying to be a good friend, I said, "Wait a minute, Tom." I went over and grabbed the limb and pulled it back to give him room to take a good unhindered swing with his club. I was holding a handful of leaves and on his downswing, the leaves pulled loose. The limb hit him broadside and he dubbed the ball about three feet. He beat the club into the ground and never looked up as he said, "Preacher, don't ever offer to help me again." Laughing so hard, I had a hard time trying to convince him that it was an accident, that the leaves broke in my hand. He never let me forget that incident and told everyone that I was not to be trusted.

I grew up with the strange ritual that required relatives, friends, or neighbors to "sit up with the corpse" when one of the family members died. I remember that my dad did this often when a member of one of those country churches passed away. One of our deacons at Northside had died and men were signing up to "sit" with the corpse. No one volunteered for the hours of 1:00 a.m. to 4:00 a.m. One of the deacons said, "Ask the preacher to sit those hours." When they asked me, I responded positively. After all, I was always looking for some quiet hours to study and this would be ideal. I arrived at Corley Funeral Home a bit before 1:00 a.m. and relieved those who had been sitting. After walking through the adjoining rooms, I settled on a nice comfortable couch across from the coffin where our deacon lay in repose. The quiet was eerie! Every so often, the silence would erupt with a muffled "buluup!" sound. This caught my attention to the point that I got up and walked over to see if the sound was coming from the coffin! It was not. I waited, listening. And then it sounded again and seemed to be coming from the hallway. I cautiously crept down the hall and stopped at the chamber that housed the organ. The strange "buluup" noise seemed to be coming from back of the organ chamber near a door that led to the preparation room where the director embalmed the body. I do not know why, but curiosity caused me to proceed forward. At the door, the "buluup" sound came again and was right under my right elbow! I looked down and found the coffee pot percolating! Somewhat relieved, I sat down and drank a cup, even though, up until now, I had never been a coffee drinker!

Mr. Corley got into a bad habit of calling on me to conduct services of anyone who did not have any church affiliation. After a couple of years of free service, riding with him to a cemetery for another free funeral, I brought up the subject. "Why do you include fees to pay the organist, florist, singer, and others, but nothing for the minister who spends time visiting the family and who takes a couple of days from his duties as a minister to his own congregation?" He was thoughtful for a moment and then said, "When we get back, I have something for you." When we got back to his establishment, we went up the elevator to a very large room of coffins on display. To one side was a row of suits, arranged in various sizes and colors. "Take your pick!" I politely declined his generous offer!

My extracurricular assignment from the Baptist Association in Navarro County was to find money to pay off the property across from the Navarro Junior College and raise money to build a Baptist Student Center on the land. I visited all of the various associations and large churches in areas outside of Navarro County where some of their youth were attending the Navarro College. I made appeals for each to include our project in their annual budgets on the basis of how many students they had at Navarro Junior College. We started building within two years, and I had the privilege of being the first Bible teacher on campus. This was my introduction into student ministry. I found more satisfaction and fulfillment doing this than being pastor of a church. At about the same time, Jane and I were being interviewed by the Southern Baptist Foreign Mission Board in Richmond, Virginia, to go to Japan as missionaries. We were almost to the appointment phase when their requirement of a medical exam showed that I had scar tissue on my stomach. They were concerned that this may be an active ulcer or one that had healed and left scars. I went into the hospital for a week of tests and a bland diet plus a little pill that dried me up so much that I could not even prime myself to spit! The result was our appointment was deferred. This presented a problem because we had already given notice to the church that we would be leaving within six months, but now we were staying. Our relationship with the deacons had deteriorated. I had kept pushing to build a new sanctuary (which we finally did while I was there), but there were those who always seem to oppose. Their attitude was aptly expressed one night in a deacon's meeting when he said, "Preacher, who told you that we want to grow? We don't want strangers coming in here and taking over our church!"

All of this frustration inspired me to preach one of my most infamous sermons. The title was, "Why Don't You Die?" My text was the story of the two Old Testament heroes who were among the twelve that Moses sent into Kadesh-Barnea to spy out the land. Ten came back fearful and had a negative, non-believing attitude. They argued that the land was fortified and the people were GIANTS! But Joshua and Caleb were believers! They said, "When God tells us this is our land, then we need to go in and claim it! God will fight for us so we can inhabit it." The people listened to the ten and not the ones who had faith, so God told Moses, "Because of their unbelief, they will wander in the wilderness for forty years until all of the adults die off, and then I will let the next generation go in and take the land." Time has passed; it is now thirty-nine and a half years later. There are only two old unbelieving geezers left alive. The younger kids (some of them over forty years old now) are saying, "Mom, I'm tired of this hot desert, eating manna, and living in a tent! When are we going into that Promised Land that you keep talking about?" Mom shushes them and says, "Not so loud. Uncle Zeke and Uncle Ezra are the last two survivors that have to die before we can go in." Now, can you imagine these younger Israelites looking at those two old reprobates, saying, "Why don't you die so we can get on with our lives!" At the conclusion of my sermon, it was really quiet. From that day forward, I was actively looking for my next assignment.

Chapter Ten:

TYLER, TEXAS 1963-1968

Well, with the door closed to Japan and with the delivery of that sermon, I took stock of our situation. Dr. and Mrs. Howard, director of the Texas Baptist student ministry on campuses across the state, had become our friends while we were building the Baptist student center on Navarro's campus. Upon inquiry, he said "Yes, we have several positions open that you might be interested in: Texas

A & M University, Texas Women's University, and Tyler Junior College." I had been to Tyler once during the Azalea and Dogwood Trails and thought that Tyler would be worth looking into. Dr. Howard made contact with Dr. Bill Shamburger, the pastor of First Baptist Church. I met with the committee, during which a lot of serious questions concerning my positions on communism and integration were discussed. Then Dr. Shamburger said, "Norm, you were an accident, were you not?" What a question! "Sir?" I replied, questioning his question. "Well, you were born during the Depression. There were not any planned families back then!" This levity changed the tenor of the conversation, and I received their approval. I became the BSU director at TJC. Go Apaches!"

Bob and Imogene Jones, former members of our young couples' class in Corsicana, had moved to Tyler. They invited us to move in with them while we searched for a house and waited for the closing. He worked for Exxon, and they have remained our lifelong friends! We bought a nice home on a circle with tons of azaleas, plus a community rose garden in the middle of the street circle.

I jumped into the student ministry with all the gusto I could conjure up. Jane taught English at Robert E. Lee High School and played the organ at First Baptist Church. Dr. Shamburger told me, "I know you will not be here much because you will be filling in for the sixty Baptist churches in Smith County, and that is okay! Just send your wife, daughter, and tithes to First Baptist!" Moses P. Timms, the leading Black minister in Tyler, was asked what was the difference between Dr. Porter Bales, the preceding pastor of First Baptist, and his successor, Dr. Bill Shamburger? His answer: "Well, both are great doctors. The difference? Dr. Shamburger uses anesthesia when he operates!"

Upon anticipating my duties as a Bible teacher and BSU director, I had asked Dr. Howard's advice. He said, "Well, don't put all of your eggs in one basket!" "Keep several irons in the fire at once." About Thanksgiving, I called and asked again, "Dr. Howard, what do I do when all of my irons get hot at the same time?" I was having a phenomenal success. What a blessing and how different from the past four years when it was like pulling teeth to get something done through a deacon board. Now, with students, when I suggested an idea, I had to hold them back! They were so anxious to do something! Our student center was a two-story building with two sections on each floor. The first floor had a classroom with a seating capacity of sixty students (all four of my classes were filled to capacity every year). On the opposite side was a lounge, library, prayer room, secretary's office, and my office. Downstairs was a kitchen and recreation room with two ping-pong tables. We added several vending machines in the hallway connecting that facility to our assembly room with a stage. This was also known as "Domino Hall." I was working my student secretary to death. One great day, the president of Smith County Baptist Association, Carolyn Holbrook, met me coming out of a Bible class. She said, "You need help! I have never seen so many students, and it is impossible to get in touch with you." I explained to her that we did not have money in the budget to hire a full-time secretary. She said, "Are you willing to take volunteers?" My answer: "Anything!" This wonderful lady enlisted the help of about eighty ladies who were retired and experienced secretaries. Each volunteered to donate a half-day once a month or once a week. I now had a full docket of qualified ladies to take dictation, keep the fiscal records, and supervise all areas of the building every hour of the day! What a Godsend!

This year at the B.S.U. we were privileged to have several ladies from the Tyler area donate their time and effort in the assembly room and office as secretaries and receptionists. These "school-moms" gave not only of their time, but lent many a helpful shoulder, guiding hand and box of brownies for our welfare. To each of these fine ladies we owe a great debt and wish to express our gratitude.

Seated: Mrs. N. E. Halbrook, Miss Rita Cartwright, Mrs. Milton Parker, Mrs. Jess Johnson. Standing: Mrs. Joe Coleman, Mrs. Billy Partridge, Mrs. Jake Beer, Mrs. Virginia Wilks, Mrs. J. E. Henderson. Not Pictured: Mrs. Wand Alexander, Mrs. Helen Baker, Mrs. Ruby Ballard, Mrs. Mary Berryman, Mrs. Emily Bissell, Mrs. Dickie Burton, Mrs Sandra Butler, Mrs. Otto Cain, Mrs. Sallie Clark, Mrs. Mary Ann Coolidge, Mrs. Rachel Corley, Mrs. Betty Dunlap Mrs. Sarah Hicks, Mrs. Alice Gilbert, Mrs. Janyce Gist, Mrs. Dorothy Gossett, Mrs. Martha Feagin, Mrs. Jo Ferrell Mrs. Ellen Ellett, Mrs. Jerry Jones, Mrs. Linda Kennington, Mrs. Eloise Lawler, Mrs. Henrietta Minsky, Mrs. Joan Norris, Mrs. Gloriana Parchman, Mrs. Ruth Patterson, Mrs. Louise Phillips, Mrs. Zella Reed, Mrs. A. P. Roberts Mrs. Norma Jean Sanders, Mrs. Beth Smith, Mrs. Flo Stevenson, Mrs. Carolyn Stroud, Mrs. Margaret Thames, Mis Shirley Thedford, Mrs. John Wood, and Mrs. Dorthy Wren.

My rescue lady, Carolyn Halbrook, and a few of the six dozen that she enlisted to work as volunteer ladies in the BSU. I also want to mention here one of the faithful ladies who ministered to the students: Martha Feagan, my dear friend for many years until she passed away after I returned to Tyler in 1991.

Our promotion and advertising on campus was high quality. I did not allow hastily scrawled signs with magic markers to be posted on campus. I insisted on bright flourescent colors of poster board, and many times, we silk-screened special promotions. I preached and led singing in the sixty Smith County Baptist churches and enlisted and advertised for special qualified leaders who were high school seniors that there was a place for them at Tyler Junior College with the Baptist Student Union ministry. Green Acres Baptist Church was especially helpful in training me and my helpers to use their printing machine. This was a tremendous help. I continued to perform a lot of magic for sweetheart and stewardship banquets. One invitation came from the First Baptist Church in El Paso, Texas (about a twelve hour drive from Tyler). I thought that I could drive my VW, do the show, and still get back in time to do another program in Shreveport the next night. When I told the pastor after the program in El Paso that I intended to spend the night driving so I could get back before noon the next day, he looked at me and said, "You have not seen the weather report, have you? There is a bad snowstorm right now that came in behind you and it is not safe for you to try to drive through that!" I did not think it could be all that bad. It was worse!!! Before long, the only way that I knew that I was still on the highway was to stay between the top of the fence posts, which were barely visible! The snow was bad! My wipers froze and the defroster only kept a small six-inch section in the lower left-hand corner of the windshield clear of ice. I could lean over the steering wheel and squint through that small space to see blinding snow all night. About 2:00 a.m., somewhere in the desert, I had a flat tire! Freezing, I tried to use the jack to raise the car in order to change the tire. The jack merely sank down in the more than 18 inches of snow. I scrounged the ditch area and kicked snow until I found a good-sized rock to put under the jack. After what seemed like an eternity, I was on the white road again. I drove into Tyler about 4:00 p.m., showered and changed clothes, and made the two-hour trip to Shreveport for the magic show. I have limited my magic shows greatly since then, especially those far away.

Our first Christmas seminar at the Howard E. Butt Foundation ranch in the hill country blew my mind. I drove my VW into the beautiful "Hill Country" for the first time. For some reason, the hood flew up and my new suit and two sport jackets (Christmas presents) blew under the tires and ate holes in the left sleeve arms of the coats. I came to the ranch and no one was around. There were signs pointing to "Laity Lodge," so I followed these to the river and a dead-end! After looking around, and with a sense of consternation and dismay, I discerned a small sign in the middle of the river pointing upstream. Cautiously, I crept inched my VW into the water and found it to be a rock bottom less than a foot deep. I ventured from one sign to another for half a mile and found an exit sign. On top of the hill was a beautiful "Frank Lloyd Wright" designed lodge overlooking the river. Looking down from the balcony, catfish larger than me were visible beneath the water. The inspirational speaker for this week was Frank Laubach, former language missionary and author of books such as, *Games With Minutes*. He had gone into many tribes that had no written language, listened to them, and identified words and objects that he could relate to. He would eventually create an alphabet, a dictionary, and a visual language for each tribe.

We were enjoying our nice little house on a circle in the Tanglewood division with beautiful azalea bushes everywhere. Lori was in preschool. We decided to build a small wading pool in the shape of a grand piano and a concrete patio around it. As Christmas approached, we wanted a real tree flocked with snow. Since I had enjoyed such success in using an Electrolux vacuum sweeper to paint our mobile home in Greenville, SC, I decided to try an attachment for flocking our tree with lots of artificial snow. Instructions on the snowpack advised placing plastic down to catch the residue of spray. We had chosen a lovely tree, a foot taller than myself. After about two hours of work, I finished around eleven o'clock that evening and left to go inside, clean up, and go to bed. Jane and Lori were already asleep. Inside, I heard a distant clap of thunder. In my underwear, I went back to the patio and deducted that I could pull the plastic with the tree on it under the covered portion of the patio. Holding the tree with one hand and pulling the plastic with the other, I slipped on the "snotty slick" artificial snow, pulling the tree down on my bare body. So frustrated that I had ruined my beautifully flocked Christmas tree, I got up and tried again. The result was a harder fall and more damage. By the time I got the pathetic-looking tree under the patio overhang, I could have passed for the Abominable Snowman! I did not want to make a mess on the carpet, so I banged on the door to wake my wife for help. When she came to the door, she began to laugh hysterically at the sight of my plight. At the time, I did not see what was so funny!

I never gave up on continuing my education. After college and seminary degrees, I went back to Southwestern Baptist Theological Seminary to get a Master of Divinity degree in Christian Education. Then, while at Tyler, I drove to East Texas State in Commerce every Saturday morning to get a master's degree in counseling. This schedule required getting up at 4:00 a.m. and driving two hours to the campus to begin my first class at 7:00 a.m. (I hesitate to mention it, but on two of those Saturday morning drives, I dozed while driving my VW and barely averted hitting a bridge abutment by steering to the ditch. My guardian angel must have been on the job because I landed in heavy grass and my VW had grass sprigs in every crevice). One of the requirements was a history class, so I signed up for Russian history. Dr. Moon was the professor. His singsong lectures pronouncing Russian names was more than my mind could comprehend for two hours early in the morning. I asked how he was going to grade us, by tests or term papers? His answer was, "maybe one test," and that was it. Another very difficult course was a math course on statistics, the median, the mode, and the mean. I was completely lost in this class and noticed a lady in the class seemed to know the material very well. She was a librarian from Dallas. I appealed to her for some tutoring, which she graciously offered for an hour or more after each class. I passed both of these courses. Another course was on ESP, or Extra Sensory Perception. I was interested in writing my thesis on the ESP of the Bible, i.e., incidents in the Bible such as the witches of Endor and how King Saul sought out soothsayers and witches and prophets to foretell the future. My interest was to compare the two spirit worlds, like demon possession vs. the Holy Spirit of God. My reading required devouring volumes of psychical research of strange events that occurred all over the world. This included hair-raising and unexplainable events that pushed beyond the physical and tangible. A lot of it tended to be devil worship and the manifestations of satanic forces. Having completed all of the hours needed except the thesis, the thesis oversight committee would not approve my thesis to research and write about the ESP of the Bible because it was a theological subject and not related to secular psychology.

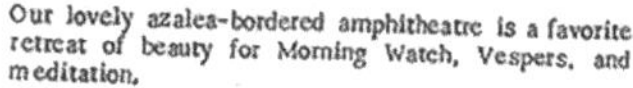
Our lovely azalea-bordered amphitheatre is a favorite retreat of beauty for Morning Watch, Vespers, and meditation.

Judge Jack Skeen as a hard-working BSU student shoveling dirt to make our dream of an amphitheater become a reality next to our student center.

When I got to the campus, I adapted my vision of doing missions in Japan where I contemplated the question, "How do I reach or have any influence on the ten million people in the capital city or the one million students there?" I reflected on Jesus' ministry, where He did not enlist the masses but spent His time with the twelve disciples and gave them the job of multiplying themselves among the masses. Within two years of our work at Tyler Junior College, our Greater Student Council boasted of the leadership of every organization on campus and included a representative from the dean's list, each sorority and fraternity, cheerleaders, football, basketball, track, dorm captains, etc. I also organized the first Fellowship of Christian Athletes. Coach "Babe" Hallmark invited me to become the chaplain of the football team. He had me lead in prayer before each game. He always advised me, "If we are behind at half-time, it probably would not be a good time for you to come to the locker room when I 'talk' to the team." The coaches entrusted me with a key to both gyms in order for our Fellowship of Christian Athletes to have a place to meet and play games. We took several athletes to the national FCA retreat in Colorado each year. Coach

Wagstaff was a prince of a coach! I slipped into a practice one day, and he was so upset by the way the guys were playing and goofing off. He used a couple of cuss words, then looked over and saw me sitting there. Without missing a beat, he turned to the team and said, "Now look what you made me do! If you had been doing what I told you to do, I would not have embarrassed myself in front of the preacher!"

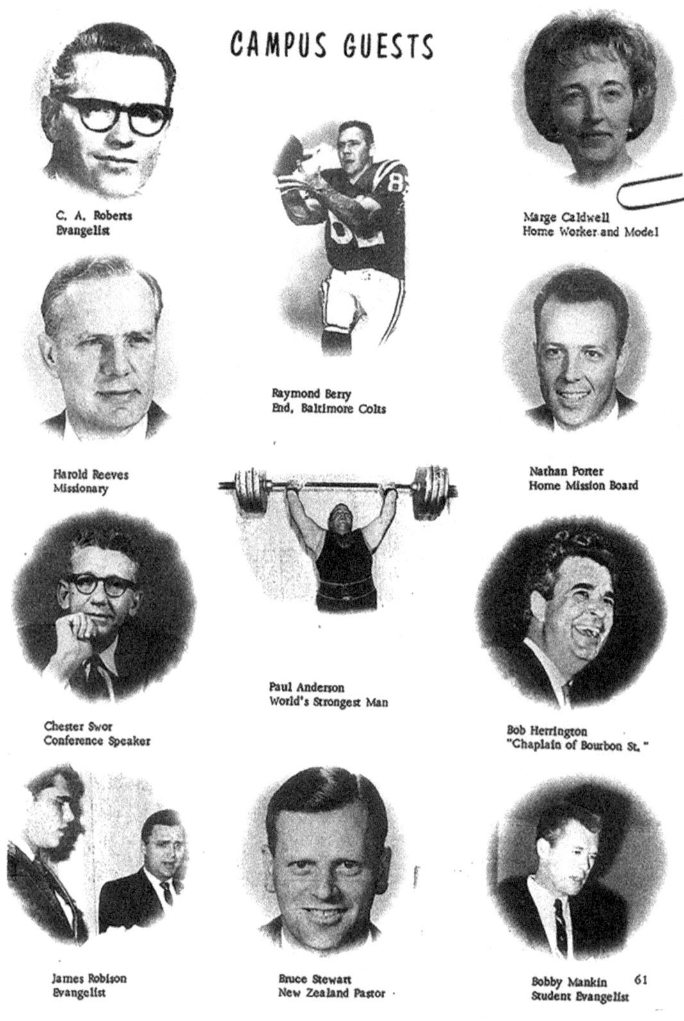

Some of the invited guests the BSU provided for special events on TJC campus

B.S.U. members are active in organizations all over the T.J.C. campus. Some of the activities participated in are represented by the following people:

Suzi Moore	Sophomore	Cheerleader	Homecoming Nominee
Ken Nunnelee	Freshman	Cheerleader	BSU Freshman Council
Vicki Britton	Sophomore	Head Cheerleader	Homecoming Nominee
Ted Thames	Sophomore	Cheerleader	BSU Executive Council
Maxine Ashendorf	Freshman	Cheerleader	Homecoming Princess
Bennie Portwood	Sophomore	Cheerleader	BSU Executive Council
Janie Routt	Sophomore	Singing Apaches	Smoke Signal Editor
Sheryl Irby	Sophomore	BSU	Smoke Signal Business Mgr.
Peggy Moore	Sophomore	Apache Belles	Morning Watch Chairman
Ann Hensel	Freshman	Apache Belles	Dorm ChaplainVaughn
Jan Hensel	Freshman	Apache Belles	Sans Souci
Dianne Davenport	Freshman	Apache Belles	Dean's List
Robert Collins	Sophomore	Apache Guard	Indian Mascot
Pat Haynes	Sophomore	Apache Yearbook	Co-Editor
Lanna Kay Weaver	Sophomore	Pow Wow	Apache Shield Editor
Jo Nora Cates	Sophomore	To-Kalon Sorority	Secretary
Gail Farris	Freshman	Pow Wow	Campus Beauty Candidate
Marsha Adams	Sophomore	BSU	President
Linda Hill	Freshman	Assoc. Youth Pianist	Dean's List
Karen Owers	Sophomore	BSU	Phi Theta Kappa
Linda Alexander	Sophomore	Apache Belles	Miss Tyler
Susie Itria	Freshman	BSU	Sigma Sigma Beauty
Paul Jival	Sophomore	International Student (Thailand)	
Nick Jival	Freshman	International Student (Thailand)	
Mike Ball	Sophomore	Student Senate	President
Sherwood Moffett	Sophomore	Student Senate	Vice-President
Steve Jones	Freshman	Student Senate	Freshman Class Vice-President
Corky Meeks	Sophomore	Youth Committee	Vice-President Youth Committee
John Loggins	Freshman	Band	Secretary-Treasurer
Donnie Gentry	Sophomore	Football	Dean's List
Robbie Albright	Freshman	Football	Most Valuable Player
Dennis Williams	Sophomore	Football	

58

BSU Greater Campus Council

We enlisted ALL of the leadership on campus, including sports, academic, spirit, fraternities, etc. Pictured above includes Donnie Gentry, future Tyler ISD superintendent; time and space will not allow me to comment on the success of each of these, but their successes are impressive!

Executive Council

First Row: Cecilia McRuiz-Summer Missions, Sharon Parker-Posters, Nancy Spence-Dorm Devotions, Gail Fairris-Apache Shield, Sandy Clark-Enlistment, Linda Hill-Communications.

Second Row: Jo Lynne Walker-Smoke Signal, Libby Jones-Worship (Tuesday Morning Watch), Judy Coleman-Education-Navye Isabell*, Diana Hewitt-Worship (Friday Morning Watch), Candy Mayo-Vespers, Nancy Trammel-Fellowship, Prissy Hearn-Community Missions (Convalescent Home).

Third Row: Ken Nunnelee-Fellowship-Jerry Warren*, John Loggins-Community Missions, Robert (Bob) Osborne-Faculty Advisor, Robbie Albright-Intramural Sports and F.C.A. Representative, Johnny Mahomes-Vice President, Ben Pegues-Evangelism.

Fourth Row: Rev. Max Pool-Pastor Advisor, Bruce Snider-Summer Missions, John Driggers-President, Danny Wills-Music, Ronnie Horton-Host, Steve Jones-Drama, Norman Ferguson-Director.

Baptist Student Union Executive Council

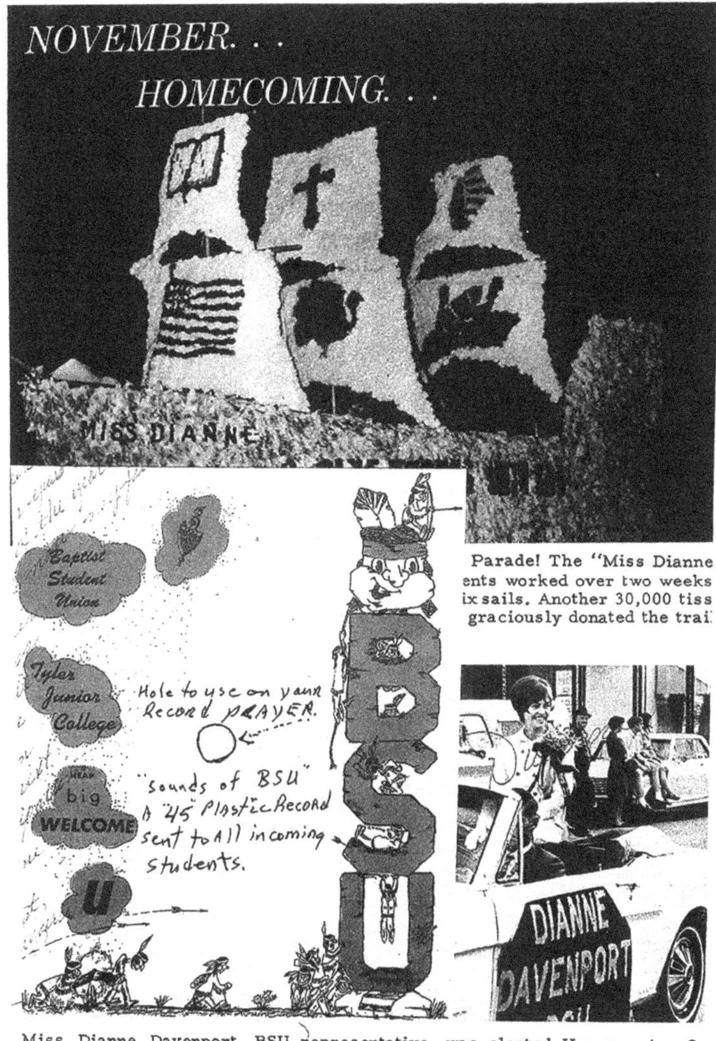

NOVEMBER. . .
HOMECOMING. . .
MISS DIANNE
Parade! The "Miss Dianne
ents worked over two weeks
ix sails. Another 30,000 tiss
graciously donated the trai
Baptist Student Union
Tyler Junior College
big
WELCOME
U
Hole to use on your Record PLAYER.
"Sounds of BSU"
A "45" Plastic Record sent to All incoming students.
BSU
DIANNE
DAVENPORT
Miss Dianne Davenport, BSU representative, was elected Homecoming Q
by the TJC student body. Mr. Jimmy Rex escorted the Queen and drove
convertible in the parade.

BSU Homecoming, featuring Diane Davenport and the BSU winning float

This belief is the core of my success wherever I have gone: REACH THE LEADERS!

I learned this from Jesus, who only trained twelve disciples who became apostles, and they changed the world. Sadly, I fear today that anti-American and liberal professors have hijacked our colleges to indoctrinate our youth. Now, after college indoctrination, these

American-hating youth have been taught that conservatives and capitalists are wrong. Professors have warped their minds against God and anything Christian. They have campaigned to ban the Ten Commandments, Christmas, Easter, or prayer in any public place. Government is put forth as the answer to everything. They scoff at our belief in God. Our youth are being brainwashed to believe that they are entitled! Somehow, the world owes them everything; a free education, a high-paying job that does not involve physical labor, health insurance for any and everyone (even people here illegally), and a nice retirement without earning it. They do not believe success is up to their own initiative, hard work, and personal ambition; rather, they want the people who have worked and become successful to share with them their hard-earned money without doing anything to earn it. They demand reparations for crimes of our ancestors two hundred years ago. Does that mean Japanese babies today should have to pay reparations to the United States when they grow up for the Japanese attack on Pearl Harbor?

The TJC vice president called my attention to a student from Thailand who wanted to come to college but needed a work scholarship. We provided the funds. First came Paul Nivalsantekorn. He was custodian, yard man, and filled the vending machines. As the year progressed, he asked if it might be possible to provide another scholarship to his younger brother, Nick. We made it possible. They were so great! Besides school and work at the student center, they secured a job at El Chico Restaurant. They earned enough money to buy a very old car. With great pride, they had me take a picture with my Polaroid camera in front of their car. This picture was to send home to their parents to show how successful they had become since coming to the United States. Observing them as they cleaned up the yard one day, I picked up a piece of paper. Nick ran over and took it out of my hand. "No! You are 'professor'. Do not do my type of work!" Another time, we had them over to the house for dinner. As they left for their car, I gave them the same old Texas or Southern saying, "Ya'll come back." They turned around and came back. Standing before me, I said, "Did you forget something?" "No, you said to come back." Both became Christians during their time here and joined First Baptist Church. Paul went on to Texas A&M and Nick went to Baylor. Back in Thailand, years later,

Paul established a tech training school, and Nick founded a liberal arts college with the presence of the Thai princess at the founding. When Summer and Heather were in middle school, Nick visited us in Tyler. He told them, "We would not be Christians today, nor could we be doing what we do today, had it not been for your father. If you ever want to come to my school, at no cost, you will live in our house and receive a free education." One other significant foreign student found Christ on one of our retreats down on the Brazos River at Latham Springs. His name is Tony Tadasa. He is now head of the small business department, teaching classes, on the West campus of TJC.

Dr. Jenkins, president of TJC, called me to come over to his office. When I arrived, he was gracious and complimentary of our work. He said, "I'm a Methodist, but I really like the way you Baptists are influencing our students for the good. I wanted to ask you if there is anything the school could do to support your Christian outreach?" I told him that I would like to have a special guest each year for a week to speak each day to our students on campus. No attendance requirements would be required. He then asked if I had speakers in mind. I told him that I had been in touch with Paul Anderson, the weightlifter who had just won the world weightlifting championship in Russia and was a dynamic Christian who would give some great demonstrations of his physical abilities as well as his testimony. I confided in him that we did not have the money in our budget to bring him. I told him it would take $1,500 to get him to the campus and pay his speaking fees. He reached into his desk and took out his personal checkbook and wrote a check for $1,000 toward getting him to come on campus. We did, and he was the talk of the campus! We also had Raymond Berry, professional football player, the next year. The following year, we had a "converted Jew" professor from Oklahoma University to speak on how our bodies and the laws of nature did not evolve, but was the direct result of God's omnipotent and creative powers.

In appreciation for your spiritual guidance and devotion to TJC, we dedicate the 1968 Apache to you . . .
Norman Ferguson

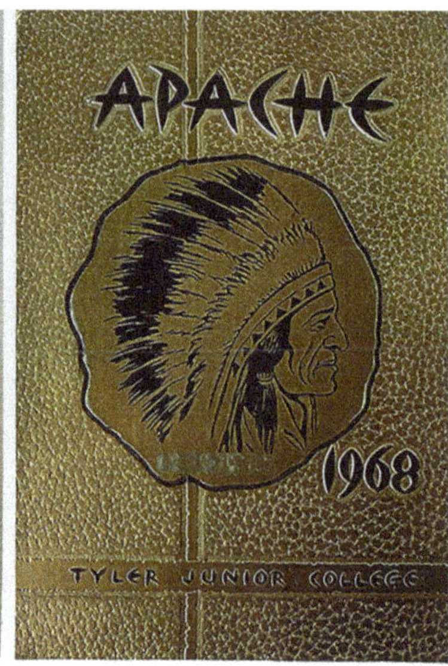

The 1968 Apache, Tyler Junior College yearbook surprised me with the dedication page! What an honor!

As I reflect on living so long, there are a couple of surprising honors bestowed on me that shocked me at the time. The first was my last year at TJC in 1968, when the editor of The Apache yearbook came into my office with a complimentary copy. She insisted that I open it. The dedication page was a full-blown picture of me in my office (complete with my flat top hair cut), with my mouth open, talking! During my four years in Tyler, all of my Sundays were booked by the 57 Smith County Baptist churches to supply and fill in during a pastor's absence. Linda Hill was a very proficient student pianist who accompanied me when I was scheduled to sing. After two years, TJC was growing and needed more dorm space. We wanted a larger house, so I applied to the Savings and Loan company located on the corner of Broadway and the Loop (now replaced by On the Border restaurant) for a building loan. The president of the S & L company lived on the back of the lot that I wanted to build on. During the application, he said, "Norm, that addition has certain requirements and stipulations. How big of a house do you plan to build?" I told him, "A five-bedroom, three-bath brick house." Then again, he inquired, "How many kids do you have?" So, I told him two (having recently adopted Bradley), but we plan to have more one day!" "Yes," he said, "but most people wait until they have more to build." So I told him my plans. "The school needs housing for more students. We plan a two-bedroom on one end with a small kitchen and ample bath, then our three bedrooms and two baths on the other end." His only other question was, "Are you going to have boys or girls, because I have two college boys. If you board girls, you better be prepared for these two boys to spend a lot of time at your house!"

Insert Image 15 Caption: The house that Norman built: 5 bedrooms, 3 baths Tyler, Texas

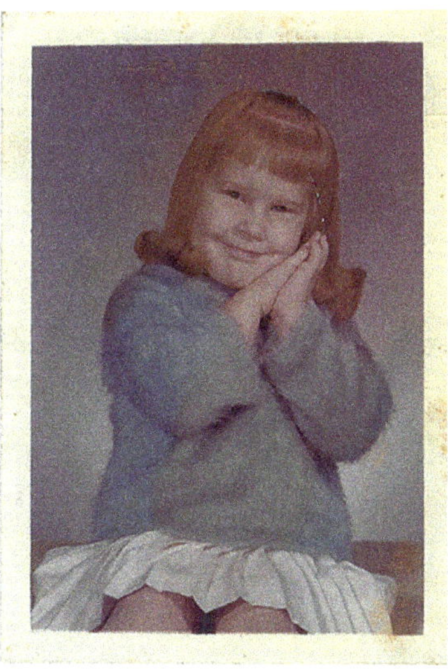

Daughter Lori Lynette and son Bradley Wayne

Some of my students would surely describe "Norm" as the most creative producer of the authentic "haunting" of a combination of a hayride and a Halloween party. Resourceful help coming from members of our "Greater Council" made these events possible. Planning required locating two large tractor-trailers with drivers and lots of hay! Then we spent weeks inspecting possible locations for the haunted house. One of our young ladies volunteered for us to use an abandoned estate, which her great-grandfather had been developing in the 1920s. He died in the middle of the construction when the Great Depression hit. It featured a lake, a three-story brick building (with dock coming into the lower part of the house for their boat), a large swimming pool, which over the years, had cracked, but still contained water on the deep end. An attic and patio was on the top level of the house. This was a dream come true as far as locations go! Admittance to go on the hayride and Halloween haunted house was one can of soup per person–any variety of Heinz 57. We always had over 100 cans of soup as they read off the names as the cans were opened. The cooks even opened some cans of chili. Max Poole secured a large black kettle in which to mix all of the soups together to form the "witch's brew." We served each a bowl of soup with crackers. Max also found several tombstones for our graveyard, complete with ghosts, who appeared under black lights coming out of the graves. An electric fence was constructed along the sloping path from the witch's brew to the haunted house. Inevitably, many of the students, or their dates, would touch the hot wire and scream with pain at such a lurking surprise. Chaperones had to caution those who got shocked not to use profanity! Next, they walked into the graveyard and witnessed ghosts coming out of graves (covered with sawdust and shavings). A professor with scuba gear volunteered to submerge in the water next to the dock under the old house. When a group led by BSU "tour guides" came onto the dock to peer at the chained up monster in the storage closet at the end of the dock, the "sea monster" would emerge and grab a student by the leg. The monster in the closet would take a flash picture of the bug-eyed fearful group. The melee and screaming resulted in a hasty retreat on the dock and a couple being pushed into the water (no harm done). Next, they visited the main floor with the mummified person in the coffin. We had secured the coffin from Burks, Walker, and Tippitt Funeral Home. I remember calling and asking Mr. Tippit if we could borrow an old beat-up used casket. His response: "Well, we haven't had any caskets returned lately, but we would be willing to loan you one." It became a donation, and we used it on many occasions. TJC's science department loaned us a replica of a human skeleton. To advertise, we placed the skeleton between the hearse driver delivering the casket and drove around campus showing students to advertise the party. Back to the scene: the top floor was filled with wadded-up paper until it was neck-deep. Each couple was challenged to go into the paper mountain and search for goodies; candy bars had been thrown into the mountain of paper. A person would be excited to yell, "I found a Snickers candy. Eventually, the "zombie" hiding under the mountain of paper would grab a couple and panic ensued. Out on the balcony, we offered a prize to the bravest of each group–a nicely-wrapped gift! When they reached out to receive it, the package containing an old Model T coil, which stored non life-threatening electric power would shock the daylights out of them!

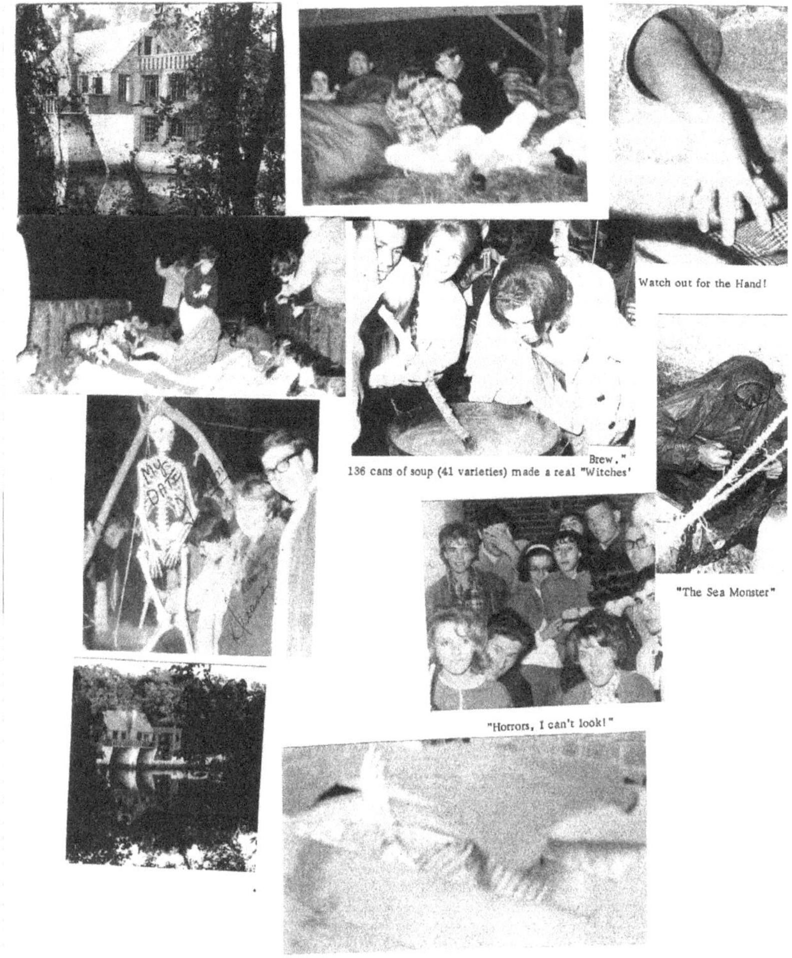

BSU Halloween @ TJC

Dr. Howard and Mrs. Howard announced that they were taking a group of BSU directors to Europe during my last summer at TJC for six weeks. We were greatly blessed to have Smith County Baptist Association pay the $5,000 for us to join them with fellow BSU directors for a mind-boggling tour of 15 countries. I had put together my only book: "Norm's Nutty Notes," which was a compilation of stunts, skits, games, and songs for my class of church vocational volunteers and workers with youth. I instructed my student secretary, Anita Majors, to print 2500 hundred copies of the book containing over 200 pages. She had to collate, punch holes, and assemble, complete with plastic binders. She accomplished this while I was in Europe those six weeks. She did a beautiful job! We received orders from Germany plus every state in the country. I do not think we made any money because we only sold these for $5.00 each to cover the cost of the paper for one of these crazy books. I signed a contract with Word Publishing Company to publish it, but could never verify the sources of many of my skits. This essentially put it on the shelf and prevented me from marketing the volume. My book did meet a lot of urgent needs at this time and received a lot of praise from those who used it.

Publication of "Norm's Nutty Notes"

There are so many stories to tell during each phase of my life and the people who influenced me. I would be very negligent if I failed to mention how grateful I am for the friendship of the BSU director who preceded me and taught psychology at TJC while I was there. Leo Rudd adopted me. We did revivals together in Timpson, Tenaha, and Chandler. I had funerals and filled in for him during vacancies in churches. He was so gifted in creating alliterative sermon outlines. The other special friend was Rev. Max Poole, my pastor advisor for the BSU. He went with us on nearly all retreats, campus events, and our annual trips to Glorieta, New Mexico. On one such trip, a couple of the students needed to get back early. He volunteered to drive his car and bring them back a day early. They were driving straight through that night to get home. About daybreak, the girl in the back seat woke up and noticed a sign on the side of the road: "Welcome to KANSAS!" She exclaimed as she sat up. Sure enough, Max had gone north at a junction in Abilene. With his dry wit, Max acknowledged his mistake with this quip: "But we were making such good time!"

Tyler Junior College integrated while I was the Baptist Student Union director and Bible teacher. Joe Carroll, minister of music at First Baptist Church, agreed to start a BSU choir. At the beginning of my second year at TJC, three Black students were admitted to the campus. All three were in my Bible classes and also in our BSU choir. Johnny from Lindale was one of these Black students and became our vice president. The choir was invited to sing at the Smith County Baptist Association's annual meeting. We began to get threats from various pastors and even the president of the First National Bank not to bring any Black students to the meeting. Our BSU choir was adamant and said, "If our Black friends cannot go and sing with us, then none of us will go!" The topic was to be discussed at the next pastor's conference. A heated discussion ensued! Fortunately, Mabel Hill, the Associational Women's Missionary Union president, was present. After hearing the discussion, she rose to her feet and addressed (or redressed) the pastors: "What a bunch of hypocrites! You urge us to pray for our young men and women to go to Africa and India and give our money to missions to take the gospel to all nations? Now you debate whether these same people we go around the world to witness to can even sing at our annual meeting?" You could hear a pin drop!

Our BSU choir sang at the annual meeting and was applauded by all. Thank the Lord for gutsy Mabel Hill. Her talented daughter, Linda, was so very helpful as a piano accompanist and student secretary.

Max Poole, pastor advisor, an energetic supporter

Jane and I had kept in touch with the foreign mission board and had an invitation for a luncheon in Dallas. We went and met Dr. Sammy DeBord, a retired missionary representing the board. After the meeting, I went up and introduced myself and asked if he had any information about my old Youth for Christ director, Jack Patterson, who had gone to Columbia, South America, as a missionary. "That's strange that you ask. He is my pastor now at the Hatcher Memorial Baptist Church in Richmond, VA." Dr. Sammy told Jack Patterson that he had met us while in Dallas. I got a call from Jack the next week. I told him about our trip to Europe, and he suggested that we drive to Richmond, leave our car in his care, and spend the night. He would take us to Dulles Airport to catch a plane to New York for our trip. He impressed on me his dire need for an associate to help him in his new church. I gave him our European itinerary. To my surprise, there was a telegram at every hotel that we checked into quoting Paul's message to the Macedonians: "Come over into Macedonia and HELP US!" I think we saw every castle and museum in Europe and fared well at five-star hotels in every country. My companions raved about the wine and beer in each country. They wanted to know why I never drank with them. I told them of my experience with Toots while growing up and vowed not to taste anything with alcohol in it. Their reply: "Norm, you are 35 years old! Why don't you just take a taste? One taste will not make you an alcoholic!" So, one night, I agreed to have a glass of red wine with them. I tasted, made an awful face, and almost spit it out! It was so bitter! I said, "Something is wrong with mine!" They said, "It came out of the same bottle as ours." Conclusion: one must acquire a taste for wine and beer.

Upon arriving in the good old USA, the first thing we got was a good old American hamburger! Dr. Patterson met us at the airport. He informed us that a small reception had been arranged for us. It turned out to be a banquet with the pulpit committee as we fielded many questions. They kept asking me what it would take to get me to move to Richmond? I was not very interested in leaving student work and told them that I could not possibly think about it until after the school year got under way. About mid-Thanksgiving, I called Jack and asked how things were in Richmond? His reply: "Terrible! The young man from Texas that we have been waiting on to come and help us has not agreed to come yet." I told him that up until this point, I had not even made it a matter of prayer, but promised that I would do so for the next few days. A couple of days later, he called and said, "Bob Harrington, the Chaplain of Bourbon Street is coming for a revival the first week of December. Could you come and lead singing for the revival?" We did, and the people were so receptive and gracious. Bob Harrington was the most entertaining preacher I have ever heard!

Chapter Eleven:

RICHMOND, VIRGINIA 1969-1973

We finally agreed to go back to Tyler and resign the BSU and sell our house. Ellis Heflebower, with one of his Mayflower vans, was at our house the first week of January 1969. All of a sudden, we were in completely new and foreign surroundings. Rain, snow, and clouds prevailed until April. A Texan with no sunshine for three months can get to be very depressed! I thought of going to the airport and get someone to fly me above the clouds to give me assurance that the sun was still shining! One day, we had a surprise visit from our wonderful benefactor, Dr. Halbrook, with his wife, Carolyn, and family. They spent a couple of days with us. I thought, "I wish Carolyn were here to help me organize helpers like she did for me at Tyler Junior College!"

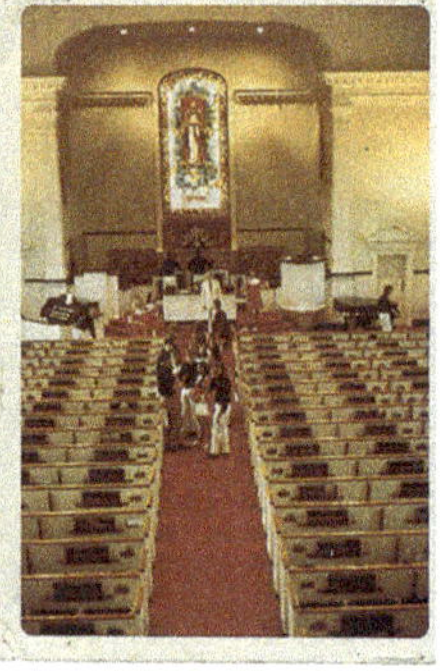

Hatcher Memorial Church, Richmond, Virginia

We had eight to ten active youth. There were not any music activities for junior high, high school, or college students. Jane was the master musician, and as my accompanist, she covered for my lack of training in conducting choir rehearsals.

I organized and promoted! Gradually, we involved students of all ages. As we grew, we had to have more activities and a lot of sponsors. First, we had a high school choir. Then, the need for a group of junior high students clamored for a choir.

As an enticement, I organized: "Teen Treats T'ween Tune Times," which came to be, "Teen Treats." This group meeting was scheduled between the high school choir and the junior high choir each Sunday evening. Mothers and other volunteers provided snacks and drinks as we scheduled "outstanding" popular youth (and adults) in the Richmond area to come and speak or perform. This really gave all of our programs a boost! Jane organized several ensemble music groups: "The Selah Singers," "The Treblettes," plus "The Five and Ten company," an entertaining group of dancers, comics, and singers. Our choirs became the focal point of the youth program. We went on ski retreats, beach parties, and bus tours to Texas, performances of the "Good News" musical at the Mosque, and on television.

Hatcher youth choir

Hatcher youth ministry

Our Sweetheart banquets were very popular as we went "all out" to decorate and provide an authentic atmosphere for each theme: "Neptune's Underwater Venture," "A Three Ring Circus," and "Dog Patch, USA." I could write a book on the preparation and effects of each of these banquets, but let me comment on the last one, which is centered on the hillbilly characters of Daisy Mae and her cartoon companions. As usual, Bennie Dunkum provided us with all kinds of support needed, which included ideas, resources, and oftentimes, unexpected surprise jokes and humor! At this banquet, I was at the microphone, and a couple of strange men walked in and came upon the stage asking to speak to Norman Ferguson. I tried to get them to one side, but they insisted on speaking to me about the rumor that we had an illegal still producing moonshine whiskey. I pointed to the Mountain Dew makeshift still with curling copper wires coming out of a barrel and said, "Is that what you are talking about?" "Yes." We need to confiscate that and have it tested!" I assured them that it only had the soft drink Mountain Dew in it. "They took a glass and said, "Ok, you come with us and we will go have this tested for alcoholic content." By then, I was in panic mode. These guys were serious. Thinking fast, I said, "Do you all have a search warrant?" "Oh, yes!" and they produced papers signed by a judge. My faithful attorney, Bennie Dunkum, and our guest speaker, a local judge, sat at the head table. I appealed to Bennie. He took the papers, handed them to the judge, and they concurred that the papers were legal. The agents got on each side of me and proceeded to escort me out of the banquet hall. Once outside, they confessed to Bennie's scheme and allowed me to go back into the banquet.

On a ski trip to Pennsylvania, we took two busloads for fun in the snow. There was plenty of snow when we arrived, and we were excited about hitting the slopes the next day. It rained all night! Only a few patches of snow remained by sun up. This was not good. We had eighty teenagers shut up for three days with nothing to do. We located some other activities in the area, and some of the youth wanted to go to a skating rink, so we had the bus drivers take them. It was about to get dark and was time for them to return when Bennie hatched up the next plot. We got a key to the bus driver's room and dressed Craig, Bennies' son, in a negligee and a girl's wig. We covered him in one of their beds with only his head showing. When the busses returned with the group, they parked the busses and started to their room. I yelled a "Thank you" to them. They acknowledged and said, "Good night." As they turned the key to their room, the first one entering suddenly backed out of the room as he bumped into the other. I saw them talking with one another, so I went over and said, "Is everything ok?" "No, there's a girl in our room!" So I said, "Well, did one of you invite her in?" "Oh, no! We are both married!" So I suggested that the front desk had made a mistake and overbooked the room and put a girl in there. So, one of them said, "Yes, and I am going to talk to them and get her out of our room! During this, Bennie had gone to his room next door and called the front desk. He made a brief reference about a joke being played on our bus drivers. "Please go along with our joke." So, when they got to the front desk, the clerk addressed them, "Yes, may I help you?" "Yes! There's a girl in our room!" The clerk said, "What do you want me to do about it?" Their reply in unison: "So, get her out!" The clerk said, "I'm sorry, we don't get involved in domestic arguments like this!" The two were really upset, and as they were coming back to their room, Craig, in his negligee and wig, ran out of the room and back into the hotel lobby. We stood around discussing this strange turn of events. I said, "The motel has scheduled some entertainment for us in the bar area, come and go with us." Bewildered and confused, they agreed. Bennie had gone ahead and talked with the drummer in the band and made the final move. During the performance, the drummer grabbed the mike and said, "Did anyone lose a key? This crazy lady was running through the lobby and dropped this one," and he read off their room number! A year later, we were at a hockey game and one of the bus drivers yelled at me from a tier above us and said, "Norm, please come up here and tell my wife what happened on that ski trip!"

The summers were packed with activities for our youth. I needed help! I asked the mission board for two summer missionaries. This was a program that I discovered as a BSU director. Several of our students at TJC had gone with the Home Mission board to all parts of the country as summer missionaries. We had good luck in Richmond, and some outstanding help came. One of their main duties centered around a program we initiated called CAT (Children's Activity Time). This was like Vacation Bible School every day for the entire summer. It provided supervised crafts, games, Bible stories, and recreation for grade-school levels. It was a welcomed activity by parents of these young kids. One outstanding young man, Rick Pribbernow, was assigned to live in a volunteer sponsor's home. The sponsor agreed to house and feed these young people throughout the summer. Rick lived on a different time schedule. He came in late, played loud music, and upset the volunteer sponsor. An urgent request came to move him to another house. I inquired among my previous volunteers, and Madge Brimmer agreed to take him until I could find someone else. After two or three days, Madge called and said, "Don't move him! I love him!" And they became lifelong friends. Years later, Madge came to stay with us one winter at our motel in Florida, and Rick worked across the street at Northwood Baptist Church.

There was an old large three-story house with a basement and an attic on the parking lot behind the church. We converted it into our coffee house and this mushroomed into something for which none of us were prepared. We had ping-pong and a boxing bag on the first floor and drinks and ice cream concoctions on the second floor served by youth (they also sang, played guitar, and witnessed). The top floor was a spacious attic where we installed the gift of a black eight-lane racecar track. Outside, we had basketball and volleyball. Eventually, this expanded from Saturday night to Friday night also. Soon, it required us to build an eight-foot fence plus issue plastic membership cards to get in. To become a member, each one applying had to have two Hatcher young people sponsor them. Our neighbor, Mr. Harris, took us to court twice for disturbing his sleep. We closed every night at 11:00. Bennie Dunkum went with me to court. The judge heard the complaints and then proceeded to lecture, not me, but Mr. Harris, "I sit here and have troubled youth come before me all day, and once in a while, a club or a church tries to offer a program to help these teenagers. Then, people like you start complaining instead of getting in there and helping them!"

I would never assume that my programs were a success because of my efforts alone! Just like the eighty volunteer ladies that helped me at Tyler Junior College, I could not have done this job without a myriad of volunteers for Teen Treats, seminars, camps, retreats, coffee houses, etc. Here are a few of those great warriors: Ray Cooper, Madge Brimmer, Bennie Dunkum, Byron Bowden, Anita Caston, and Virginia Hoover. I remember these as being my right-hand helpers! But I really want to try and list some, not all, but at least the last names of many supporters and volunteers (please forgive if I leave many out): Baldridge, Bolton, Clary, Cozens, Dagenhart, Duke, Early, Farmer, Fergusson, Gary, George, Gibson, Glass, Greenwood, Fords, Garnett, Harris, Heflebower, Herbaugh, Higgenbottom, Higgs, Hoover, Howe, Inge, Ingram, Jones, Lee, Llwellyn, Lloyd, Lowry, Lynn, Martin, Mattox, Meador, Moore, Munn, Owen, Patch, Patterson ,Payne, Pedigo, Photakos, Pierce, Rettig, Riddle, Schooles, Smith, and Zimmerman. Expose "Nosy Nora", a.k.a. Darlene Tanner! Her sister, Deborah, was a beautiful and gifted young lady who went to University of Richmond and married a very successful football coach. I would never be able to list all of my wonderful youth by name. Suffice it to say, those great teenagers were the heart of my ministry in Richmond (I apologize for the lack of names here, but most of my records and pictures were lost in my divorce)!

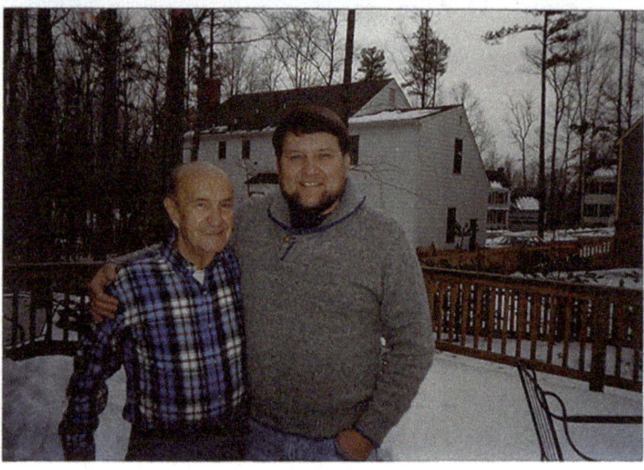

Bennie and Alma Dunkum, Norm's enablers

I think it would be appropriate to give Bennie Dunkum the title of "Norm's Enabler!" He was my go-to person with all of my ideas! I do not know whether he ever became a member of Hatcher Memorial church as they lived on the other side of the James River in another county. He had three vintage 1968 Buick convertibles that he, his beautiful wife, Alma, and his son, Craig, shuttled back and forth almost every day of the week. I met him at his Bull and Bear club in downtown often (he never allowed me to pay for a meal). Whenever I asked him a question, he would light up with a twinkle in his eye and say, "Well, I think you have three options..." and he would proceed to lay out all kinds of creative ideas.

On one of those conversations, I told him that we needed some kind of Sunday School class for newlyweds. I explained that Dr. Patterson and I were performing weddings every week, but we did not have any kind of ministry in which to get them involved. He had a bewildered look on his face and mused, "Do I understand you correctly? You are proposing, trying to entice a young couple who have just gotten married, are enamored with each other, having sex every day, and staying out late on Saturday night, and you want me to find a way to get them out of bed to come to a Bible class at 9:45 on Sunday morning?" He looked at me and said, "As an attorney, that is the most ridiculous and possibly impossible task that I have ever had put forth in a question." In a few moments of quiet, he said, "But I like a challenge...let's do it." We used Hatcher's plush wedding reception lounge with adjoining kitchen in which to meet. Bennie and Alma were my co-teachers. He had several overnight retreats for young couples, and we made use of his converted chicken house along with their nice swimming pool. One night, he told the couples, "Ok, here are poles, rolls of wrapping paper, wire, and tape. Now make your sleeping tents. I will provide the air mattresses."

One time for our Circus-themed Sweetheart banquet, Bennie secured a baby elephant to be there for the occasion. On an all-church picnic, he located a client farmer to donate a small pig for us to use in the "greased pig" catching contest. About 100 grade-school kids went after that poor pig until one finally caught him. He took the squealing pig home with him. The boy's dad called me at 2:00 a.m. to yell, "Come and get this #%&? squealing pig! I did so in the middle of the night and reunited the pig with its family the next day.

We instigated a summer outreach ministry with competition from four teams of church members, where each group would meet for visitation assignments and then come back to the various home headquarters for homemade ice cream. One evening, I was trying to get from one of the homes to the second to check the results. It was pouring rain, and I went down into a low place where a small creek ran under the road. I was going about 45 mph when I hit a creek stream out of its banks. My VW immediately began to float. Thankfully, it stopped against the concrete railing. The water on the driver's side pushed against the door and I could not get out. I finally rolled the passenger window down and crawled out to sit atop the VW. I was ready to jump as far as I could in the stream of rushing waters when I remembered that my new golf clubs were in the back seat. I crawled back through the window and retrieved my clubs and wadded to safety, but my VW was ruined.

About my second year at Hatcher, I got a call from the minister of music at First Baptist Church. They had received a large donation for a new pipe organ and he wanted to sell us their Aeolean Skinner 53 rank pipe organ for $35,000. I told him that we did not have the money or the chamber space to install such, but if it came to junking it, we would be interested in salvaging it. In May, he called again and said, "It's all yours for nothing, but you will have to have it completely out by September first." A couple of ignorant members opposed accepting it and convinced a vote against it in the monthly business meeting. A large group of our musicians did not agree, and we made arrangements with Mr. Ramos, an 80-year-old organ builder, to dismantle it so long as we could provide the muscles to transport and store the huge bellows, chests, and pipes as well as the five-rank console. We took all of the seats out of one of our old school busses and enlisted forty to fifty kids to "party" every day all summer long to haul those thousands of parts to an old vacant Presbyterian church building, plus an area in our old chapel balcony. Custodian Julian Gary was not too happy with us. The teenagers were sent home every night from a very hard day's work, looking like they had been working in the coal mines! I had to get busy and find a person who would contribute $40,000 to build a matching organ chamber so we would have room to install sections of the organ on both sides of the choir. Miss Daisy and an anonymous donor provided the funds to build the organ chamber plus the funds to install the organ in the two chambers. Over a year later, we again engaged Mr. Ramos to begin the installation. I think we paid him $10,000 to take it out and another $10,000 to reinstall. The installation was completed after I left. The Aeoleon Skinner Pipe Organ Company came and tuned the instrument. Today, Hatcher enjoys the music from one of less than a dozen of such organs on the East Coast.

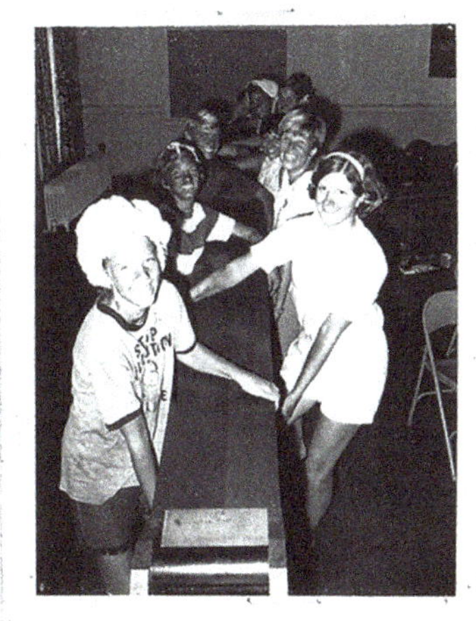

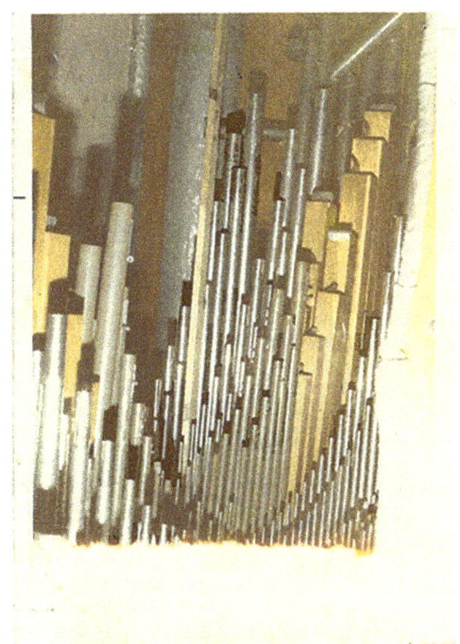

Hatcher youth moving the parts of a 53-rank Pipe Organ from First Baptist in Richmond to install at Hatcher.

It seemed that the nominating committee approached me every year to take over the high school Sunday School department. I gave them some stipulations: I would choose the teachers and curriculum, and I wanted access to the Chapel basement to remodel as we desired. To my amazement, they agreed. Byron Bowden and Anita Caston were outstanding help. Anita designed and engineered the supergraphics on the walls of the basement; we built a stage for performances and speakers, plus connections for a TV show featuring the news from three of our high schools. Byron Bowden provided us with two video cameras to loan to our reporters to take to school and interview athletes and campus leaders with breaking news on their respective campuses. The people they interviewed often showed up on Sunday mornings because they were going to be featured on our live TV "breaking news" segment to open our hour of Bible study. Since Byron was an Air Force guy and owned his own plane, I asked and he agreed to transport by plane all of my newly recruited workers in the high school youth program to Tangier Island in the middle of the Chesapeake Bay. We brought all of our workers together for a two-day retreat. I gave them my vision for reaching and teaching high school students. Basically, the 10th graders would study Old Testament stories, the 11th grade would delve into the New Testament (half a year on the life of Jesus and the other half on the missionary journeys of the apostle Paul), and seniors would study a course that we outlined on "Preparation for Life" (this included sections on college education, technical training for a vocation other than college, dating, birth control, life insurance, how and when to buy a house and/or a car, and how to keep records to prepare for financial success and security). This was a winning strategy, and there was a lot of excitement every Sunday morning. I remember visiting Byron's Old Testament class when he told me that Craig Dunkum was going to do a live enactment of Moses striking the rock in the desert in anger to produce water. His students in the class had designed the papier-mâché' rock to actually produce water when he struck it! It was awesome and inspiring!

Nathan was born while we were in Richmond. Brad grew and became the entertainer in kindergarten at our Hatcher Memorial School. Part of my associate pastor's duties was to oversee this part of our education program. The personnel committee finally got another choir director for the adult choir, and I was more than ready to give it up. Speaking of Brad, we took him to trick-or-treat around the neighborhood on Halloween night. The next morning, the Ecks (family next door) called and said, "Brad's over here trick-or-treating again this morning!" One Sunday, as Jane was preparing dinner and I was reading the Sunday paper, Brad was sitting in his youth chair, and Nathan was in the high chair. Every time Jane placed something on the table, Brad would crawl onto the table and try to swipe some of it. I politely told him to wait until all of the food was on the table, then we would have the blessing, and eat when everyone was seated. This happened about four times. The next time, I reached over and grabbed a shoulder and pushed him into his chair. I said, "Sit!" Brad's lower lip protruded in a pout as he answered, "I'm a'sittin', but I'm standing up inside!" This concept from a five-year-old was so revealing.

Our youth choir was invited to sing at the Eagle Erie and other great venues, like the State Evangelism Conference. The speaker for the Evangelism Conference was Dr. Carl Bates, who was not only the pastor of First Baptist Church in Charleston, North Carolina, but also the president of the Southern Baptist Convention. A few days after our performance, I received a call from him complimenting us on our great choir. He wanted me to come and be interviewed for Minister of Music for his church! I assured him that I was not qualified. He said, "I heard your choir. That is the kind of music I want in our church!" "Yes, sir, but I have not had the education to do that. You have people in your choir with degrees in music who are much more qualified than me! I would never feel comfortable in that kind of situation." I view that as a great compliment for the youth choir's performance, not my musical ability. I did get great private voice lessons while at Bob Jones University and God has given me many opportunities to sing, and I have really enjoyed singing!

All good things come to an end. The end was gradual for both our marriage and our ministry. Jane was very unhappy that the church was not paying her. She came before the committee to request the same amount of money as I was making, and she was probably worth it. She spent more time in rehearsals with her music groups where, evidently, her heart was. She provided teen babysitters with Lori, Brad, and Nathan most of the time. We had heated discussions over it. I purchased a cabin on the Rappahannock River. We would leave after church on Sunday night and come back early Tuesday morning in time for staff meetings. Chairman Worth Schumann would have no part in paying her. I began to research options to get out of church work even though I did not want to admit it openly. I discussed this with Pastor Jack a couple of times and told him of my plans to buy a motel in Florida so that if I did get a divorce, I did not want to harm the church with that kind of damaging news. It seemed that Jane's desire for kids was first during those years that she was having all of those miscarriages, but once we had children, she did not seem interested in teaching them or staying at home with them.

I secured the aid of a Jewish realtor, Louis Kessler, who had been to Florida several times and knew of some of the opportunities in the West Palm Beach area. He told me of the Granada Inn. The possibility of purchasing such resulted in Bennie and I spending three days at my cabin on the Rappahannock River, drawing up the contract to purchase the Granada (more on that transaction later). My last Sunday at Hatcher, Bennie again had a surprise for me. Two policemen came down the aisle and served me with a "cease and desist" complaint for leaving all of my friends and co-workers. They also presented me with the 1888 locomotive brass bell that had been in the chapel and used in that first church building to ring every Sunday morning as a call to the residents of the Lakeside community to come and worship. It has been the center of my coffee table all these years. It was dirty and black until a young man in California asked me to perform his wedding ceremony. I found out that he polished brass and copper, so I made a deal to conduct his wedding free of charge if he would polish my bell. He made it look like a new penny!

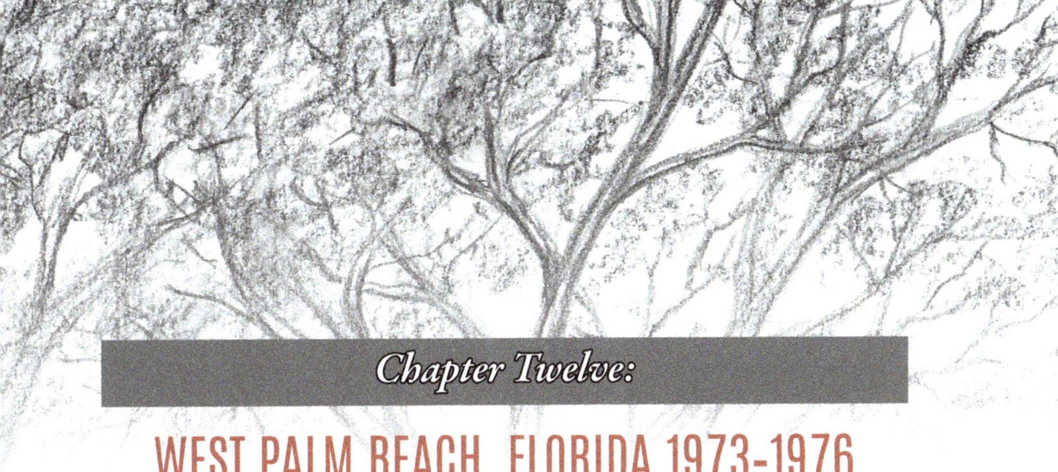

Chapter Twelve:

WEST PALM BEACH, FLORIDA 1973-1976

We sold our house and the river cabin, and I flew to Miami with my contract to purchase the Granada Inn. Louis Kessler, the owner of the motel, and several attorneys (all Jewish) met with me to go over the contract and close the deal. As I looked around, I told them that I felt a little out of place since I was the only Gentile in the room. After looking over the contract, one of the attorneys said, "I see you must have had a good Jewish attorney draw up this contract. Everything is in your favor!" Louis remarked that I was a "Gentile with a 'shagish' cup," which he interpreted as "a Gentile with a Jewish head." On the day set for us to occupy the motel premises, Bennie flew down to be with me. Louis had insisted that he be my first client to pay his motel bill. I confided in Bennie to be close by when Louis came in for a big surprise. When this exuberant realtor came in and wanted to pay his bill, I made it out and showed it to him. He turned red in the face and said, "That's more money than I have ever paid for a room here in all my life!" I calmly told him, "The motel is now under new management." He sputtered and complained. I said, "Louis, I may buy you a steak dinner, but this is what you are going to pay." Bennie walked up and asked, "Well, Louis, do you think this young preacher is going to be a successful motel owner?" Louis: "Yah! He will be very rich if he treats all his customers like he is treating me!"

Well, the first week surprised me with new expenses! Both the electric company and the water company served notices that I had to pay deposits on my new accounts. This totaled over $2,500, and I was already broke from using nearly everything at the closing. Somehow, we managed. Little did I know that the challenges would get bigger!

Jane stayed in Richmond until her teaching ended in June, along with Bradley and Nathan. Lori and I got in my VW to travel to West Palm Beach and take over running the motel. We lived in room number 9, next to the office. While living in that small room, we remodeled and refurbished it. Trying to solve where we would live when Jane and the boys joined us, I decided to knock on the door of the house facing 38th Street, across the alley from the back of the motel. When I knocked on the door, a lady answered. I introduced myself and told her that we had recently bought the motel and were looking for a place to live. I was wondering if she and her husband (who was a professor at Palm Beach Atlantic College) would be interested in selling their house? She had this strange look on her face, then finally answered, "Please come in! Let me get my husband." When he came in, I began to explain the situation to him that it would be so convenient to live directly behind the motel. He then asked me, "Who told you that we were interested in selling our home?" I told him, "No one, I was just hoping!" He said that he had taken another job out of the area and he had not even notified the college yet. Then I said, "Well, it still may not be possible for us to manage because we used most of our money to buy the motel. "Could you live with a purchase that would allow us to take over the mortgage, then pay you over the next two years in balloon payments for your equity in the house? He replied, "Yes, we do not need the money at this time." Talk about God providing! He is so faithful!

Buying a motel in Florida was one of the greatest steps of faith that I have ever experienced! The furniture was old! The mattresses stunk! None of the air conditioners worked well! The TVs were a constant headache! The doors had jalousie glass panels that were easily broken into. The sprinkler system did not work. The swimming pool was an everyday challenge to keep it clear with the right amount of chlorine to pass inspection! We needed new laundry machines as well as the need to replace threadbare towels, sheets, mattresses, and bedspreads. Our approach was to take one room at a time and do a complete renovation with new carpet, TV, air conditioner, mattress, carpet, etc. I spent a lot of time repairing the sprinkler system, cleaning the pool, and redesigning the fountain (complete with an automatic water-filling apparatus and a gas-flaming torch on top of three layers of cascading water. It became the most attractive motel on the strip of motels along Highway Number One.

One of the first rooms that we refinished was room 5. I checked a couple into the room on the second day it was open and they came back to the office, and said, "We wanted a room with a TV in it." I said, "There is a new TV in that room!" When he argued with me, I went to see for myself, and surprise! The first customer that we had rented it to the day before had stolen the TV off of the wall.

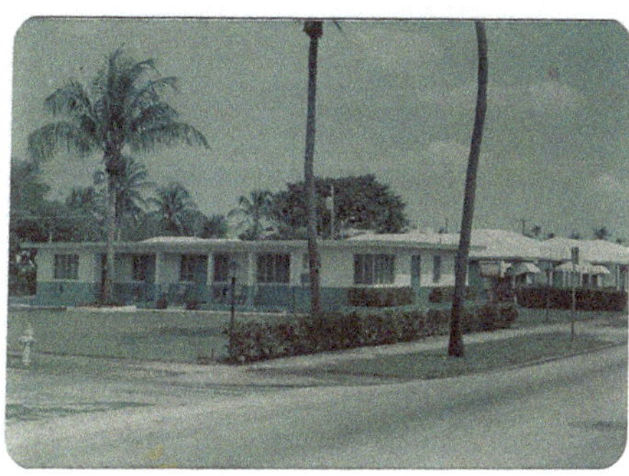

The Granada Inn, West Palm Beach, Florida

The big gas crunch of 1973 caught us that first full winter that we were the owners of the Granada Inn. Half of our income for the year was during those critical months of December through March when the "snowbirds" from Canada and all states up north flocked to Florida for the winter. Well, the gas crunch fixed that!

No one came! In order to survive, we sold family memberships to families in the neighborhood to swim in our pool! This provided us enough income to pay the mortgage (held by the former owners who would be happy to re-take our motel with all of our improvements). We finished the remodeling of all 15 rooms and five apartments by the end of the second year. We even hired a maid or two to help clean the rooms. I was on a retreat with Dr. Jess Moody and his assistant, Barry Schahn, about seventy miles up the coast from West Palm Beach, when Barry called me over and said, "Norm, your motel is on fire!" I retorted with, "That's not a funny joke!" He finally convinced me that he was not joking!

I jumped in my car and was coming south on Number One Highway, exceeding 100 mph when I passed a parked state highway patrol car among the trees in the median. I topped the next hill where there was an exit. I took it and found my way through all kinds of back roads to find my motel in ashes. The roof was torn off. Pieces of furniture were stacked out in the parking areas and all of the carpets and rooms were soaked and smelled like burnt toast, streaked with soot. The insurance company ripped us off and only gave $29,000 toward the $79,000, plus what it cost to rebuild and replace all of the furnishings. I rebuilt all of the doors to the fifteen rooms with a solid panel of wood and security locks. In some ways, the fire was a blessing in the fact that we now had all new facilities and furnishings.

Nathan was my big assistant at age three. In papering a room, I would cut the wallpaper trimmings and let them fall to the floor. He would pick them up and go to the other side of the room not yet done and stick the scraps on the wall. When I would go to that side and take the scraps down to put permanent wall coverings on, he would yell, "I've already done that wall, Daddy!" He was like a shadow following me in all the jobs that I had to do at the motel. Brad was really showing promise as a swimmer at the YMCA as he was in the first grade and beating kids in swim meets as old as fifth graders. I regret we did not follow through in keeping him in this sport! Lori became an unpaid employee at an early age...checking guests in and answering the phone at the front desk.

It was about this time that I began to get involved in the community and tried being on staff for a year at Northwood Baptist Church. I was invited by Coach Bill to be the chaplain of the Northshore High School football team and got to know a number of the football players and their families. Jess Moody became my very dear friend during this time, as well as Barry Schahn. The Denton family and the Fowler family stand out as being our very steady friends during these years. Jim Fowler loaned me equipment to build my backyard fountain that featured rocks that glowed under black light. He also gave me some of the materials to build a huge monkey bar set as one of the escapes out of the five-level tree house in a very large mango tree. It featured a slide from one level, a ladder, monkey bars, a rope, and a fire pole from the very top level. Lori, Brad, and Nathan had a lot of friends in the neighborhood wanting to come over and play. We had to put a fence around our property to control the flow. Years later, various confessions let me know that there were some days when our kids hid out in the tree house to keep from going to school.

These four years of owning a motel taught me a lot about the motel and business, in general. I decided to take a course in real estate to perhaps use my knowledge to market some of the Mom & Pop motels in the area. This really opened up a whole new venture in my life. I became a part-time real estate representative and enlisted motels for sale under a nearby broker. I found that nearly all of these small motels carried two sets of books. There was what income was reported to the IRS and then there was a record of the actual money made (which was always substantially more than reported). It is almost impossible to sell a motel for what it is worth based solely on what is reported on the income tax report. Chain motels are required to keep better electronically generated records. This is why foreigners are buying up all the Mom & Pop motels and do little maintenance or upkeep...they hide all the income! I took enough education courses to earn my GRI degree in real estate.

Dentists have never been high on my friends list. I had never been to a dentist until I was in Southwestern Baptist Theological Seminary in Fort Worth, Texas. While studying there, I was living in Midlothian,

Texas, as the minister of music and youth at the First Baptist Church. We did not have classes on Mondays, so I looked up the local dentist, Dr. Payne, to check out some of my tooth decay. He did not believe in any kind of pain medications or shots to deaden the mouth before doing any drilling. I thought this was the normal procedure for all dentists, so every Monday, I went with fear and trembling to his office to be tortured. He could not see well and the drill would slip off the tooth and bore into my cheeks and gums. I did not go back to a dentist until I was in Richmond, VA. I found a dental school at Virginia Commonwealth University in Downtown Richmond. They were slow, but at least they used Novocaine shots! My parking tickets cost more than the dental charges. The professor in the dental school had to approve each procedure, and during one of these examinations, he asked if it would be all right for him to point out something to the students. I agreed. As the dental students gathered around, he pointed to a raised spot on my tongue. "Who knows what this is?" he asked. One bright student responded with, "That is a taste bud." The doctor agreed and said, "Do you know why this one is enlarged?" No one answered. So he showed off his knowledge: "When this taste bud is enlarged, it is a sign of a beer drinker, or someone who likes hot spicy food...is that right, sir?" I told the professor, "Well, you put me in a spot since I am a Baptist preacher and do not drink beer, but I do like hot spicy food (the students really teased him about his great knowledge).

Now in Florida, I needed work done on my teeth again. I found a fellow Texan, Dr. Terry Hornaday. He and I got along very well. He had a new young associate just out of school named Dr. Lamerough. For some reason, he drew the assignment to work on my tooth that needed a root canal. This process began in February and was not completed until July in the year of 1976. I had a weekly appointment...he was really slow! In the meantime, I spent a lot of time with Dr. Hornaday talking investments and politics. He and I met with Sandy, who was a salesman with all kinds of charts and core drillings that he had bought from oil companies in Columbia, South America. These showed the mineral content and the gold content of the core drillings in each location. He was enlisting investors. Terry Hornaday, Herb Geller, his attorney in North Carolina, and I invested $10,000 each in a gamble to strike it rich in South American gold (more on that later)!

It was right here in Dr. Terry Hornaday's office that I was coming upon a fork in the road of my life. I was so unaware how this fork in the road would change the direction of my life!

WHICH
WAY?

LIFE'S INDELIBLE MOMENTS

Norman Wayne Ferguson

Part II 1976–2020?

With the celebration of our 150 years of freedom from England & the constitutional establishment of freedom of religion, speech, and press in the United States of America in 1976, I was thankful that somehow I had survived the ownership of the Granada Inn through the gas shortage, the devastating fire, and the vandalism of everyday neighborhood gangs that constantly destroyed our property.

I was in the dentist's office, which has not been my favorite place to hang out. I was impressed by the beauty of the dental assistant, and I frankly told her so. She dropped her instruments and left the office. When the doctor came in to do the work on my tooth, she remained out of my line of vision. I do not understand why, but her lovely smile and sparkling eyes made an indelible impression on my mind. I could not get her image out of my thoughts. She was always there. Days went by, and suddenly, as I was driving by a florist shop, I turned around and went in. I ordered a dozen roses to be sent to Ginny in care of Dr. Terry Hornaday's office. The young saleslady asked if I wanted to write a note to accompany the flowers? I said "Yes." She gave me a card. I wrote: "Went to the dentist to lose a tooth, instead, lost my heart!" I did not sign it. The next week when I kept my appointment, Rosalie was at the receptionist's desk and said, "Mr. Ferguson, I thought you had been to college?" What kind of question is that? I began to feel that maybe my Texas accent really was bad. Maybe I sounded like a country hick with no education? So, in defense, I replied, "Yes ma'am, I have four years of college, two years on a master's degree, and four years of theological seminary." Her retort was, "Well, you don't spell Jenny with a 'G'...it is a 'J'." That was the defining moment when I realized they had matched my handwriting on the flower note to the handwriting on my records! I sat down in the dentist chair. Someone came up behind me and placed a gentle kiss on my cheek. It was Jenny. She said, "Thanks for the nice flowers. That was very sweet and thoughtful of you!"

This did not help to get her out of my mind! One afternoon, I went to the parking lot at 4:00 to wait for her to get off work. Dr. Lamoreaux was so slow. She did not come out of the office until after 7:00. When she finally appeared, she was dressed in this cute, all white tennis outfit. She was somewhat startled to see me standing beside her Maverick and said, "What are you doing here?" So, I told her that I really wanted to know more about her. I suggested that we go for lunch sometime. She was quick to say "No, I am going through a divorce and not interested in seeing or dating anyone!" I assured her that no harm could be done in a restaurant while we ate and talked. She kept insisting on leaving to go play her tennis match. I kept insisting on getting together for lunch. Finally, she said, "Ok, I will meet you at the Greenhouse this Saturday at noon." I agreed and thought that she had probably told me this to get rid of me. BUT, Saturday noon came, and she showed up. We must have talked for two hours...our chemistry was electric! Forty-four years later, it still is!

I found her route to and from work and tried to intercept her for a quick exchange of words. I left tennis balls on the antenna of her car with the numbers "143," which I used to sign on everything that I sent to her. Interpretation: "I love you." Obviously, each number represents one of the three words. I knocked on her door as a fresh fruit and vegetable salesman to get to see her for a moment. I confided in my good friend, Bill Denton, about my feelings. We discussed the possibilities of infatuation, or the "43-year-old panic," etc. None of it helped.

One day, while I was in the motel office, my old friend and fellow basketball buddy, Jim Smith, in Virginia called and said, "I see you are coming back to Hatcher for a revival with Dr. Jess Moody soon." I told him that I was and asked if he was still racing cars or airplanes. He said that his wife made him give up the car racing, but he still flew his plane. Jenny was going to fly to Nantucket to visit her twin brother, Jeff, the same time that I would be in Virginia. I asked, "What about a trip to Martha's Vineyard in your plane?" He said, "Sure." So the plans were tentatively set. I went to Virginia a few days early to visit friends and stay with Bennie and Alma Dunkum. Bad weather and snow prevented our flying, but Jim volunteered to drive...so we took off and went through some rough weather to get there, but arrived in Hyannis Port. I called the restaurant where Jeff was working and asked to speak to Jenny. When she got on line, she was in shock to learn that I was close by. She grabbed her bag and hopped on a twin-engine plane and flew from Nantucket to where we met her. We headed to Virginia by car, passing through New York and Pennsylvania. We enjoyed one another's company, infatuated with each other throughout the long drive, until we arrived at Richmond, Virginia. Jim and I dropped Jenny off at the airport in order for her to fly back to North Palm Beach, Florida. I stayed behind to lead the singing for the revival with Dr. Jess Moody.

Jane, my wife at the time, was not happy with Jim taking me on a trip. A week after we got back to Florida, I was closing a sale on a property near Lake Okeechobee, and met Jenny afterward. Jane called my broker and began to figure out that I was seeing someone. She packed a suitcase of my things, set it outside, and locked the doors. She changed the locks and closed all of our financial accounts at the bank.

Chapter 13:

NORTH PALM BEACH, FLORIDA 1976-1981

I found a small apartment, moved in, and placed my real estate license with the Gallery of Homes. The bank would not loan me even $50.00 because I was a risk with a possible divorce. The honorarium for our being in the Hatcher revival was $2,200.00, and Jane deposited it into her account and would not give any of it to me. I confronted Betty, the maid, and took the keys from her, jumped the desk, and opened the cash drawer. I took $800. This was much less than my share of the honorarium from Hatcher's revival. Without any income yet, I really needed a few dollars to tide me through the next several days. These were tough days financially and emotionally. Jane threatened to take the lives of the children if I did not move back immediately. She thought that she could cut off all the finances and starve me to come back; a bad mistake on her part. I refused to meet her unless her sister Martha was present. I asked Martha to keep a check on the kids: Lori, Bradley, and Nathan. Jenny was steady through all of this, even when Jane went to Dr. Hornaday's office and tried to get her fired. My only means of transportation was an old Dodge Dart in which the motel used to haul chlorine. I was later able to trade it for an old 1967 Buick convertible. I had it painted a much too bright yellow! When we picked the kids up to take them with us for an evening out together, Jane would follow and bang the back of my old convertible with her Lincoln Continental! She was totally unhinged! She hooked up with a much younger male across the street, and the owner of the Queen's lodge. She had him accompany her to Hatcher Baptist Church in Richmond, Virginia, to show off her good-looking young trophy. She later married the mayor of West Palm Beach and immediately divorced him after their honeymoon. Jenny and I tried to ignore all this and enjoy our time together. I rented an apartment and shared it with a young man who waited tables. We rarely saw each other because our shifts were different.

When I was thrown out of my home and business, my main concern was Jenny. I asked her to accompany me to the Everglades for the weekend. She agreed and I called her mother Jeanne and told her that her daughter, Jenny, was going to be with me for the weekend and not to worry about her. This was the first conversation that I had with her mom. Later, I made a luncheon date with Jeanne and gave her a detailed account of my background and assured her that I really did have honorable intentions concerning her daughter. That weekend, Jenny and I had time to really talk at length and get to know one another. I told her, "Since we seem to be getting serious in our relationship, there are a couple of things that you need to know about me." She looked at me and said, "Like what?" "Well, I'm older than I look!" She said, "Well, you're only 3 or four years older than me, aren't you?" I said, "No, I'm 17 years older than you." Her shocked response was, "Oh my gosh! You are old enough to be my dad!" Then she said, "You said a couple of things...what else?" So, I said, "Well, I am an ordained Baptist minister." "Oh, dear! I'm dating a priest! That must be a mortal sin!" I assured her that a priest does not get married but ministers can and do." I really did not know whether she could handle much more and did not know if the relationship would continue. We rode horses on that weekend and grew closer to each other. We found that both of us were interested in sports. So, the next few months our spare time was spent jogging, playing golf, tennis, basketball, and throwing the football.

JENNY! When I met Jenny in 1976, she was a very pretty lady. Why do I love her? She has become my lovely wife, a devout Christian with unbelievable faith! She is a doting mother–but firm in discipline. She is a talented children's choir director, an effective and beloved Spanish teacher, friend to everyone, and a special friend to her co-workers. She is a talented cook, creative artist, thoughtful and generous to a fault, but most of all, she is my faithful companion, confidant, and friend!

I persuaded her to get her real estate license and move to the Wilcox Gallery of Homes. It was difficult for her to leave our friend, Dr. Hornaday. Since he was a pilot, he continued to ask us to go on flying trips to various locations to eat out with him.

Thankfully, he always footed the bill.

With the money from Jenny's first real estate closing, we decided to take a short vacation to the Bahamas. Those were three of the most awesome days of my life! I had never enjoyed being with someone so much as we jogged, swam, and shopped at the basket market. We kept an eye on our small amount of cash and saved enough for the taxi back to the airport. When we arrived at the airport and tried to check in, we were confronted with a forgotten $6.00 each boarding pass tax. We simply did not have it. We did not have any money or credit card to spend another night in a motel. No one was sympathetic with our plight. The plane left without us! We sought out the American Consulate and appealed to him for the $12.00 needed to get on board the plane to fly home. He reluctantly agreed to give us the cash. I took his name and address. We called

Jenny's mom "collect" to delay picking us up at the airport. I mailed the $12.00 back to this wonderful Good Samaritan. He was so surprised! We were not the first of many who had borrowed money from him, but he said we were the first to ever repay him for his generosity. We exchanged Christmas cards for about ten years. By the way, we still have some of those priceless straw baskets that we purchased on that trip.

During that year, we came to be close to Rosalie and her family. Her brother, Phil Romano, owned several restaurants in the Palm Beach County area: Old Mother Shuckers on Military Trail, The Pasta House in Lake Worth, and one of his most successful at the time was Romano's 300 on Palm Beach Island. Jenny's sister, Jill, was the vice president; her twin brother Jeff worked there as well as Jenny's ex, Eddie, who was the purchasing agent. Phil took out a million-dollar policy on Jill shortly before her tragic death in her Porsche (many questions have gone unanswered as to this being an accident). Phil received "double indemnity" from Jill's death and used the money to go to Texas and begin a new franchise called Fuddruckers Hamburgers. He also began an Italian restaurant franchise called Romano's. Let me give you the background as to how Phil chose the name for his first franchise. The girls in Dr. Hornaday's office liked to play tricks on any new girl who came to work in the office. They would tell her to go out into the waiting room and call for the next appointment. These were the names they would make up to embarrass the new girl: "Mr. Shitlips, please come in," or "Mr. Fuddrucker, the dentist is ready to see you." At Phil Romano's house one evening, he listened to his sister, Rosalie, and Jenny laughing about these funny tricks that they had pulled on innocent new girls. He liked the name Fuddruckers and decided to name his new chain of hamburgers with that name.

Fuddruckers restaurant

Phil Romano's investor, Jed Cassuba, was a developer and business partner in Phil's restaurant businesses. Jed's brother-in-law, Nick Raisch, another investor, was an outstanding football player for Notre Dame in the 1950s. Jenny and I became friends with him. My attorney friend, Bennie Dunkum, from Richmond, Virginia was coming for a visit, so I set up an all day get-acquainted schedule to socialize and eat together with the powers that be on Palm Beach and the area. Starting with breakfast, Jenny and I escorted Bennie to meet and spend time with about ten of our outstanding friends. Nick and his wife were one of those gracious hosts. Their house was on land that extended from the Intracoastal Waterway to the Atlantic Ocean. He took us to his gymnasium, wine cellar, and such luxuries that I had never seen before. All of these visits lasted until after midnight. Bennie was impressed!

One of our friends was the owner of a pizza shop. He had been placed into the witness protection program and moved from New York to the North Palm Beach area to start life over again incognito. I met a whole new stratum of friends during this first year with Jenny.

On a visit back to the Granada, I found the old candy machine turned around facing the wall. I asked about it, and Jane said it was broken and she was junking it. I took it, repaired it, and painted it. Ollie Wilcox got permission for us to place it in the building. This one little candy machine was our lifesaver on many occasions. With little income between real estate closings, we often needed to get gas in the car to take clients to see property, or buy a couple of hamburgers, or get some quarters to go to the Laundromat. It was almost like magic! There was always just enough to do the very basic necessity at the time. God works in mysterious ways! I was pressed into getting gas to show a very rich client from Italy a property on Worth Avenue in Palm Beach. He and his wife rode in the back of my bright yellow Buick. He told me his Philippe watch was not working properly, so I volunteered to take it to a watch shop. He politely declined. A crooked banker busted that million-dollar deal the morning we were meeting to have the closing.

Another time on a holiday weekend, a call came in with an urgent request to see some property pronto! Ollie, my broker, asked if I could take him to look at some properties. I went to the candy machine, got some coins, bought gas, and took him to see some houses in the \$50,000 to \$60,000 range. He was a nice Black gentleman and had a lady friend with him. The first house was a 3-bedroom 2-bath home for $58,000.00. He looked through the rooms and we ended up on the patio in the backyard. I asked him. "Do you like this house? Or do you want to look at some more? He said, "No, this one will do." He took a paper bag from beneath his arm and dumped a bag of bundled hundred dollar bills onto the table. He invited me to count out the $58,000. I was in shock! I had never seen so much cash laying out in the open! I told him that we needed to go back to the office and write up a contract. He said, "You mean I can't deal with you? Am I going to have to get an attorney and all of that?" I told him that with his cash, it would not take long to close the deal. He picked his money up and gave me the girl's phone number. I called day after day and for weeks...no answer. When I would talk to the girl, she would say that he disappeared that night and she never heard from him again.

My divorce dragged on for months! Impatient, I finally urged my attorney to call Jane's attorney to get together for an agreement. Jane kept interrupting me when I talked about what I wanted in the settlement. Her attorney sent her out to the waiting room. I assured her attorney that she could have the motel and all eleven of my life insurance policies that I had accumulated. She wanted custody of the three children and I agreed with the stipulation that she would take care of all of their expenses–including their college education expenses (my three children were never afforded this opportunity). We had purchased the five-apartment complex across the street within the past year and furnished each one. The apartment complex was still mortgaged to the max, but I wanted it for a rental property. The attorney thought that was a fair arrangement, so we settled.

Jenny took to selling real estate like a pro! She paid attention to all of the details. Ollie Wilcox had a fifty-foot sign across the entire length of our sales room featuring a toilet commode: "THE JOB IS NOT FINISHED UNTIL THE PAPER WORK IS DONE!" Jenny was in contention every month for the "Realtor of the Month" and made "Million-Dollar Salesperson of the Year" three years in a row. She attained this distinction by selling FHA & VA homes for $25,000 to $40,000 each to reach a million dollars in sales. I moved into commercial real estate and had some great success in getting deals signed, but invariably, attorneys and bankers proved to torpedo nearly every deal.

One for $650,000 closed but it took me two years to sue and receive my commission.

About the five-apartment complex that I received out of the divorce proceedings, Jane confiscated all of the furnishings out of the five apartments. The rooms were bare when I took them over. I still had three credit cards in my possession, so I went to various furniture stores and bought beds, chairs, tables, etc., to furnish the apartments. My cards only had a $1500 limit on each. Now suddenly each card had about $6,000 charged to each of them. A credit man with the card companies called and told me how much I had gone over my credit limit. When he told me, "You cannot do that!" I calmly told him that I already had! I explained my situation to him and told him that I was going to pay back every penny plus interest. Every month, he called and I would tell him how much I could afford to pay on these debts. It took two years, and when I made the final payment, he said, "If you are ever in Atlanta, please call me! I want to meet you and take you to lunch!" After many headaches with renters, I finally got an offer from the Northwood Baptist Church located just across the street to purchase the apartments. The sale netted me a much-needed $12,000.00.

The first Christmas with Jenny, we collected a ton of pinecones and various kinds of nuts: walnuts, hazelnuts, pecans, almonds, etc., and some dried flowers. We proceeded to drill holes in these and make Christmas wreaths for all of our friends. Our fingers were raw from making these. We still have ours and the one we made for her mom. One night while we were working on these wreaths with Jenny's next-door apartment neighbors, I was really upset. I was complaining a good bit about how my ex had sold all of my tools, including a De Walt radial saw that my brother-in-law, Charlie Eidson, had given me, worth about $2,500.00. She sold it for $100. I then told them that I was afraid she was going to sell the 1888 locomotive bell that sat on top of a train and was installed in the first church building of Hatcher Memorial Baptist Church. It rang loudly to call worshippers to church during the 1920s. I said that I had gone by and got the numbers off of the garage locks and that *I* had keys made to get into the garage. The problem was the fact that the bell was too heavy for one person to move. By this time, Jenny's neighbor, who had probably had a few too many beers at this point, jumped up and said, "Hell, let's go get the damn bell!" We drove from North Palm Beach to the Granada Inn and pulled into the alley behind the garage and apartment complex above. It was hard to keep from making noise. The dogs began to bark with excitement, but we finally opened the gate. We got into the garage and wrapped a towel around the clapper of the bell to prevent it from ringing. My friend grabbed one side of the bell as though he was going to take off with it. It did not move! He grunted and glared at the bell and cussed a bit. Damn, that thing is really heavy. Bit by bit, and inch by inch, we scooted it into the alley. Next, was the exertion needed to get it into the trunk of his little car. He and his girlfriend, plus me and Jenny, all got some kind of grip on the housing of the bell, and on the count of three, we made a swing for the trunk. On about the third try, we landed the bell on the bumper. His bumper was badly scratched by now! We rolled it gently on its side and into the trunk. I do not remember when or how we got it out of his car!

Jenny and I started attending the Chapel in the Sun, which met in the Holiday Inn on Singer Island with chandeliers made of Seagram's Seven liquor bottles. Rev. Barry Schahn was the minister. On our first visit, he saw us come in as we slipped into the back row. After the song, the pastor said, "I see my friend, Norm Ferguson, has come in, and I am going to ask him to lead us in prayer." I prayed and we sat down. Jenny was aghast! "Did you know he was going to do that?" "No," I answered. "Well, he better not do that to me!" Going out after the service, I teased her by telling Barry what she had said. Months went by, and gradually Jenny began to understand that her faith is a personal thing between a person and their Lord who loved us enough to lay down His life for us. She made a profession of faith (I later baptized her in California). She really surprised Pastor Barry one Sunday when she said going out the door, "Well, I think I'm ready now!" Puzzled, he looked at her and said, "Ready for what?" She said, "Well, if you call on me to pray, I think I can do it now!" And so he did one Sunday as he asked, "Miss Jenny, would you please dismiss us in prayer?"

WEDDING IN LEYSIN, SWITZERLAND 1978

Switzerland Wedding in Leysin's seventeenth-century church

Switzerland window flower boxes

We had been attending the Chapel in the Sun for about a year when Pastor Barry Schahn said, "Norm, we have a group of forty of your friends going to Leysin, Switzerland, for a ski trip. There is a beautiful 17th-century church there that we have permission to use. This would make a beautiful setting for yours and Jenny's wedding. I said, "Ok, let me ask her." In a nice romantic setting, with a soft whisper, I said, "Jenny, how would you like to go to Switzerland and get married? There was a long period of silence. I thought that maybe she had not heard me, but then she said, "Well, the Switzerland part sounds good." I answered. "No, no. It is a package deal" (she accuses me of bribing her with the trip to get her to marry me)! Among the forty friends who accompanied us was one girl who sang and played the guitar. Several gave us their advice on how to be happily married, and many took pictures. Everyone preceded us out of the church. When they motioned for us to exit, we found they had formed an arched gauntlet with their ski poles and made us run under as they pelted us with snowballs. Back at the hotel, the local bakery had baked and decorated a beautiful cake for the entire party. It was a storybook wedding (this entire trip set us back $695 each)!

Let me tell you a bit about the skiing. We went up the gondola and dozens of little kids, no more than 4 to 6 years old, were going down the slopes. We said, "Well, it can't be too difficult!" So, we went back down and got our togs and skis. Returning to the top of the mountain, I told Jenny (like the gentleman that I am) to go first. She disappeared over the ridge! I inched toward the edge and began to snowplow in zigzag fashion down the steep incline until I found her piled up in the snow. We went a bit further, and at a very sharp bend, we both plowed into a vertical snowbank and jammed our skis into the snow wall. There we were, side by side, stuck about four feet up in the bank and neither of us could move. We laughed so hard trying to free ourselves to get back on track. It took us an hour to get down the slope that first trip.

Now, I had skied in Colorado, North Carolina, Pennsylvania, etc., but this was my first introduction to giant MOGULS! I fell from one mogul to the next for what seemed to be a half-mile. By the last day, my hip was so bruised I could not bear to think of falling on it again. So, when I came to the moguls, I decided the best approach would be to go straight down as fast as I could and get it over quick! I marveled at how fast I was skiing! Barely hitting the tops of the moguls, I began to think, "If I wipe out at this speed, I may not live!" Sure enough, I catapulted into what seemed like an orbit and rolled forever in the snow. As I lay there half conscious, a stream of people came by and dropped off my gloves, my toboggan, my bent poles, one of my skis, etc. I could not bear to put weight on the left leg. The calf was so pulverized and bruised where the safety strap holding the ski to my leg caused it to whip around and severely bruise it. It took six months to heal!

One of my commercial listings working real estate was the Howard Johnson motel in Juno Beach, Florida. There were two of us in the commercial division of Wilcox Gallery of Homes, Jim King and me. I did not enjoy his company! He was very self centered and suggested shady tactics when dealing with customers. However, he became heavily involved in stitching together a plan for us to buy the Howard Johnson motel and we would become managing partners. I enlisted the big investors together from my friends at the Chapel In the Sun, namely, Ed Hawkins, Gordon Grey, and Zell Davis. Ed was the heavy hitter. He was a retired racecar driver and had sold his once-owned race track to Hollywood actor, Telly Savalas. Howard Johnson required someone of his net worth to make a viable purchase of the property. We secured a first-mortgage loan on the 36 rooms and property. Extra acreage with the motel was owned and we secured a second mortgage commitment on that. We still needed a $75,000 third mortgage to make the deal fly. Jim and I threw our commissions into the deal to each buy one-fifth of the ownership. We searched everywhere, but could not find a way to close the deal. While I was working on some of our remodeling jobs on the Intercoastal Waterway and the one in Riviera Beach, Jenny was showing a young man some properties. When I got home, she told me of this strange encounter with a young man in a very expensive car with tinted windows. As they looked at various properties, he asked her, "Are you investing in any of these properties yourself?" She told him about our Howard Johnson deal and the fact that we had not been able to find an investor willing to put up $75,000 for a third-place mortgage. As they were parting, he handed her his card and said, "Have your husband go to Miami and talk to this gentleman. I think he can help you." I was skeptical, but Jenny said, "What does it hurt to go and check it out?" So, I drove to Miami. This was not in a very affluent neighborhood! The buildings were poor and rundown and in the low-rent district of Miami. The office was nothing elaborate, but small and reeked of smoke! When I went in, there was no receptionist, but a rather large gentleman with his feet on his desk, smoking a cigar. Without taking his feet off the desk, he asked, "Yeah! What can I do for you?" I handed him the card and told him that the young man who gave me the card directed me to come and see him about a $75,000 loan. He immediately sat up and his feet hit the floor. He asked a few questions. He wanted to know if I had any reservations about taking offshore money for the loan. I told him that if he had a cashier's check at the closing, money would be money! He told me to call him about three days before the closing was to take place. I was full of questions, so I said, "How long will we have to wait for the committee before we have an answer as to whether we will get the loan?" He said, "We don't have committees. You got the loan when my boss gave you that card!"

There must have been 35 people assembled in the bank at 10:00 a.m. in Riviera Beach, Florida for the closing. The owner of the motel and his son were there with their attorneys, both realtors were there, representatives from Howard Johnson were present, our investors were present, and numerous bank people were running around with arm loads of papers. There was not any third mortgage guy with a $75,000 cashier's check present yet! The banker was ranting that he did not realize we had so many other loans and liens with mortgages on the property and so many investors. He was a befuddled old gentleman who seemed to be out of his expertise. We had lunches brought in, and I was making calls to Miami every little bit. About 2:00 p.m., our Miami attorney came in and sat down beside me. He wanted to know what was going on and I told him the banker was holding the process up. He stood up and took off his coat, exposing his large frame with suspenders holding his pants up and said in a very commanding voice, "I don't know about the rest of you, but I have other business to attend to. Here is my cashier's check for the third mortgage in the amount of $75,000. Why is the bank griping about other mortgages? They have the first-place lien, so the bank is assured of getting their money before we get ours! Start the papers around! Let's all sign these and get this deal done." Papers started shuffling and everyone signed. We became the proud owners of the Howard Johnson Motel in Juno Beach at about 7:00 that evening.

Jenny received one of the worst sunburns of her life draining the Howard Johnson swimming pool, scraping and sanding the concrete walls, and painting the HJ logo onto the bottom of the pool. I replaced the weeds in the lawn with new Saint Augustine grass sod. Jim King and his girlfriend moved into the motel and took over as resident managers. I did not object at the time because I had plenty of other responsibilities.

With Jenny's background of snorkeling in Key Biscayne and swimming in the ocean, she signed me up for another precarious and exciting adventure. We began scuba diving lessons. The best place for us to practice putting on our tanks and gear was at the Howard Johnson swimming pool. We made several simulated dives getting accustomed to breathing underwater with our oxygen tanks on our back. In the boat, we repeated getting into the water with our life jackets inflated. Once we were comfortable, we let the air out of the life jacket, and with our goggles and masks on, the belt weights around our waist would pull us downward. After a few trips like this, I noticed that nearly everyone else would sit on the back of the boat and fall into the water backwards without their life jackets inflated. Holding onto their mask, they would immediately sink. I decided to try this newly learned method. Upon flipping backwards into the water, my mask and tube filled with water. I was already underwater and struggled to get back to the top. I was drowning and no one noticed! With strenuous and desperate strokes, I broke surface where the boat captain was close and pulled me in. I rested a minute. He said, "Follow the anchor rope and pull yourself down to join the group." Again, after long minutes of pulling as hard as I could, the group never seemed to get any closer. Suddenly, I ran out of air and immediately made an effort to get back to the top of the water. Again, the man on the boat asked, "What's wrong?" I told him, "I'm out of air!" He laughed and said, "You cannot be out of air, you just got in the water a few minutes ago." I went to the back of the boat and sat on the ramp. He inspected my equipment and indeed found the oxygen tank valve shut. He said, "I saw you struggling. The rope got under the knob of your oxygen tank and every time you pulled on the rope, it turned the knob and shut your air off." I finally joined my group. The diving teacher pointed out the Moray Eels in their holes below with teeth barred. We hitched a ride on some very large sea turtles. Suddenly, he held up his hand with caution. He gingerly stirred the sand ahead with his swim flipper. It looked like the entire ocean floor moved. A giant Manta Ray glided gracefully away. Looking at the oxygen that was left in my tank, I knew that we had to go back to the surface after a 90-foot dive. I pointed to my watch and indicated to Jenny that I needed to go back up. She could not understand why I had used so much air. She still had half of a tank! She wanted to stay and try to catch one of the monstrous lobsters we viewed up close. The scuba dive instructor announced that our last dive would be at night. After such a "fun day," I decided to gracefully decline that last dive.

The workers at our Howard Johnson motel began to confide that my partner, Jim King, was not honest. He had confiscated three of our new TVs, kept the money from the vending machines, and checked in people to several rooms per night without going through the cash register or listing them on the books. My co-owners did not believe that I knew what I was talking about. One night, the young night manager alerted me to Jim's absence. I went in, took the books from the safe, and made copies of all of the entries, then took the books back. Jim did not know that I had done this. I found that he had not paid any sales tax, and because I was a partner, I ended up paying all of the back taxes after kicking him out. When I gave the facts to my fellow owners, I said, "Don't take my word for it. Go interview the people who work for us at the motel." They did.

When they talked with the young man at the front desk what he thought about Mr. Jim King as a manager, his reply: "Well, if there was going to be a hanging of Jim King, there would be one hell of a fight as to who gets to hold the rope!" Convinced, they bought Jim's portion of ownership. I learned a hard lesson. Never go into partnership with ANYONE again!

While we were trying to put the motel deal together, I made a stop at the Dairy Belle, a former Dairy Queen that was owned by a little Christian lady for about 27 years. I was a regular customer of hers, and she had the best ice cream in the area. If she was not busy, we would sometimes talk. On this particular day, she remarked, "I want you to buy_my store." I laughed and said, "You meant to say you want me to sell your store?" She repeated, "No, I want a good Christian to buy my store and treat my customers fairly. I know that you would manage it well." I looked at her in disbelief and said, "Well, thanks for the compliment, but I have been through a divorce and I could not raise $100 dollars if my life depended on it." She replied, "This is a good investment and will make you money. You can pay for my inventory out of each month's cash flow. I will work for you at minimum wage until you are comfortable running the business. I am tired, getting old, and I need to retire." We went over some figures and shook hands. I drove back to the real estate office where Jenny was working. She looked at me and said, "Is something wrong?" So I told her that I had just bought the Dairy Belle! She started asking, "How? With What? Have you gone crazy?" This little ice cream store became a much larger income staple than we could have imagined. It was similar to the little candy machine we depended on so often, only it generated a lot more money.

Dairy Belle Ice Cream store, Riviera Beach, Florida

Jenny's mom was a travel agent. We were coming back from visiting my parents in Oklahoma and were driving in North Carolina when Jenny spotted an out-rigging store and had me park. When she came out, she said, "We need to get a motel for the night. We are booked to go whitewater rafting in the morning at 6:00 a.m." We got to the edge of the Nolichucky River the next morning to meet our guide, the two other couples, and instructions for the trip down the river. Both of the other couples were old and almost feeble. Our guide instructed us how to sit with our legs locked under the raft tubing and "draw right" or "draw left" with our paddles instantly when he yelled out. Here is how the brochure describes the trip: "Whitewater rafting the Nolichucky is an experience that challenges rafters with extreme rapids in an impressive wilderness setting. The Unalaska Mountains provide an incredible backdrop as you paddle from North Carolina into Tennessee in the steepest river gorge east of the Mississippi."

My fears from having just seen the movie *Deliverance* and hearing shots during the trip kept me tense the whole day! Yes, the view was spectacular! It was a thrill a minute or more! We turned over and bumped down the rapids with our life jackets. We were accompanied by another group in a raft.

After ours capsized and jammed up against a boulder, the other group pulled to the shore and came back with ropes. They stretched ropes across the river. Our guides made it to our raft by hanging onto the overhanging rope. It took hours to free our raft from the force of the strong current pounding it against the boulder. Our water and dinner in a cooler had been lost when we capsized. Back in the raft, Jenny and I, along with our guide, were almost on our own as we tried to keep the raft upright. It was dark when we finally finished docking and were relieved to get on the bus to take us back to North Carolina. My arms and shoulders have never ached or hurt so bad! A few years later, we took Summer Joy and Heather on a bit more tame river near Seneca, South Carolina, to enjoy this exhilarating experience!

Family white water rafting down a "more tame" river in South Carolina

This was a time before cellphones. The forerunner was a pager, and mine was at my side, constantly going off. One time the call was from my partner on the First Street remodeling project in Riviera Beach. The next call was an inspector looking at our Intercoastal remodeling project, or one of our carpenters, named John Brinson, who was working on six of the Howard Johnson motel rooms at a time. We were upgrading each unit with new bathroom fixtures, tile, and flooring. Some days, it was the Dairy Belle needing a refrigeration man, or someone did not show up to work. Often, it was the office wanting us to take someone to look at real estate. We definitely had too many irons in the fire. Every time the pager would go off, I had to find a phone to contact the person calling. One call blasted the message, "Mr. Ferguson, please call the sheriff's office." I figured someone had dialed the wrong number, so I ignored it. They called again! I took a break to knock on a neighbor's door to use their phone to call the sheriff. "Mr. Ferguson, we have your boys here. We caught them stealing a baseball glove from Wal-Mart and they are here in custody. Would you like to come and bail them out?" Those were not the kind of calls that I wanted to hear! Bradley talks about the time he took a bowling ball to the bridge overpass from Riviera Beach to Singer Island and let it roll down into the business district at the bottom of the bridge. It hit a building like a bomb and did a lot of damage. Fortunately, no one was hurt. The kids disappeared from the scene pretty quickly after this foolish prank.

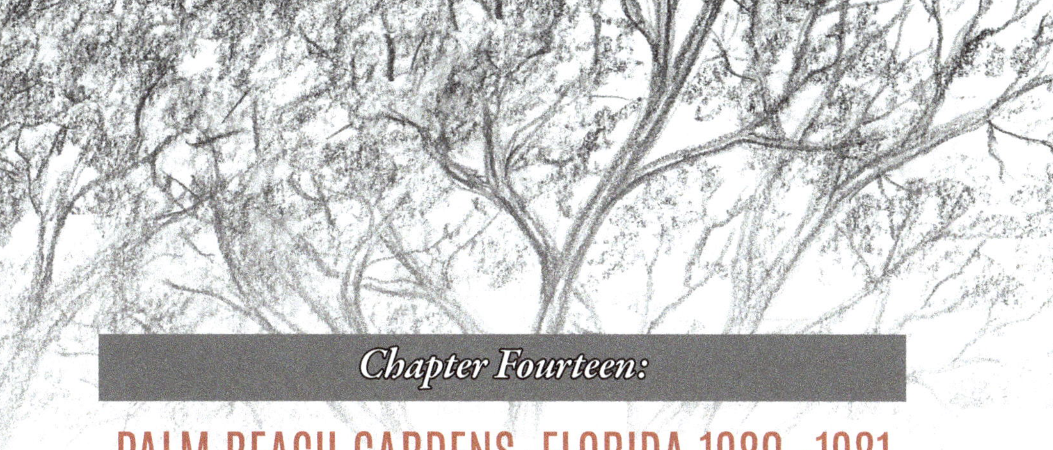

Chapter Fourteen:

PALM BEACH GARDENS, FLORIDA 1980 -1981

Life was really busy and often hectic. We were trying to survive and talked about having a nice home of our own. We witnessed many great distressed sales as they would come on the market, but we were in no position financially to purchase any of them. One of our associates, Chuck Stelli, listed a home in his Palm Beach Gardens neighborhood and posted it on the office bulletin board. When I spotted it, I immediately drove over to have a look. It was a very nice 3-bedroom, 2-bath home on an inside corner lot with a very large back yard. This was enhanced by several fruit trees and some tall pines. The mortgage was an assumable VA loan. I grabbed Jenny and took her to look at it. Then, I petitioned our broker, Ollie Wilcox, if he would waive the broker's commission for a salesman's personal home and he said "Yes." With our sales/buyer's commission, we got our home with almost no money down. What a Godsend! This was a nice little neighborhood, and soon, our friends, Joel and Sylvia Sharpton, moved into a house down the street. They acted as Summer Joy's godparents and babysat with her often. Sylvia loved rocking Summer Joy until she would drift off to sleep. We got busy & remodeled our home and took pride in our dwelling. Jenny and I did not have much furniture, and I had lost all of my tools in the divorce. God provided! One of Jenny's listings of a home for sale was that of a little lady in her 90s. Her husband had passed away and now she was selling her home to fly to California to live with her sister. She was selling everything! Jenny and I moved through each room and noted how so much of her furniture would fit into our new home. I told her that we really did want to take most of the tools and a lot of the furniture as well as knickknacks. I think she adopted us. She said, "You mark all the things that you want. I will set a price on them and you can pay me out of your commission when we close the deal on the house." Her sister came from California for the closing. We had set all of the new furnishings up in our new home on 4444 Birdwood in Palm Beach Gardens. We told the two sisters that we wanted to take them to lunch after the closing. After the meal, we asked if they would like to see where we had placed all of their precious belongings. Their excited response was "Yes!" It was so much fun to see their approval and exclamations and compliments about how we were going to continue to make good use of their heritage; one bed we still have was handmade by these two ladies' great grandfather. This precious home was the stage where we witnessed Summer Joy take her first steps. She was standing in the kitchen, trying to keep her balance. Teetering to the left, she staggered her first step, but did not fall! She followed quickly with about a dozen steps into the utility room before she toppled over!

Just after moving into our new home, I stopped at the bank in North Palm Beach. When I came out and got into my little Ford, it would not start. I called for help. They could not figure out the problem, but agreed to tow it to their shop and do a diagnostic test to locate the problem. About a week later, I went by to check on the progress, and was shocked that the business had used a teen to take my entire engine apart. They demanded $1500 for the work done and another $3,000 to reassemble. When I asked if they found the problem, they replied "No, but whatever it is will be corrected when we reassemble." We scrapped up enough money to get the car released and towed to our new home on Birdwood. The trunk and seats were loaded down with buckets of parts. Across the street lived a very Good Samaritan who was a mechanic for the Palm Beach Gardens Police Department. He noticed our dilemma and offered to help. He showed us what the first step would be to reassemble the car. After work each day, he would inspect the work that Jenny and I had done on the car and advise us to the next step. About two months later, we got the car back together (minus a few parts left over). We turned the switch, and WOW! IT STARTED! We immediately took it to a car dealer and traded it in.

Another memorable event happened while Bradley was sitting in the Florida room. Jenny and I were working on a nice canopy with several lights to hang over our bed. A thunderstorm suddenly developed. Lightening hit one of our pine trees. The bolt of lightning then plowed a ditch from the tree to the corner of the house and blew the fascia boards off at the corner of the roof. Brad was sitting next to that window and came running into our bedroom with eyes the size of saucers, yelling and asking, "Did you guys hear that?" Most of the lights blew out in the entire house. This happened the day before our Open House event.

About this time, I had secretly contracted for a young man who worked for us at the Dairy Belle to restore a 1968 red Volkswagen convertible for Jenny's birthday. Unfortunately, on his way to surprise her with the beautiful restored VW, he had a wreck! This ruined the surprise and we had to have all that work done over again!

As some of our remodeling projects began to be completed and the real estate market went into a slight slump, I secured a job working for a construction company in one of the many building projects going on in the Jupiter area. Working late to finish, pouring a large foundation, an inexperienced crane operator knocked me off of a 15-foot wall with the concrete bucket as he swung it around and hit me. A few days later, a spear-shaped piece of one-inch roofing plywood slid off of the roof and stuck in the ground about a foot from where I was working. Not long after that, I was on a scaffold inside the house and a roofer above the partially-covered roof squatted down, causing his hammer to come out of the loop in his belt and fall. The hammer claws hit me in the head. I tumbled off of the scaffold and onto the floor, unconscious and bleeding. When I woke up, I was in an ambulance going to the hospital to get sewn up. Jenny's reaction was, "Let's start spending more time at the Dairy Belle. I think we are getting ripped off when we are not there." This proved to be true by hundreds of dollars a week.

Ed Hawkins, our Howard Johnson partner, was also on the board of a Christian camp in the Adirondack Mountains in New York. He secured reservations for Brad and Nathan to attend. We flew up and notified Shirley Locke Anderson (Jenny's friend who owned property in Key West and West Palm Beach) that we were coming to visit her in Brattleboro, Vermont. As a professional and well-known artist, she had promised Jenny that she would paint a portrait of her if we ever came to visit her. When she left Florida, it was in order to buy her childhood farm home and restore it. We dropped the boys off for three weeks of camp. Shirley started painting the portrait of Jenny. After three days of watching the paint dry, I became restless. I took the rental car and checked out the countryside. After driving aimlessly admiring the countryside, I came across a yard and barn sale. The yard sale had a sign that read, "Player piano for sale in the barn." I walked down to the barn and found an old timer sitting there. I asked how much he wanted for the old piano. He said, "A hundred dollars." I asked, "Does the three boxes of player rolls go with the piano?" "Yep," was his answer. I proceeded to qualify myself and told him that I was visiting Shirley Locke Anderson and that we were out of state from Palm Beach Gardens, Florida. I asked, "Would you be willing to take a check since I don't have cash with me?" He looked me over for a bit and finally said, "Well, you look to be a pretty honest fellow, so I'll take your check." I wrote him a check for $100 and headed back to the farmhouse. Jenny wanted to know where I had been, so I told her, "I found a player piano and bought it for $100.00." She laughed and said, "No, you did not! Quit telling me fibs. Remember, we flew up here. There is no way you could get a piano from here to Florida." I assured her that "It was too good of a deal to pass up." She really thought she had married a lunatic. I got on the phone and found a Ryder truck that I could rent one way for $750. When I told her that, she said, "Oh, that makes a lot of sense! You are going to spend $750 to get a $100 piano to Florida." So I had to tell her the rest of my plans. "There are so many antique sales going on around us, we can fill the truck up with antiques and sell them when we get back to Florida." Her eyes lit up with the prospect of antique shopping. Shirley assured all the people we bought things from that we were good for repaying them after we got back to Florida and sold the items. One large roll-top desk sold for enough to pay for our entire trip. We had many other unique things, like pump organs, sewing machines, iceboxes, etc. We canceled our airplane tickets since Jenny insisted on staying with me in the hot Ryder truck with no air conditioning. We had 1500 miles of bumpy roads ahead. It was August, and she was seven months pregnant. We picked up Brad and Nathan and started the long tortuous journey home. Jenny had her feet up on the dash with the window down trying to stay cool, but I could tell she was miserable. To tease her a bit, I would periodically reach around the two boys between us and gently punch her on the shoulder. "What?" she would ask in an irritated response. I would smile and say, "Isn't it a joy to be pregnant in the summertime?" We finally made it home, and the antique sale was a great success. One lady came to look at the large roll-top desk. She said that it was much too large for what she needed. Then she said, "But I want to buy your back-loading antique ice box!" I assured her that it was my wife's pride and joy and that it was not for sale. She offered three times what we had paid for it. I said, "Lady, you caught me when we really need the money. Take it, do not leave your address or phone number, or my wife will be coming to get it!" Sure enough, forty years later, Jenny has not let me forget my mistake of selling her icebox!

We thought the delivery date for the baby was to be about the end of September, but was delayed until October 12th, Columbus Day. On that Sunday morning, Jenny woke me up and said, "My water broke." I jumped out of bed and was rushing to get her to the hospital when she said, "I need to go by the Dairy Belle and write the payroll checks before we go to the hospital." When we checked into the hospital, they took X-rays. The doctor was called in. I was faithfully doing my duty as a Lamaze coach to try to keep her calm and remind her to take deep breaths. When the doctor came, he announced a change of plans. "The baby is breached, so we are going to do a C-section to assure the safety of you and the baby." All of Norm's Lamaze training was not needed! Jenny began to cry. The doctor and I tried to assure her that she would be ok. She said, "I know, but I was hoping to watch my Dolphins play football this afternoon, and now I will be asleep!" Talk about a true Dolphin fan! In the delivery room, the discussion turned to naming the baby. Jenny said, "What are we going to name the baby?" I replied, "Well, if it is a girl, I think we should name her Summer Joy!" I do not think we imagined that this name derived from a teasing would be literally fulfilled by this little lady! She has brought JOY to so many!

The C-section surgery was a success but it cost an extra $1500 to get Jenny and Summer Joy released from the hospital. We had not planned for this and were not prepared to pay. One of our dear friends and investors in the Howard Johnson motel, Gordon Gray, and his wife,

Edie, graciously loaned us the money to bring the girls home from the hospital.

Shortly after that, Summer Joy became a vibrant and vital part of our lives! What more can one ask for? We had a new home, a new baby, and we were the owners of an ice cream store, a motel, and good health. God is good! ALL THE TIME!

Brad and Nate came to stay with us often, as well as Lori. We helped Lori get a couple of good jobs, but she was not ready or willing at this time in her life to settle down and work. She preferred to stay out all night and party. She experienced a couple of tragic deaths of two of her friends. I will leave that for her to tell you about.

Jane had married a body-building Canadian teacher who loved sailing and beach volleyball. He latched onto Jane and convinced her to purchase a 53-foot sailing vessel in which they could travel to almost any place in the world. According to the boys, Ray was intensely disliked. He was self-centered and mistreated them. I will spare you the graphic details. From the boys' account, Ray's treatment was one of the reasons that Brad chose to live with one of the Granada Inn's maids along with her son; a very pathetic situation. Then on a trip, she asked Brad (aged 13 at the time) if he would like to meet his real biological mother. He said yes, so she dropped him off in Corsicana, where Brad found a city full of relatives. Roxy, his biological mother, then asked if he wanted to meet his biological father? She took him to Gilbert Sutherlin's farm and introduced them. Brad ended up living there on the farm for his teenage years. The positive part was that Gilbert taught Brad how to move houses and level them. He taught him how to weld, to build, and to operate large pieces of equipment. The sad part was that he did not like Brad and would never compliment him no matter how hard Brad worked. When he died, he did not leave Brad anything! Jane has also made the statement that "Brad is not in my will." Jane asked us to take Nathan to live with us as she was not able to supervise him, and he was failing in his grades. We tutored him and had him making good grades. He became a student patrol officer at school. He was on the bowling team and proud of his grades. Brad came periodically, but did not get along well with our neighbor who had a swimming pool. He threw nails into the neighbor's pool to cause rust to form on the bottom. This was in retaliation because the neighbor had called the police when he observed Brad doing wheelies on our lawn-mower in the street. This is also when we began to find bits of weed stashed behind the toilet and in the closet by our boys. When we made a move to California, it did not seem possible to take them with us. This was difficult and heart-wrenching to see how neglected the boys were. What happened to our divorce agreement that Jane would provide and take care of them through school and college? At the time, we had a new baby and were facing unknown challenges in the job ahead.

Because of the many dangerous and unguarded bodies of water in Florida, we enrolled Summer Joy in "teach a baby to swim" at nine months of age. She was taught to turn over on her back and kick if she fell into water. When she came to the edge of the pool, she would turn over and hold onto the side for up to five minutes with both hands. I think this introduced her to one of her great loves, swimming. It was also a great benefit in her fight against her later health problem.

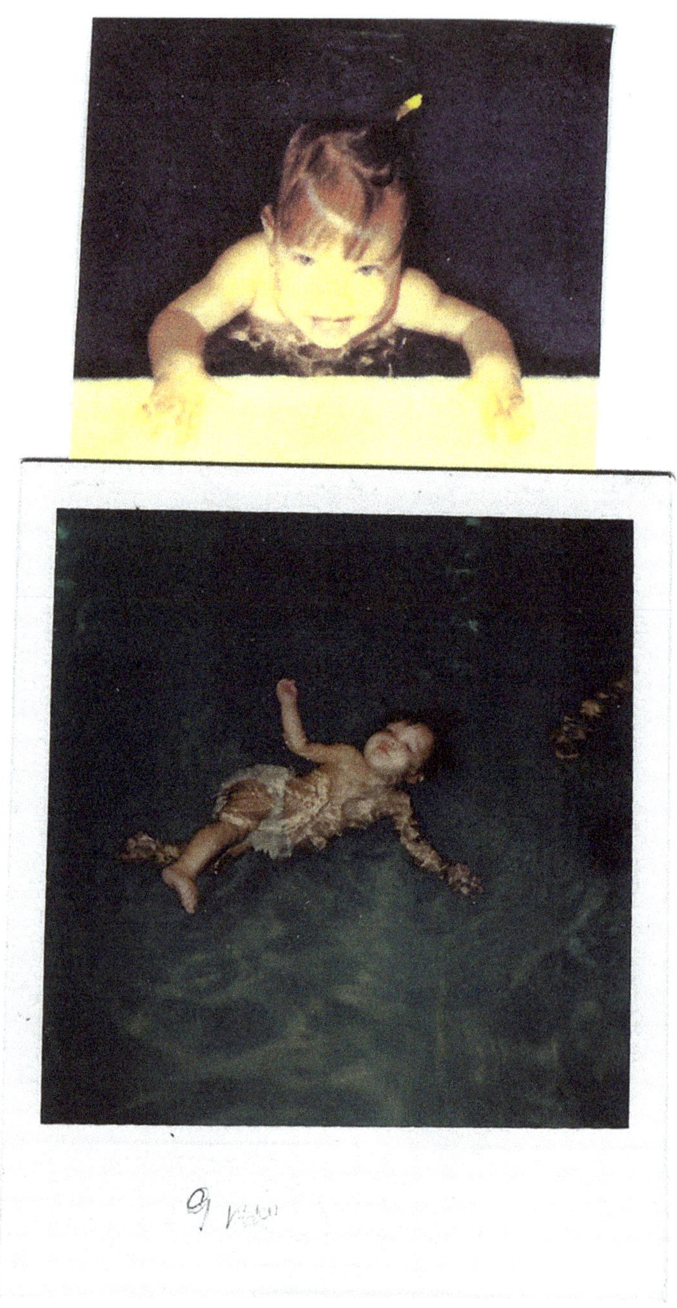

Summer Joy's swim lessons at nine months of age

She was the center of attention at the Dairy Belle, and spent hours jumping up and down in the jump swing mounted above the door leading to the cooler. The large double sink was her personal swimming pool. She used her little personal vehicle to find the box that contained broken ice cream cones and helped herself. When she could get someone to put ice cream in one of the cones, she would jam it to her mouth and hold it there until her face turned blue! Brad and Nate became two of our student employees. We noticed a problem with bad cans of whipping cream. Half a case would have no gas to make the whipping cream come out. We discovered that the employees were using the gas to make their voices sound funny. We did not think it was funny!

On one occasion, I got a phone call at 2:00 a.m. from the police that our Dairy Belle's large window had been smashed with a trashcan. They asked me to come and let them in because they thought the vandal was still inside. I arrived and opened the door. The policeman and his dog went in. The dog went straight to the cooler. As the dog was straining at the leash to tear into the looter, he was trembling with fear and came out without any resistance.

Insert image Dairy Belle

We also had two thefts of my briefcase with the day's cash money inside. This was over $1,000 on each occasion. The first was during a rainstorm, and I pulled in under the awning to jump out and go back into the Dairy Belle to retrieve something that I had forgotten. Less than a minute later, I jumped back into the car and immediately noticed that my briefcase was gone! The other time was when I had to go to the airport and meet someone. When I parked, I took the briefcase with the day's money in it and placed it in the trunk of the car. Evidently, someone was watching because when I came back 30 minutes later, the trunk had been pried open and my briefcase was gone!

The Chapel in the Sun sometimes met in Zell & Gloria Davis' home situated on the lake of beautiful Singer Island. This is where we were first introduced to Big Chuck Connors, affectionately nicknamed by his Brazilian church people as "Bwana." He had served on Dr. Jess Moody's staff at First Baptist Church in West Palm Beach and had developed a Christian missions ministry building churches all over Brazil; more than 100 such churches. He enlisted volunteers to pay their own way to go and help build these churches. After raising enough money to buy and ship the materials to build another church, he would take 10 to 15 people and construct another church structure made of concrete blocks

"Bwana" Chuck Conner

Brazilian pastor, Norton Lagges, Barry Schahn, and Norm

(we were destined to become more involved with Chuck years later). One Sunday stands out in my mind as a "red letter" day. It was when the United States Hockey team was playing the Russian team. The odds of the USA beating the Russians were almost zero because the American team were amateurs and college students. The Russian team was made up of older professional players. After church that Sunday morning, Barry invited us to their house to watch the game on TV. I have never been so excited and more proud to be an American than when we won that game. It was an epic moment in sports' history!

My old neighbor behind the Granada Inn, which backed up to my old house and faced the other street, was Herb Geller. He and I had both invested with Sammy in the gold venture in Columbia, South America. Dr. Hornaday was a third investor.

Herb also negotiated a land deal in the mountains of North Carolina that we bought into as another investment. Herb, plus Scott Carter, our attorney in North Carolina, and I decided it would be a good idea to make the trip to Columbia to check out our investment. We flew into Bogota and rented a private plane to fly us into a small field near Medellin, close to our gold mine. Upon landing, the plane hit a large rock in the dirt runway and blew a tire. We swerved and the plane went erratic and out of control. I thought we would flip, but the pilot brought it to a stop safely. The only building at this airport was a tin barn where a chicken was tied up by the leg near the door. The pilot was able to make some calls to get a new tire flown in. He told us that we would not be able to fly out until the next day. We hired a taxi (all of the taxis were 1955 to 1957 Chevrolets). I asked the driver how many miles he had on the old car and he motioned that the speedometer had turned over and over and over! We finally arrived at the gold mine after discovering the cab driver was taking us the long way around so he could charge us more! The perimeter of the gold processing acreage was lined with soldier-type guys brandishing rifles and ammunition belts across their chests. We identified ourselves and were given a tour. More than a hundred laborers were busy working. Bulldozers and backhoes were scooping the gravel and dirt from the riverbed and placing the wet gravel onto troughs with water running through. A sifting process shook the gravel and separated out the larger rocks and gravel. At the very last process, there were lots of flecks and small stones of gold.

We were shown how expensive the process was and told that there was a need to have more investors. We received word that a possible investor was in the city of Barranquilla. After conferring together, we got a flight into that city. We had booked a motel by the name of The El Goff. When we got off of the plane, we were getting our baggage and my buddies had already headed to the street. As I was identifying my luggage, a young man came up and flashed under his coat to show me something. We had already experienced several con artists flashing their coats open to reveal hot items for sale. I pushed back on him and told him that I was not interested! He insisted and I pushed him again and headed to the street with my bags. Evidently, I had shoved a young drug enforcement detective! When I caught up with Herb and our attorney, about eight undercover policemen surrounded us. Little did we know that the El Goff was the main outlet for drug dealing in Baranquilla. They ordered us to open all of our luggage. When they found my bottle of Tums, they declared "Drugs!" I assured them it was for my upset tummy. They finally released us, and we found the same type of men wearing bandoliers guarding the motel. We met with our possible investor, but he was not ready to invest. We called the airport to arrange for a return flight to Bogota. They laughed and said, "The company handling most outgoing flights has been closed for over two months now. People have been on the waiting list for weeks to get a flight out of here." We went to our room and found the window open. The ceiling was black with mosquitoes! We fought these varmints and swatted them–killing thousands. We asked the desk clerk to wake us at 3:00 a.m. and made our way back to the airport. At the desk, Herb slid a $100 dollar bill to the girl and told her that we really needed to get a flight out TODAY! She took the money and said for us to wait close by. Eventually, at about 9:00 a.m., she had seven open seats with reservations that had not yet been claimed. She nodded for us to come to the desk. We were in the process of getting our 3 tickets when a man came up claiming five of the tickets. That left only two available. Herb and the attorney gave me their cash and credit cards and jumped on the plane, leaving me behind to find a way out. After wondering around trying to find someone who could speak English, I found a 12-year-old kid who could speak some English. I showed him a $50 dollar bill and told him that he could have it if he would help me get a plane ticket out so I could fly to the United States. He stayed with me all day and all night! We went back into town and talked with different people. Each time, they would ask for five or ten dollars in order to share any information. A day later, we had been without sleep for 36 hours when we got a first-class ticket for about $300 to Cali. In the meantime, Herb and our attorney flew into Miami and Jenny was there to meet them. She asked, “Where is Norman?” She was incredulous and would not believe that they had left me in Columbia. She went back to North Palm Beach, awaiting some kind of communication from me. I arrived the next day in Miami and called her to come and get me! My interest in gold mines decreased greatly after that trip!

Herb Geller had been divorced, and when he found a new young lady willing to tie the knot, he asked if I would perform his wedding ceremony. I told him that I did not have a Jewish ceremony in my book of ceremonies. He said, “Oh, that’s ok, just make one up and we will stomp on the wine glass at the end.” I went to the bride-to-be and said, “Do you have anything that you would like to include in the ceremony?” “What do you mean?” she replied. So I told her that Herb told me to make up a ceremony and they would add the breaking of the wine glass at the end of the ceremony. She smiled and said, “Yes, I would like to have an input.” The day of the great event arrived with about 50 guests at their apartment. There was a beautiful winding staircase with many of the guests standing on it for a bird’s eye view of the wedding. After the processional and everyone was in place, I came to the part of the ceremony for each to pledge their vows to the other. I said, “Herb, do you promise to get up every Sunday morning and serve your wife breakfast in bed?” The silence was deafening! I heard a whisper, “I’ve never heard that in a ceremony before!” The blood drained from Herb’s face. His eyes were as big as saucers. I waited with a stone face. He stammered out, “I do!” After the ceremony, he cornered me and said, “You dirty dog! How could you do that to me, I am your friend!” I replied, “Herb, that was payback for what you did to me by leaving me in Columbia!”

Dr. Jess Moody became a very good friend while I was in Florida. He would come by and pick me up on his motorcycle or in his Mercedes car to invite me to go with him for a ride and have lunch together. Since I was a minister but not on his staff, I think perhaps I made a good listening post where he felt comfortable knowing I would not gossip. On one occasion, I took Jenny to the airport to meet him. When he got off of the plane, I introduced Jess to Jenny. He looked at her and said, "Honey, do your eyes bother you?" Surprised, she said "No, sir." He said, "Well, they sure do bother me!" A couple of years later, he called from California where he had become the pastor of the First Baptist Church of Van Nuys. He later moved the church and renamed it the Shepherd of the Hills Church.

Chapter Fifteen:

UNITED COMMUNITY CHURCH, GLENDALE, CALIFORNIA 1981 -1983

This call from Dr. Jess Moody was to advise me that there was an opportunity for me to get back into the church ministry. "Norm, you have rested long enough! There is a church here that needs your leadership." He asked me to contact Dr. Stuart McBirney, pastor of the Glendale United Community Church. I did, and flew to Glendale to look the situation over. I was surprised at what a large organization was involved. In addition to the church, there was a theological seminary, plus a national patriotic television ministry known for fighting communism worldwide. I negotiated the salary and terms of moving. I told him that I had to go back and liquidate our Dairy Belle business, our holdings in the Howard Johnson motel, and our home. This all happened within a month, and we moved by the first of the year. Jenny's brother, Jeff, and their mom, Jeanne, drove the Ryder truck with our furniture from Florida to California, pulling Jenny's red Volkswagen convertible behind the truck. They made a stop in New Braunfels, Texas, to visit one of Mom Mom's old golf buddies. She was the owner of a famous restaurant near the tubing industry on the Comal River.

Jenny and I made the trip in our car with baby Summer Joy. We stopped for an evening meal in Cloudcroft, New Mexico, and Jenny overheard a couple talking next to us. They had been snowmobiling and were going to go on a night ride later in the evening. With Jenny's adventurous spirit, she was insistent that we spend the night so we could go experience this. I refused to put Summer Joy on one of those monsters. We stayed in the car with the heater on and the motor running. They were gone for over three hours. They were required to wear a slick jumpsuit and follow the guide. They went airborne over moguls and steep inclines. They weaved in and out at breakneck speeds. Getting confident on a half-pike, back and forth, she was caught off guard when the guide made a sharp turn. Her hands were frozen and the nylon jumpsuit caused her to slide off! The snowmobile plowed into a small tree. This cost me $130.00 extra for damages when they got back. I was so relieved that my daredevil wife was okay!

This move to California was another step out on faith, but it was exciting to see how God works things out! My life verses from teenage years have always been my favorite promise; Proverbs 3:5-6: "Trust in the Lord with all your heart. Acknowledge Him and He will direct your path."

We found California to be beautiful and exciting! I remember asking Dr. Jess Moody before we moved, "What is California like?" He said, "Well, it is like a granola bar...a lot of fruits, nuts, and flakes out here. But most of the people are normal, and the climate is close to perfect." He told me that owning the first house that he bought in California netted him a profit of $50.00. When I questioned him about such a small profit, he corrected with, "Oh, that was $50 per hour from the time I purchased it until the time I sold it."

We found such wonderful people and quickly made friends with the ones who needed to be ministered to. I became very active in the Downtown Kiwanis Club, where I developed a whole set of new and gifted friends from all walks of life. Great opportunities and rewards came from this membership. During our tenure there, I probably gave over 200 of my "Tips for Success" motivational talks to various service clubs. While there, I also performed magic shows for their "Ladies Night" banquets. I was invited to join the famous "Magic Castle" in Hollywood, but we moved before I was scheduled to perform. After leaving California and moving to Alabama, this Kiwanis Club sent me an "Outstanding Citizenship Award" for performing at over 50 service clubs within a six-month period. I never received any remuneration for these talks, but I so thoroughly enjoyed entertaining that I think this could have become a satisfying career!

Minister of Prestidigitation, Norm, doing a magic show.

Jenny was happy to be in California. She grew up around the beaches of Key Biscayne. Now in California, she had time and opportunity to get back to the beach with Summer Joy and several other mothers with their little siblings.

Upon arriving with the truck full of our things, we were shocked to find the cost of housing! Driving around to view what was available, we lucked upon an old house (does God equate the word *luck* with His providence?) where workers and their trucks were visible. I stopped and found the owner. I asked if they were going to rent or sell the house. He said, "When we finish, we will put it up for rent." I asked, "How much will the rent be?" The answer: "$750.00 per month and no lease required." I explained that we had just arrived from Florida and we needed to unload our furniture as quickly as possible. They agreed that we could indeed move in if we did not mind having the workers finish their jobs. This older couple proved to be a great blessing in our lives. They were up in years and had owned this land when it was acreage. He developed the houses all around the four streets that encircled their own home, which included about two acres in the middle. Our old house was built in 1906. It had very large rooms and a partial basement. A backyard gate gave us access to the owners' property with a variety of fruit trees: avocados, persimmons, peach, pear, plum, apple, orange, lemon, and some of which I was not familiar with.

The United Community Church of Glendale was a very unique experience. The church had bought properties through the years to close streets, build a seminary, and a large television ministry. Many volunteers read all of the daily newspapers from all over the world to find and clip out articles on the spread of communism. Dr. McBirney was one of the foremost newscasters on the evils of communism. He daily exposed them on his large TV ministry. The offerings coming in to support this ministry was largely responsible for money to develop all of the other programs. The sanctuary was a modern heptagon-shaped building in the round, and was elevated at different levels from the pulpit upwards. Sound and lighting were the latest available. Before and after Bible studies, donuts and refreshments, along with coffee and juices, were served in a large fellowship hall that opened up to the outside where ample tables and chairs were set among the trees and manicured grounds. Many decisions for Christ were being made each week, especially under the dynamic leadership of our youth minister, Mike "Bo" Boshears. He engineered a program of music with a live band of youth, competition with ridiculous games, and testimonies of various young people! I learned so much about youth ministry during this time. We scheduled a baptismal service, and I had about 16 people to baptize. When I stepped into the baptistry, I froze! The custodian had failed to light the furnace to heat the water before the service. With teeth chattering, I told the people to be baptized and those who had come to witness this event that we would need to postpone the baptism until next week in order to have warm water. One young man said, "I'm in the service and I am shipping out tomorrow for Vietnam. I think I can take the cold water!" So, I proceeded to baptize him. By the time he came up out of the water, several of the young men and women were in line saying, "We don't want to wait either." Jenny was in this group. So, I finally got to baptize my lovely wife!

There was always a lot of excitement around us in California! You never knew when you would go by a shooting scene for a movie. Traffic was rerouted while camera crews were making a movie. We stood in lines to get tickets to Disney, Knots Berry Farm, Universal, the Jay Leno show, etc. The beach was close by. An outing was scheduled for a get-together on the beach with friends and their families pretty often. We attended the Rose Parade each New Year's Day and went to

Pasadena (next to our city of Glendale) for the Rose Bowl Football game and fireworks displays. Jenny was getting acquainted with driving on twelve-lane super highways and gaining confidence in navigating her way around the metropolis in her little red Volkswagen convertible. She pulled into a pharmacy parking area and, suddenly, there was a low-flying helicopter hovering above her. A policeman appeared on the driver's side and told her to "keep your head down." He rested his gun across the windshield of the car. Police cars came down the sidewalk, and she was terrified! Thankfully, they arrested the foiled robbery suspect, and she was allowed to drive away unscathed. Her knees shook for a while, and I noted a bit of quivering anxiety when she told me all that had happened to her. Some nights, we would wake up with the bed jumping around on the floor from a little earthquake." On our way to Monterrey, Jenny was driving and woke me, saying. "Something is wrong with the car! It feels like all four tires are flat." At that moment, the radio music was interrupted with, "Folks, we are in the middle of an earthquake!" This was in Coalinga, CA, close by where we were driving. At the next exit, the bridge had collapsed on a car in the lane going the opposite direction. On our way back, we took the very beautiful and curving coastal highway along the Pacific Ocean.

One of the inspirations for a sermon on faith came to me as we watched hang gliders jump off the cliffs in La Jolla near San Diego with what looked like a kite strapped to their backs. On other trips, we visited the great sequoia redwood trees, and had wonderful times skiing in Big Bear and Mammoth. We pined for gold. We made a trip over to Vegas, etc. Yes, we definitely got to see and enjoy a lot of what California has to offer.

Meanwhile, on two occasions, Dr. McBirnie had me transport him in my car and drop him off about half a mile from our church. He told me not to disclose any of this with staff or members. I thought it strange but wanted to please the senior minister. He assigned me the task of "Balloon Sunday," where we encouraged the members to write an encouraging word about their Christian lives or how to become a Christian. We would then exit the sanctuary, and each person would tie the missile to a balloon inflated with helium gas. It was always interesting to discover where these balloons ended up and who responded. The next day at staff meeting, Dr. McBirnie began to criticize the event.

I had pictures to prove him wrong, and did so. I thought I was going to get fired for debating his criticism, but I gave the honest truth. Staff members wanted me to apologize because he might fire me. At the next meeting we had, I explained to him, "Dr. McBirnie, I am a Texan and I was taught when someone shoots at you, do not ask questions! Shoot back! That is what I did when you shot at me by saying something untrue about me!" We seemingly had an amiable agreement, at least for the time being.

A habit among the seven staff members began to develop. About mid morning, we started gathering at Big Boy's restaurant for coffee and a snack. It became a sharing time of all the rumors and gossip surrounding the newspaper articles of our senior minster. He was being investigated on a number of shady deals, including the purchase of a multi-story retirement home for three and a half million dollars. It was a government loan, and he was trying to buy a property for half of its value and evicting all of the senior residents, then doubling his money. There were problems in the seminary and in his TV ministry. The truth came out that years before this, he had been run out of San Antonio, Texas, as the pastor of the First Baptist Church and the president of the Southern Baptist Convention, for infidelity. He came to California and started over. Why did I not know all of this before?

It got so bad we began to think that the only way for the church to survive was to ask him to resign and let him concentrate on his TV ministry about communism. The other six thought that I should be the one to confront him and tell him this. Reluctantly, I agreed that I would go and deliver the message. When I met with him, he was belligerent and told me, "This is MY church! I built it! It is in my name! You cannot take it from me! You may leave, but I am not leaving!" He then asked if I would resign immediately, and I said, "Yes, I cannot work with you any longer!" So I signed my resignation. I left the office and told the other staff members what I had just witnessed and done. They were in shock! News of my resignation spread like the wildfires of California! Spontaneous group meetings of various ministries within our church began to meet, and the chagrin of many was expressed. Many of the church leaders asked if they could come to our house for a meeting. We met. During that historic meeting, they suggested that we have a mass exodus from United Community Church and start a church of our own. The minister affiliated with the TV ministry was not in this group, and Dr. Bob was very hesitant to go along with it.

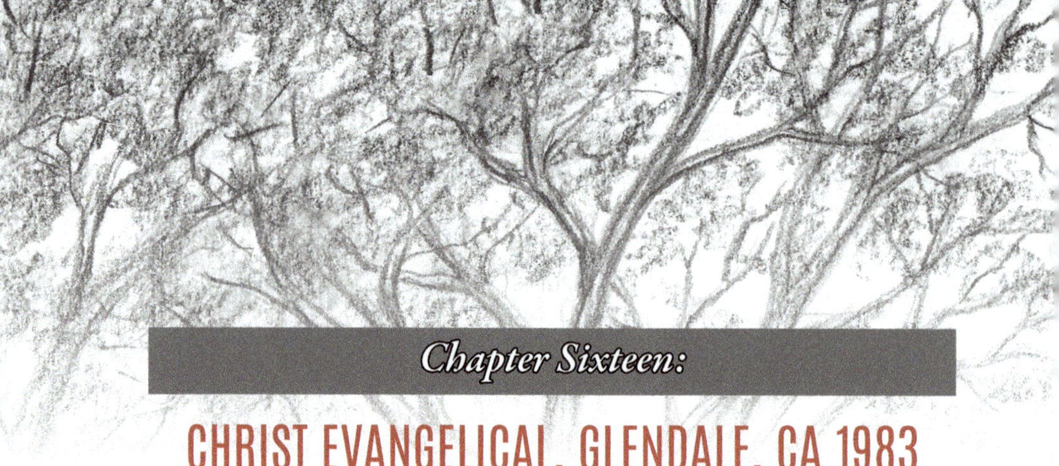

Chapter Sixteen:

CHRIST EVANGELICAL, GLENDALE, CA 1983

A school was located that we could rent for Sunday School classes and an auditorium for worship. We set the date for "The Exodus" on a Sunday, two weeks in advance. On that July day, Dr. McBirnie found over three hundred of his members missing, including the choir, nearly all of the Sunday School teachers, the complete youth ministry, and all of the staff, with the exception of one. We compared it to the Israelites leaving Egypt, and credited God for giving us wisdom and courage to leave such a flawed situation. It was a lot of work to organize a church overnight. We had to come early each Sunday to set up chairs, prepare for Bible classes, and solve all kinds of logistics for a nursery, plus organizational problems. At times, I felt like we were trying to make a statue with silly putty. We were organizing a new congregation while it was in flux! Now I see that the Lord was directing and giving us His leadership day by day.

My salary was cut in half, and the five other staff members actually got a small raise. The deacons tried to put all of us on equal footing. We all longed for some kind of meeting place, but with the heavy staff salaries, we could not afford to buy property. At one of my Kiwanis Club meetings, I was seated next to the minister of the Seventh Day Adventist Church of Glendale. I mentioned the difficult time that we were having by meeting in a school building each Sunday. He turned to me and said, "Our denomination was in your shoes a few years ago and were fortunate enough to have congregations like the Baptists, Presbyterians, Methodists, and others sympathize with our problem. Many of them allowed us to use their facilities on Sunday because we only needed to meet on Saturday, our Sabbath, when their buildings were not occupied. So, I think we should return the favor!" We worked out an agreement to use their beautiful facilities and only pay for utilities and janitorial services. What an unbelievable answer to prayer! It took hundreds of hours for the staff and members to develop and agree on some by-laws and a constitution. We had to get past disagreements of an Assembly of God staff member, a Methodist, an Episcopalian, a Baptist, and another dozen that I never knew what affiliation or background from which they came, but the splitting of theological hairs on syntax and the structure of a sentence was way too detailed for me!

One particular Sunday we designated as "picture day" for the church on the steps of the Glendale Seventh Day Adventist church, now known to us as The Christ Evangelical Church. I was in the street with my camera, directing everyone to get into photo position, when Jenny came up and whispered, "I don't mean to rush you, but my water just broke and I need to go to the hospital soon." We left for the hospital, and I think half of the church members followed. All of them were anticipating Heather Jill's debut! She did arrived with a full-grown head of dark hair! This was such a perfect time to have our second child, and Jenny was blessed to be free from working. She could devote all of her time to being mother to our two precious girls.

Jenny was able to make the flight back to North Palm Beach a couple of times from California to visit Mom Mom. On one of those flights, Jenny's sciatica flared up and caused her such pain she lay in the aisle of the airplane to find relief. When she got to North Palm Beach, she started daily trips to the chiropractor for treatments. This caused a long extended stay in Florida. I used this time to go on a much-needed diet, and created several other surprises that gave her a lot of pleasure when she finally got to come home. I crafted a frame for the stained glass gift that LeAnn Pitzer Rollins had made for us. Then, I bought one inch-by-twelve-inch oak boards to make five table leaves to enlarge the dining room table that Bob and Mary Barron had given us, as well as finding six oak chairs to match for the table. During this extended time, Summer and Heather enjoyed the very large swimming pool at the North Palm Beach Country Club where Mom Mom was a member. I could not believe that Summer Joy jumped off of the 50-foot tower into the pool! Note: swimming occupied a lot of their time as well as ours. Both were active in swim lessons and swim meets. This required us as parents to become involved as timers and lane checkers. They both sported good tans from the outdoor swimming events.

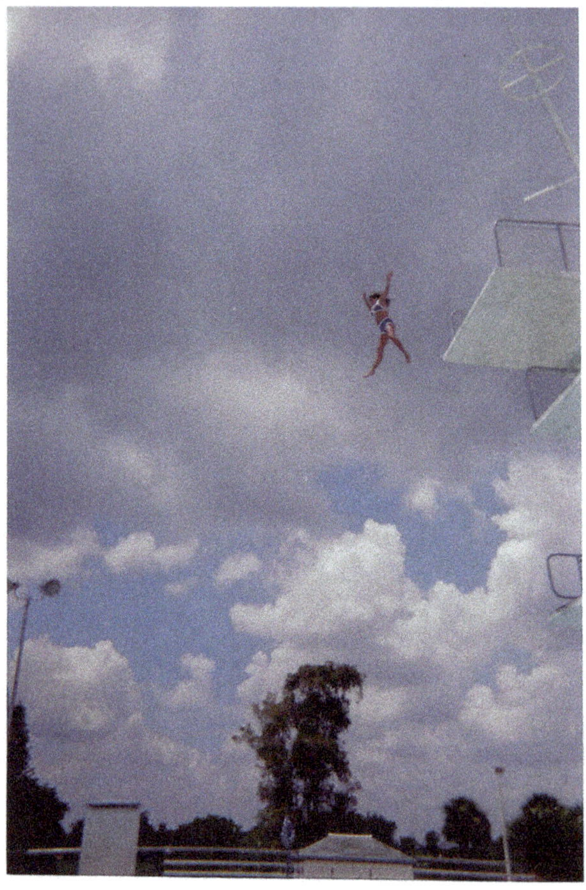

Summer Joy jumping from 50-foot tower in North Palm Beach

Many of our acquaintances and members of the new Christ Evangelical Church became lifelong friends. Moe and Luina Schidlowski (originally from Oklahoma) became godparents to Heather and were such blessings to us (years after we left California, the newspaper exposed the evil man responsible for killing several in a nursing home and our precious Luina was one of those).

Moe and Luina Schidlowsky, Heather's godparents

Please allow me to list some of these special people: Lee Ann Pitzer (a young policewoman who had a daughter. Amy was about two years older than our Summer Joy. Lee Ann married a police officer, Dick Rollins, a helicopter pilot). "Bo" and Gloria Boshears, our youth minister, was an exceptional leader and friend. John and Sharon Gramatky and their three beautiful girls have been our friends for over 35 years now. We housesat for them once, and while we were there, the upstairs water in the bathroom sprang a leak. We discovered the whole house was flooded. What a tragic mess! Thankfully, the insurance company replaced everything, but it took months for them to recover their home.

Friends in Christ Evangelical Church

Bob and Marietta Barron demonstrated the most dramatic changes in behavior that I have ever witnessed. When he became a Christian, he was a dynamo and a constant witness for his Lord and Savior. We had many great Bible studies, fellowships, and get-togethers with them. They gave us the large five-leaf oak table that seats 12 in our dining room. We still have it. Other friends included James and Ginger Burkey, Walter and Myra Kendall, Monte Gardner, Robert and Barbara Guisinger, Steve and Susan McIntyre, Gloria Monaco, John and Emily Myrick, Ralph and Jean Munger, Ken and Rosemary Thiele, and Bert and Jessie Warden.

Hazel Smith was very special! She went to the YWCA every morning to swim laps. At 96 years of age, she was the sharpest Bible scholar in the entire congregation. I would start to quote a Scripture and she would give me the chapter and verse. Her son had been serving as a missionary in France for over forty years. After one of our home Bible studies, I was accompanying her to her car, and she suddenly stopped and said, "Someone has stolen my car!" I suggested that maybe she had forgotten where she parked. She looked at me in disbelief and exclaimed, "What! You don't think I can remember where I parked?!" She had parked in a "red zone" after dark and the neighbors had called the police, who then called for a wrecker to take the car and impound it. I took her home that evening and came back the next morning to help her retrieve her car. A year after we left California, she was coming out of a nursing home from a visit with one of her friends, and a car coming around the corner hit and killed her as she was getting into her car; one of God's very special people.

We really enjoyed our youth ministry under "Bo," and attended many of the Friday and Saturday night events featuring the band, crazy and ridiculous competition, and Christian testimonies. There was some considerable debate concerning a current R-rated movie under discussion. My curiosity, along with the argument that we should know what we are talking about in a discussion, persuaded Jenny to attend a drive-in movie to view the film. After all, no one from the church would see us at a drive-in movie. We paid for the tickets, drove in, and parked next to a speaker for the window. It was a really hot night and I offered to go to the concession stand and get some ice cold drinks. Jenny nixed that idea for fear someone would recognize me at this movie. We saw enough of the movie to be unhappy with some of the scenes and decided to leave early. As I started to back out of our parking space, a chorus of voices from the car next to us yelled, "Good night, Mr. Ferguson!" This was embarrassing as the news became well circulated via the gossip channels. Somewhere, I remember God reminds us that, "things done in the dark and in secret will be exposed with His light!" Years later, we reconnected with one of those California young couples. We made arrangements to get together with Eddie and Violet Salina in Plano, Texas. As we got out of the car, Eddie greeted me with, "Goodnight Mr. Ferguson!"

As stated previously, I performed magic entertainment for a number of "Ladies Night" events at service clubs, such as the Lion's Club. This also led to invitations to present my "Tips for Success" talks to over 50 service clubs within a six-month timeframe. This talk was composed of about twelve "down-home" country, humorous tales. It was so successful I was tempted to take to the road in an attempt to become a motivational speaker. Each story that I related illustrated a trait or quality a person must possess if he or she hopes to be successful. I will share a couple of these stories with you now:

In order to be a success, you must learn to BE TACTFUL.

Two brothers were living with their invalid mother. The younger brother was mentally incapacitated. This heavy responsibility caring for both the mom and younger brother took its toll on the elderly brother over the years. One day, he informed the younger brother that he really needed some R and R, so he told him that he was going on a short trip to rest and relax. "Don't worry, brother, I will call you a couple of times each day to check on you and Mom. I will help you with any problem that may come up." The young brother nodded in agreement. On the first day away, he called home and asked, "How are things going, brother?" "Well, you know that favorite cat of yours? Well, he ran out in the street this morning and a big truck ran over him! It smashed him 'flattered than a flitter!'" Upon hearing this tragic news, the older brother fainted! When he finally regained consciousness, he picked up the phone and said, "Brother, you need to learn to be more tactful when you have bad news to share with someone!" Response: "What do you mean, tactful?" So, the older brother instructs him, "You let a person down a little bit at a time when sharing bad news. When I called, you should have said, "Well, we had a little problem with your cat. He got out and ran upon the roof. We had to call the fire department to come and rescue him. While rescuing him, he fell and it broke him up pretty bad. We rushed him to the vet!" Then, when I called back the next time, you could then say, "I'm sorry, brother, the vet couldn't save your cat!" That's how you tactfully break bad news. The younger brother listened and agreed to be more tactful in the future. Then the older brother said, "By the way, how's Mom?" Silence. And then he blurts out, "She's up on the roof!"

Another point is a story about the need to BE TRUTHFUL:

Mose was in front of the judge's bench when the judge asked him, "Why did you say at the scene of the accident that you were not hurt, but you are now claiming injuries for the insurance company to pay?" Mose's answer: "Your Honor, you need to understand the circumstances under which I said that I was not hurt. Betsy, my mule, was pulling the wagon out onto the blacktop highway and 'Ol Blue, my dog, was in the back of the wagon. About the time that we got out to the middle of the highway, a GTO came over the hill going 100 miles an hour! He hit us broadside! Betsy went flying over to the ditch on the right side of the road and 'Ol Blue slammed into the ditch on the other side. I went skidding down the blacktop! Right behind that GTO was a policeman! He topped the hill with his lights ablazing and his siren blaring. He saw the wreckage and came to a screeching halt. Jumping out of his patrol car, the first thing he heard was old Betsy just braying and bawling in the ditch. He walked over, looked at her, then took out his revolver and shot old Betsy right 'tween the eyes. Then he whirled around at the sound of 'Ol Blue howling in the ditch. He walked over and shot 'Ol Blue too! Then, with his gun still smoking, he walked up to me and asked, "Are you hurt?" **"No, sir!"**

My dad told me to always tell the truth! But life has taught me that there are times when it is wiser and prudent to know WHEN to tell the truth!

"Outstanding Citizenship" award from two Kiwanis Clubs, Glendale, CA, and Montgomery, AL

Sometimes an organization can have too many heads. This was true with our new congregation. Although I was the youngest and probably had the best experience and educational background, the other staff ministers began to disqualify me to become the senior pastor because I had been divorced. At first, we rotated the preaching duties. Ralph Hoops, the Hollywood-related preacher, tried to preach one Sunday morning while he was obviously inebriated and kept asking his wife for advice as to what he was talking about. Dr. Robert Hubbard, Sr. was much older and very reluctant to lead as he debated every issue until everyone was worn out. Jerry Davis was the "perfect" Methodist, and had a smooth and usually verbose answer for everything, always proving that the Methodist approach was the best in each and every circumstance. Jackie Pack, a former entertainer in bars and saloons, had a very dramatic and life-changing experience when she came to know the Lord. I thought she was probably the more spiritually-attuned among this bevy of ministers. The youth minister was recognized as a co-equal, but he was hardly ever included in the staff for a leadership role. As much as we loved these wonderful people and the comfortable living we enjoyed in the exotic atmosphere of California, two facts kept nagging at us: one, we were using much of the money that we had saved from selling the Dairy Belle, the Howard Johnson motel, and our home in Florida. Two, we became concerned that as much as we loved California, we were not convinced that this was the ideal atmosphere in which to raise two young girls.

Chapter Seventeen:

HOPE HULL, ALABAMA 1983-1984

An unexpected call from Barry Schahn, our former pastor at the Chapel in the Sun and minister who performed our wedding ceremony in Switzerland, informed us of this very exciting ministry in which he was involved. The Church Born in a Barn in Hope Hull, Alabama, had beginnings in a prayer meeting and a Bible study under the direction of Big Chuck Conners (Bwana). The church had called Barry to be their minister, and was growing rapidly. Barry needed me to come and become his associate pastor. I flew into Montgomery and met with the committee, and we agreed on the details. I made the mistake of allowing a high-pressure real estate agent take me to a very large and beautiful home in Fort Deposit with acres of azaleas and trees. Coming from California, the price seemed too good to be true, so I signed a deal that committed the remaining $40,000 that we had left from our property sales in Florida; big first mistake! The next problem was that I did not wait and ask for my wife's opinion; second mistake. Third mistake: it was twenty-five minutes from Hope Hull where our church was located. Well, we made the move, and in spite of my mistakes, we really enjoyed our new and different rural home with a country style of living. The move was from LA to LA; Los Angeles to Lower Alabama. The culture was about a hundred years back in time. We had a plumbing problem in the big house and Jenny called the local plumber who happened to be a Black man (90% of the people in our town and county were Black). He had a couple of kids with him, and since we were in Vacation Bible School at the church, she offered to come by and pick his kids up and take them to VBS. He looked at her like she had fallen out of a tree and landed on her head! "Where are you from, ma'am? We just don't do that around here!" Our next door neighbor, whose deceased husband had been a state senator, would often invite us over and serve us with deserts. She would remark in the presence of her maid, named C, "She is the best n... that I've ever had!"

The Lowndes Signal was the local weekly newspaper, and we found ourselves in the headlines very often. One day, Jenny took the girls across the railroad tracks to the small store about a block from our home. It was owned by Miss Bertie. Jenny had Heather in a basket on the front of her bike and Summer Joy on the back. She stopped across the street from the newspaper office under the shade tree of the Golsons to eat the goodies they had purchased at Miss Bertie's store. The featured article on the front page of the paper: "Pastor's wife and girls picnic." On another occasion, Jenny had a Sunday School class party in Hope Hull, and I attended a community Bar-B-Q in the neighborhood. The headlines on the front page: "Pastor goes to one party, wife to another!"

We really did enjoy working with our pastor, Barry Schahn, and Big Chuck. The church had many talented musicians. Kitty Weller was a very efficient and wonderful secretary. She teased us a lot about taking off to go to Grandy's restaurant for coffee. She carried the bulk of the load by keeping things running smoothly during our big growth time. We developed a very effective visitation ministry and helped Chuckie (Big Chuck's young son) start and develop a band as a part of our youth ministry. This musical group was later an enormous asset in our production of the "Singing Christmas Tree" in Fort Deposit. We were enjoying this time and everything was going well. The services were very unique, and the big barn was being filled every Sunday. There was an altar call with an open invitation for people who had prayer needs to come to the altar, which was made of bales of hay. This was reminiscent to the beginnings of the church. The pastor would then pray an intercessory prayer for those petitioning the Lord with their requests.

Jenny had the misfortune of hitting a deer with our car on her way to Fort Dale School in Greenville. There did not seem to be any damage, but the next day, as I was taking Summer Joy to the doctor in Montgomery, the hood flew up and busted the windshield. I could not see where I was going and it was a scary time for a few moments.

Finally, after getting off of the interstate safely, I found some nylon strapping tape and told my very startled little girl, "There, that should hold it!" But it did not! A few miles down the road, it flew up again. This time I found an electric extension cord and tied the hood down with it. Trying to comfort four-year-old Summer Joy, who was sobbing and sniffing, I said, "Now I really made it secure this time!" She looked at me, crying, and said, "I sure wish McGuiver was here!" I was really upstaged by the TV magician who could innovate and solve any problem with almost nothing!

On another day, taking the same trip to the doctor, we stopped and got Summer Joy some food. She was always hungry, even immediately after she had eaten. At this stop, she ate two hamburgers, fries, and a drink with dessert. When the doctor saw her, he remarked about how large her tummy was. Jenny told him again (as she had told the doctor in California and also this one), "Yes, this is one of the reasons for my concern. I have questioned that she throws up a lot of phlegm and mucous, and her stool is very foul-smelling." Now the doctor looked concerned. He ordered a sweat test. He then made an appointment for us to take her to the Children's Hospital in Birmingham. The test was positive. Summer Joy had the genetic disease called cystic fibrosis! We were devastated. We learned that it takes a gene from both parents to produce a child with CF. A child may be a carrier if they only inherit one parent's gene. As we looked back into the history of both families, we found several instances on both sides of our families where a sibling had died with pneumonia. The doctor's prognosis at the time was that Summer Joy had a 25% chance to live to be twelve years old. This was really a time that drove us to trust God in all aspects of our lives. Jenny called and had one of our church members fly with Heather to Birmingham to also be tested. Thankfully, Heather did not have cystic fibrosis.

Jenny began to research everything related to cystic fibrosis. The Reader's Digest story of "Alex...a girl's diary with CF" had alerted her even in California that something was amiss. Now she searched and found a holistic doctor in Florida. She took Summer Joy to see him, and he gave her different medications; among them were small beads that we mixed with peanut butter. She then took her on a flight to Boston, Massachusetts, for testing and advice. The doctors there wanted to put her on a heavy dose of antibiotics, and keep her on these forever. We did not like this approach. The Haiglers in Fort Deposit offered us the tents and treatment items that they had used when treating a daughter that they had lost to CF. It was sadly outdated. We continued the two or three times a day, giving Summer Joy pulmonary chest poundings with our cupped hands to break up the mucous and help her breathe. Summer Joy was so patient as this came way too often. I felt sorry for Heather because she thought her sister was getting much more preferential treatment than she was because she got to sit in our laps while we pounded her back and chest! We enrolled the girls in the YMCA summer swim programs. The doctor had recommended swimming as a good therapy. This was a continued regimen for the girls as we had given Summer swim lessons at nine months of age in North Palm Beach, and every summer, the girls swam at Mom Mom's North Palm Beach Country Club pool.

I think at this point, Summer Joy began to get an early glimpse of her own mortality. When we would go to the bales of hay during the services at The Church Born in a Barn to pray, she would accompany us, kneel, and pray. She became an inspiration to many others, even as a little four-year-old believer. At home one evening, while I was studying, she came and interrupted me, saying, "Mother says she is too busy to beat me tonight. 'Go get Daddy to beat you!'" I wondered if she had used this choice of words to anyone else? I began to try to refer to her treatments as "pulmonary percussions" versus "beating" her.

Geographic distance prevented us from seeing or visiting Jenny's family very often, so we planned a get-together in Wolfeboro, New Hampshire, for the next Christmas. This included Mom Mom, Jenny's mother in North Palm Beach, her twin brother, Jeff, who lived in the Boston area. George Hutchison, Jenny and Jeff's old high school buddy, graciously invited us to occupy one of his rental properties free. Mom Mom brought her friend, Mr. Van Horn, and we drove up to arrive a week before Christmas. Here we experienced another of "life's indelible moments." In order to surprise the girls, we had purchased a large dollhouse kit that had thousands of pieces! It required the dexterity of me and Uncle Jeff working every night in the basement with glue guns to get it together before Christmas. We all had a part in cutting down a Christmas tree and decorating it with strings of popcorn and cranberries. The girls created several "original" Christmas ornaments from construction paper designs.

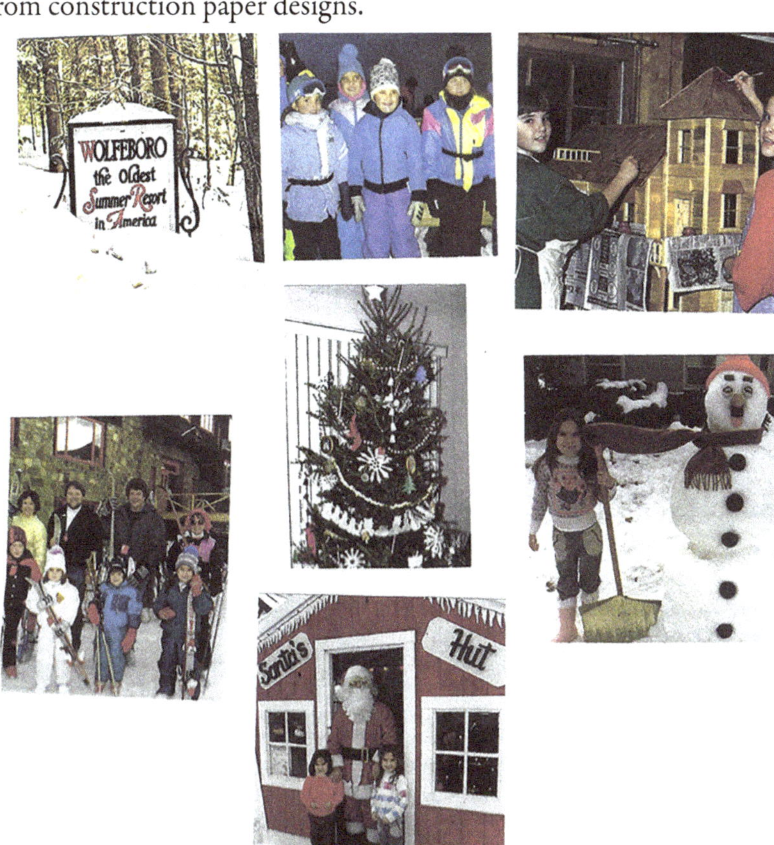

Christmas in Wolfeboro, NH

"Uncle George Hutchison" took the girls to a frozen Lake Wolfeboro, where Santa's Shack sat situated on the edge of the iced lake where cars drove across it. The girls remember this as going to the North Pole to share their wish lists with Santa. We snow skied at the local venue. The remaining time was spent cooking, shopping, and preparing for Christmas. Snow fell almost every night. This gave me an idea. I asked George if he had any deer hooves. He thought about it and came up with a couple of hooves from a hat rack. After the girls went to bed, we placed the dollhouse around the Christmas tree. Then, we took the deer hooves and went outside. We used a board to make sled marks on the roof of the porch overhang and also in the front yard. We sprinkled the yard with a good number of hoof marks in the snow. The girls had placed food for the deer and milk and cookies for Santa that Christmas Eve. The next morning, after opening the presents, we dressed the girls to go play in the snow. Out in the front yard, Summer Joy suddenly stopped and called to Heather to "come and look!" Summer started pointing to the deer tracks and said, "Heather, those are not dog tracks! Those are deer tracks, and that looks like where a sled landed!" What fun! Note: Probably four years later, Heather was in the third grade at Fort Dale Academy in Greenville, AL when the kids got into an argument as to whether Santa Claus was real or not. One of her classmates, Sam Ryals, remarked, "Well, Heather has seen the deer tracks! And Heather don't tell no lies!"

Churches are not a safe haven from the devil! He works overtime in the church to thwart God's work. Our pastor had been a very outstanding football player in Orange, Texas, where he had a bone-shattering tackle that sent him to the hospital. The doctor set the arm and left for the weekend. When he returned, Barry's arm had died! They went through numerous operations to salvage partial use. The pain persisted through the years. Barry and a young nurse began to cause gossip. The end result was that she was getting him drug medications to ease his pain. He not only had become addicted to the drugs, but they were having an affair together. When one of the members discovered the relationship, it tore up our church! Many members quit coming. Barry left, and he and Judy divorced. Big Chuck took over. It soon became evident that there was not enough income to sustain the present staff.

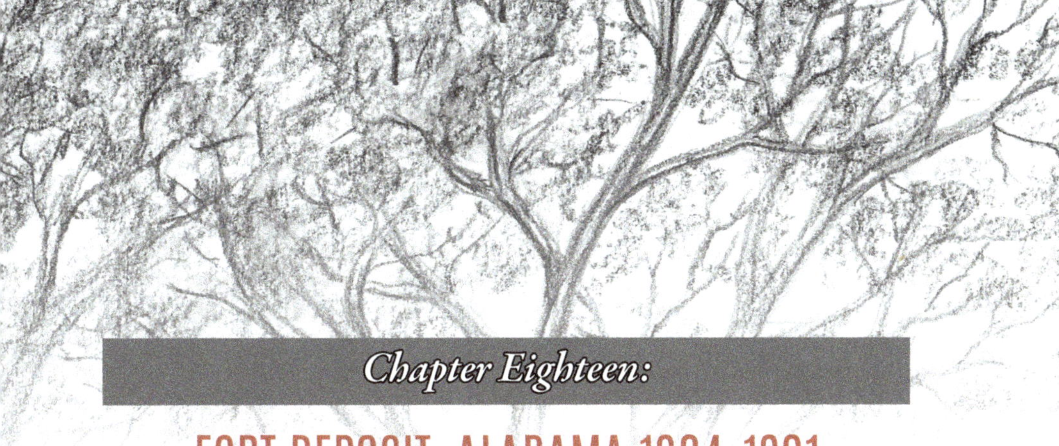

Chapter Eighteen:

FORT DEPOSIT, ALABAMA 1984-1991

I searched around and located my friend Jim Smith. Yes, the one who drove me from Richmond to Martha's Vineyard to see Jenny. He worked for Van Pac, a moving company that specialized in transporting families all over the world from one oil field to another. He convinced me to contact the company. They hired me for six months to go to the Dallas/Fort Worth area and establish an office for them. Reluctantly, I went to Texas and stayed with my cousin, Mrs. Cliff (Melody) Raborn, and her family while I endeavored to establish a business. About this time, the bottom fell out of the oil business. I was not able to get any business going. Jim Smith and one of the sons of the Van Pac owners were flying an old World War II plane. It stalled, and they crashed, killing both of them instantly. I lost a great friend that day. Still in Dallas at the end of these six months, I got a job with Barry Schahn, where he was the manager of mobile home sales.

If.... by Rudyard Kipling

If you can keep your head when all about you
Are losing theirs and blaming it on you;
If you can trust yourself when all men doubt you,
But make allowance for their doubting too:
If you can wait and not be tired by waiting,
Or, being lied about, don't deal in lies,
Or being hated don't give way to hating,
And yet don't look too good, nor talk too wise;

If you can dream — and not make dreams your master;
If you can think — and not make thoughts your aim,
If you can meet with Triumph and Disaster
And treat those two impostors just the same:.
If you can bear to hear the truth you've spoken
Twisted by knaves to make a trap for fools,
Or watch the things you gave your life to, broken,
And stoop and build 'em up with worn-out tools;

If you can make one heap of all your winnings
And risk it on one turn of pitch-and-toss,
And lose, and start again at your beginnings,
And never breathe a word about your loss:
If you can force your heart and nerve and sinew
To serve your turn long after they are gone,
And so hold on when there is nothing in you
Except the Will which says to them: "Hold on!"

If you can talk with crowds and keep your virtue,
Or walk with Kings — nor lose the common touch,
If neither foes nor loving friends can hurt you,
If all men count with you, but none too much:
If you can fill the unforgiving minute
With sixty seconds' worth of distance run,
Yours is the Earth and everything that's in it,
And which is more: you'll be a Man, my son!

"IF" by Rudyard Kipling

I worked a second job working the night shift at the Consolidated Trucking Company. We loaded trucks with merchandise from a warehouse–heavy work! Jenny and I tried to meet about every two or three months in Jackson, Mississippi, about halfway between us. All of us were miserable. In the meantime, we could not make payments on the mortgage of the big home that I had purchased when we moved from California. I went back to Fort Deposit to sign the papers, which would forfeit the house and the $40,000.00 we had invested in it. We were given a few weeks to vacate. Out of the black clouds of despair, the Bethel Baptist Church there in Fort Deposit came and told me that their pastor had left. The committee wanted to know if I would become their interim pastor. I told them of our situation. The committee got the consent of the church to allow us to move our furniture into the parsonage, which was only a couple of blocks away.

We did not view this as a permanent assignment, but week after week, the church attendance picked up and the people really showed an appreciation for us. We had gone through the winter, and in a business meeting, Sandra De Jong asked "Bunk" Norman, chairman of the pulpit committee, if the committee had interviewed the interim pastor about accepting the pastor's position. He answered that they had not. She then made a motion that the offer be made. It passed with a unanimous vote. When the committee asked if I would take the position and what would be my salary request, I assured the committee that the amount in the current budget was sufficient. This was the beginning of my longest ministry of eight years. My big mistake in making a terrible investment in a big old house was turned into a blessing by God. This was such a wonderful place to nurture our two young girls. They benefitted from Miss Josephine's piano lessons, Miss Bootsie's dance lessons, and Jenny's children's choir experiences.

We experimented with several multi-level business programs that entailed involving friends and neighbors to buy a product ad infinitum, such as Amway, Pre-Paid Legal, and a few others. This particular time of stretched finances led me to invest in the Pre-Paid Legal program. It had an attractive promise to represent a person in fighting traffic tickets! I really was in need of this service much too often myself! It also was an easy sell to the big rig truck drivers. Chester Henry was the colorful gentleman who enlisted me. I made a number of his meetings in the Atlanta area, about four hours away from us. He was always optimistic, enthusiastic, and had a good sense of humor. He was a great salesman. Many years after I ceased to be active in the program, Heather was scheduled to fly into Atlanta, and she needed to spend the night somewhere before going on to Clemson University. I called Chester, and he agreed to pick her up at the airport and give her lodging in his mobile home for the night. When he arrived at the airport, the driver's side door of his car was tied together with a rope. He got in from the passenger's side and then Heather reluctantly got in. Arriving at his place, Heather began asking why the door was crushed at the hinges. He explained that he had pulled off of the interstate highway to retrieve something from the back seat when a big truck came by and the wind blew his car door back against the front fender. Heather examined the door closely. To her shock and amazement, the edge of the front door had scratches and residue of truck paint where the truck had actually hit the door, not the wind from the truck passing. Chester turned white as he realized how close his "behind" was as he stooped over searching for something in the rear seat!

We spent many hours running a taxi service to transport the girls to Huntington College in Montgomery for dance lessons. Heather was a toddler, but picked up quickly by watching her big sister's routines. Waiting for a recital to begin featuring Summer, the background music began to play, and Heather left the bleachers. She proceeded to put on a show going through the dance routines. Everyone was thrilled to watch and began to applaud. She looked up in surprise, ducked her head with embarrassment, and scurried back to Mom and Dad in the bleachers. We also made the Montgomery trip a few hundred times for YMCA swim meets, art lessons, and so many fun activities for the girls. Even though we lived some distance away, we tried to give the girls all of the opportunities to develop their skills and talents.

We were pleased to learn that Jane had married an older man, Les Wilbrecht. This brought her some stability and happiness. It came a bit late to help Lori, Bradley, or Nathan. Lori had been in Germany and came home to spend time with us. Brad brought his new bride to Fort Deposit, but it did not last long. He re-married and returned with Marlena. They lived in the Montgomery area, but that was a pretty rocky affair. Jane had sent Nathan to Germany to live with Lori, but he would not listen to Lori during these rebellious years. He was failing everything in school, so Jane asked us to take him again when he returned from Germany. We enrolled him in Hooper Academy in Montgomery. He made the wrestling team, football team, and other activities. Jenny supervised his homework, and we got him an afternoon job working for Charlie Haigler's Auto Shop. This enabled him to finish the course he was taking in Germany on auto repairs and painting. One day, he took off in a panel truck that had been loaned to me temporarily from one of the church members. In driving to Florida, he burned up the motor. I had to fly to Florida and maneuver it at 25–30 mph to get it back to Alabama. Besides the airfare cost and trip back from Florida, it cost another $1,800 to get a motor job done on the truck. Jane and Les moved to Old Mexico. Nathan came to live with us again in Tyler. Jenny took him to Pasados restaurant, where he began to work where he was paid an extra dividend: he discovered his wife, Melinda. They married and started a business, "Lawn Rescue." They live about fifteen minutes from us in Flint, Texas. We have enjoyed our occasional get-togethers, and watched grandkids, Jordyn and River, grow up and become adults.

Back to Bethel...one cold morning, we found Summer Joy lying on the tiled bathroom floor. We asked her why she was lying down on an old cold floor, she replied, "Oh no, it isn't cold, it is very warm." Sure enough, I placed my hand on the floor and it was almost hot! Looking through a back wall panel, I discovered a veritable lake of water under the slab concrete floor in the parsonage. It took some insistence to convince some of the deacons to come and take a look. The plumber verified our worst fears. The hot water pipe in the wall had sprung a leak and posed great dangers of that part of the house sinking. This required a large concrete truck to come and pump about two feet of solid concrete under the floor. This gave stability to our dwelling.

The Montgomery Baptist Association notified me that the Southern Baptist Convention was sponsoring a worldwide evangelistic crusade, and I was invited to participate by conducting services on the San Andres Islands in Columbia, South America. Jenny drove me to Birmingham, Alabama, where I boarded a plane for New Orleans. Waiting for the next flight, I heard my name being called on the airport speaker to report to the desk. I was escorted out to the loading dock where my magic was scattered all over the flatbed truck. "Secret compartments! You must be a drug smuggler!" After some serious discussion, they allowed me to repack my magic. From there, my flight went to the Panama Canal, where I transferred for the last leg of the flight to San Andres. Going through Customs, a very large Black officer took my passport. He had a machine gun with belts of bullets crisscrossed across his chest. Looking at my passport, he discovered that Sasha and the airlines, had made a mistake in New Orleans, and so he ordered me "BACK ON PLANE!" I was afraid he was not going to return my passport. The plane took me back to the Panama Canal to spend the night. At 4:00 a.m., the motel woke me up and said, "Go board your plane to San Andres now!" Arriving early, a small bus transported me to Tegucigalpa, where I met the pastor, Rev. James C. Oliver, Jr., and his wife, Marilyn. The homes were so poor and humble. Many of the homes had dirt floors. The island generator would shut down two or three times a day. My partner, Judge Bozeman, a layman attorney from Lowndes County, taxied us around the island on a moped. I rode on the back of the small motorcycle, clutching my magic suitcase. I performed gospel magic at schools during the day, and he gave his Christian testimony. Their pronunciation for lawyer came out sounding like "liar!" He remarked to me, "These people really are on to us attorneys!" One afternoon, we did not have an assignment, so we took the moped to the beach, then decided to climb the rugged peaks of the island. The trail had trees overhanging and lots of bushes. Going under one, my friend bumped the small tree and killer ants fell on us. The sting was worse than fire ants! We ran to the edge of the cliff to jump in the Caribbean waters below, but decided suicide was likely, so we started running back down the trail. Upon reaching the water, with several people around, we had stripped down all clothes and we jumped into the water to get some relief! Back at the pastor's home, we doctored our wounds. Young boys and men took turns climbing a tower next to the church. This was a "lookout" to give a warning should any boats or planes approach from Nicaragua. They convinced me to climb up to the platform on the tower. I found out that I was not in as good physical condition as I thought. My arms and legs quivered from exhaustion and fright before I got back to earth!

I preached every night to a packed church with hundreds standing outside. There were no instruments, such as a piano, organ, or guitar to accompany the singing, but the gusto with which they sang familiar hymns was the most inspiring music that I have ever heard! Toward the end of my sermon one night, the island generator went out, and we were in total darkness. I asked the people to bow their heads in prayer to consider what decision they wanted to make for Jesus. The ushers came to the front with flashlights. The choir began to sing "Just as I Am." The aisles filled with people wanting to accept the Lord or make a rededication. I stood there, receiving people with decisions for over an hour! The choir sang a dozen invitation songs; some songs had 10 to 12 verses. The movement of the Holy Spirit was something I have never experienced before or after!

Pastor Norm showing his deacons how to hang sheetrock on the ceiling of the new fellowship hall. Jenny and Norm did a large portion of finishing the sheetrock in all of the new classrooms of the new building.

As the church was growing, we needed a larger fellowship hall as well as more classrooms. We were nearing completion shortly before our first production of the "Singing Christmas Tree." At the last minute, on a Sunday night, after the invitation closed, I made an announcement: "Folks, it looks like we are going to have to use emergency flood lights for the reception following our 'Singing Christmas Tree' performance. We do not have the money for the chandeliers or the carpet. The invitation is open for any volunteers to provide these." To my surprise, one gentleman spoke up and said, "I will donate the money for the carpet." My response was, "The invitation is still open...does anyone want to give the chandeliers?" No answer was forthcoming, so I pronounced the benediction. Early the next morning, my phone rang. It was Annie Lou Golson, the wealthiest lady in our church. She gave me her opinion: "Preacher, I do not believe it is wise to spend that money on carpet! We should buy the lights first." I explained to her that we were not at liberty to divert designated funds and gifts from the project that the giver intended. I then queried, "Annie Lou, why don't you give the lights?" Silence. Finally, she said, "I believe I will. Come and get my check." So, John Norman, the adult choir director, Jenny as the children's choir director, and I donned our rented tuxedos. We received those attending the reception following that first presentation of the "Singing Christmas Tree" under gorgeous chandelier lights and luxurious carpet. God answers prayer in the most unsuspecting ways!

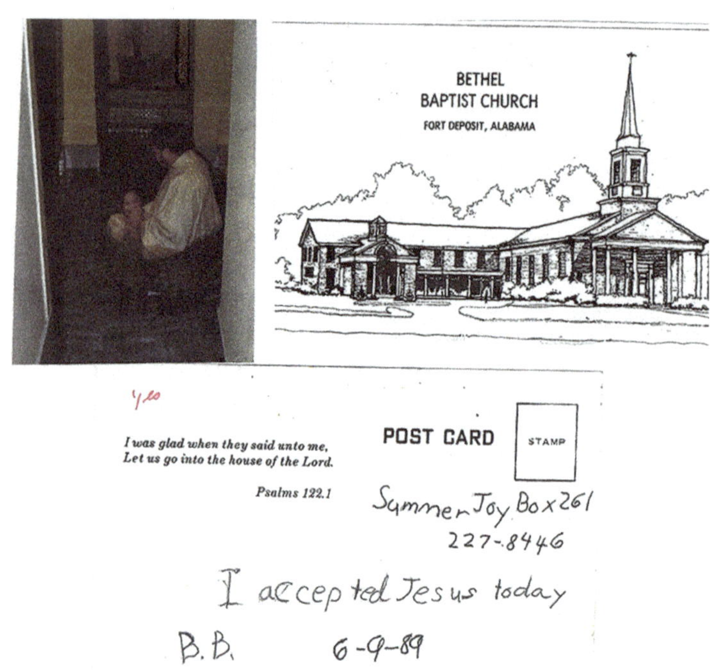

Summer Joy's baptism at Bethel

Heather Jill's baptism in Pete Norman's swimming pool, Fort Deposit, Alabama

It was a Saturday before we were scheduled to baptize Summer Joy and "Cappy" Barganier. I was walking through the sanctuary to my study when I heard noises coming from the baptistry. I walked through the choir loft and pulled back the curtains. There was Millard "Mutt" Rogers, holding his clothes and shoes over his head and walking through the waters butt naked. "MUTT! What are you doing?" Talk about shocked!

He began to explain that while testing the water in the baptistry as it was filling, he proceeded to exit through the door of the dressing room on the right. It had locked! He had no other choice but go through the water with his clothes on or take his clothes off and wade through the water and keep his clothes dry. I made a deal, "Mutt, my mouth is closed about this for the time being, but as one of my deacons, I will expect your co-operation in the future." He claims "blackmail." You decide.

On a cold February morning, Wayne Sasser interrupted my sermon preparation with a frantic phone call. "Preacher, please change into your swimsuit and come over. I desperately need your assistance! I did as requested and found that in an unguarded moment, he had driven his riding lawnmower too close to his swimming pool. He and the lawnmower tipped over into the deep end of the pool. This required both of us to get into the cold water on a very cold February day and push the mower to the shallow end. He thanked me and said, "Are you going to tell anyone about this?" After assuring him that I was passing up a good chance to make the headlines in the Lowndes Signal, our local news gazette, my lips were sealed until I could find an appropriate time to share the moment.

I raised rabbits and doves to use when doing my magic shows. One morning, the girls left the house to go to school. They both came running back into the house screaming uncontrollably! They kept pointing outside. I hurried to see what was causing such alarm. To my chagrin, bodies of all my rabbits and about ten ducks and geese from the pond next door were scattered all over our yard. A pack of wild dogs had attacked. I buried everything, and the next night, the dogs returned and dug all of these up again. I hated for our small girls to experience such a horrifying scene.

Please allow me to go back to how we came to have a "Singing Christmas Tree" program in such a small church. I kept hearing of great reviews of the "Singing Christmas Tree" in various churches. We had occasion to travel to the Bellevue Baptist Church in Tennessee, where they had performed such an outstanding Christmas event. Jenny was bemoaning the fact that she had hoped to be in a church large enough for the girls to be in a children's choir. I suggested that if she wanted them in a children's choir, she should organize one. She retorted, "I have never had a music lesson in my life!" I told her that all she needed to do in this marvelous age was to buy the music and tape, listen to it, and learn it. Then play it over a few times for the kids to learn and sing along with the accompaniment tape. After our trip to Bellevue, I came home and called several members of the congregation together after a service to see if we had enough interest to produce a "Singing Christmas Tree" event in our small town and church. When I mentioned the estimated cost of $1500 to purchase the plywood to build the risers for the choir to stand on, most of the people threw up their hands and said there was no way we could do it. The Joshua and Caleb of the group were Max Conway and Colonel "Dutch" De Jong. With a positive spirit, they engineered the building of the tree, and we enlisted Little Chuckie and his band from Hope Hull to come and handle the sound and lights on the tree.

“Singing Christmas Tree” at Bethel Baptist, Ft. Deposit, AL

Powerband

Chuckie Conner's "Power Band" as our "Singing Christmas Tree" tech team

Jenny prepared her children's choir to sing their musical. This was followed by the adult choir's presentation of a cantata. We had three nights of performances with a reception in our new fellowship hall. The church was packed all three nights with people near and far. This became an annual affair for four years. We expanded with a live nativity scene on the church lawn, set up by Tommy Bender (the cow we borrowed for the live nativity broke down our corral and went home). I cut out plywood life-sized figures of the entire manger cast of shepherds, wise men, etc., and Jean Childs did an excellent job of painting them to look realistic. These marked the path along the road to the live manger scene.

Congregation of Bethel Baptist Church, Ft. Deposit, AL

In such a small town, we felt safe with Summer and Heather having the freedom to visit the neighbors. Next door, they would visit Miss Ellis, who always had an ample supply of candy and cookies. Across the road was Mr. & Mrs. Capps, whose favorite treat was small six-ounce Coca Colas. We asked our girls to leave us notes if they left the house. These were priceless jewels: "Gon nex stor to see Ms Elis," and one simply said, "Gone somwher, be back in a minit."

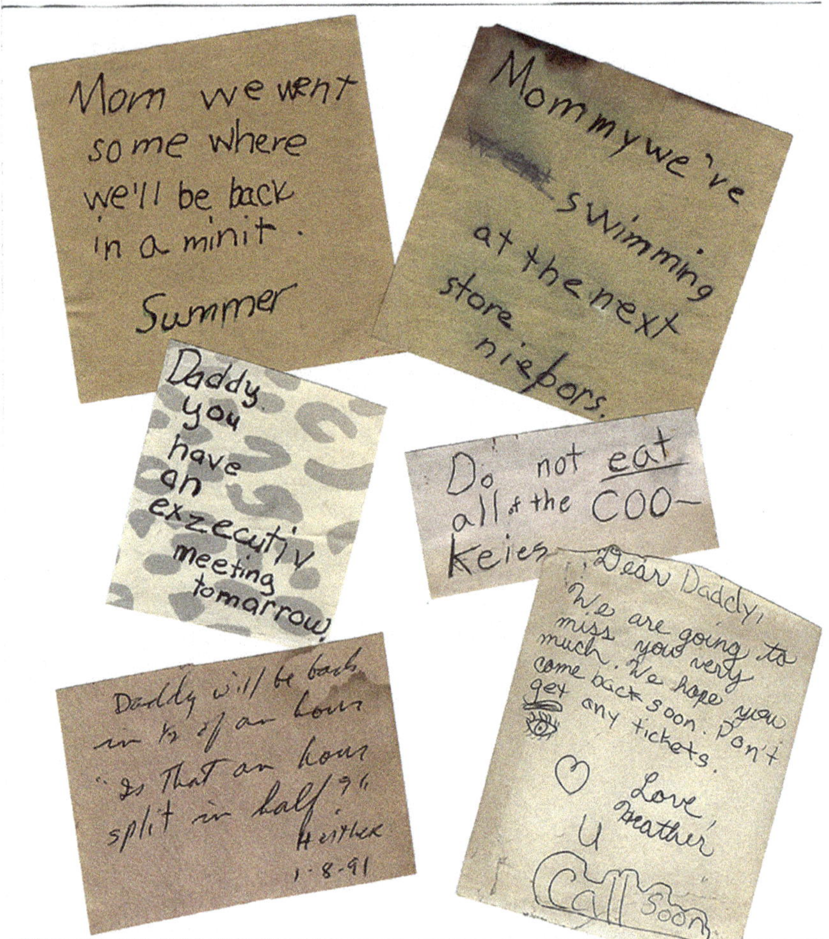

In Fort Deposit, Alabama, Summer and Heather were instructed to leave us a note if they decided to visit one of the neighbors or if the phone rang while we were not close by, to please make a note. Precious messages from our girls just learning to write. I served the girls leftover chicken smothered in mushroom gravy for lunch. Coming home from teaching, Jenny asked: "What did you eat for lunch?" Summer Joy replied, "some of that old suffocated chicken!"

Summer & Heather's notes to parents

I built a tree house for the girls (not quit as many stories as the one in West Palm Beach). It had a dollhouse capable of entertaining a half dozen friends in the top level. Another level provided an escape via hanging onto a pulley that went to another tree in the yard (a few of the kids had not developed enough upper body and arm strength to hang on for this ride). There was also a fireman's pole, a slide into a sand box, and a trampoline to jump from a lower level and get a big bounce!

A few of the parents were a bit hesitant to allow their kids to come and play in such a "dangerous" tree house. Summer Joy was the only one to ever get injured when she fractured a leg. It was a freak accident when another kid hit the mat while Summer was jumping, and this caused the hyper-extension of her leg. She got a lot of attention and mileage from the leg cast that she had during this time. Coach Autry in Fort Dale Academy was having his physical education class compete on the chin-up bar. The boys finished competing when Summer interrupted and said, "Coach, may I try?" He hoisted her and her cast leg onto the bar. She did more chin-ups than any of the boys...always the competitor! This cemented a great friendship with Coach Autry! He taxied her around on his back so she did not have to use her crutches.

Summer & Heather's tree house playground

After a few years at Bethel Baptist Church, I still had a desire to finish my doctor's degree. In March, I connected with Bethel Bible College and Seminary in Dothan, Alabama. I shared my transcripts and asked how many more hours would it require for me to complete my Doctor of Divinity or Doctor of Theology degrees. They verified the fact that I had more than enough hours already, but I had several hours from multiple schools, which did not fulfill the requirements. "You need to take 32 hours from one school (our school) to be conferred the degree of 'Doctor.'" I enrolled and took the required books and tapes supplied by the school to take home. I could study and send in my book reviews, then answer questions at the end of each course. Most of this was done by mail. About mid-May, Jenny and I delivered a couple of my assignments in person to Bethel Seminary in Dothan, Alabama. The registrar asked, "Are you planning to graduate this June 10th at our commencement?" I was quick to reply, "Oh, no! I do not think that is possible!" The girl said, "The grader of your work says they have never had anyone to answer everything so thoroughly." At this moment, Jenny had been listening and asked, "How many more hours does he need to complete in order to graduate on June tenth?" The registrar said that it looked to be about nine hours. Jenny said, "Put him down for graduation. I think he can do it!" We walked out, and I argued with Jenny about her insane idea. I reminded her that I had to prepare sermons and conduct Vacation Bible School in addition to finishing all of these requirements. I lost the argument! I spent day and night reading and typing. Jenny and the girls would come to the church about 9 or 10 each night to get their hug and goodnight kiss. I finished the last assignment and project in time to take it to Dothan two days before graduation. The family attended the ceremonies. Hundreds of people from every country in the world were there to receive their master's degree, and some, their doctor's degree. I was a bit disappointed that I was not listed in the area of those who had made the "Honors List." I was seated between a man from Africa and a scholar from Indonesia. Nearby was one from Tanzania. The president proceeded to recognize the Honor students. After the last presentation, the Dean said, "We have a doctoral student tonight who has not only had the highest grades ever in our program, but has also completed the doctor's degree requirements in the shortest time anyone has ever done so. Dr. Norman Ferguson, please come forward." My hearing is not the best, but as I sat there wondering if he just called my name, the guys on each side were punching and congratulating me. Stunned, I made my way to the stage and received my gold medallion and certificate. For a kid who barely got out of high school, I saw the words "Summa Cum Laude" on my degree diploma. What a great honor! To God be the glory!

Bethany Bible College and Bethany Theological Seminary

CERTIFICATE OF HONOR

THIS CERTIFICATE IS HEREBY AWARDED TO

NORMAN W. FERGUSON

IN RECOGNITION OF

SCHOLASTIC ACHIEVEMENT

SUMMA CUM LAUDE

AWARDED BY

THE FACULTY AND ADMINISTRATION

IN WITNESS WHEREOF, WE HAVE HEREUNTO SET OUR HANDS AND THE SEAL OF THE INSTITUTION, THIS 7th DAY OF June, 19 90.

Steve A. Shumake DRE
EXECUTIVE PRESIDENT

Carl W. Warden Th.M.
DEAN

Norm's special recognition at graduation with "Summa Cum Laude" certificate

Norm's graduation with daughters, and Norm with president, receiving his doctor's diploma

Priester's Pecan Store on the interstate was one of the larger companies that employed several of our members in Fort Deposit. Also, Benco, the large sign-making industry, owned by Bill and Lina Lou Mixon, had the nicest home in Fort Deposit. We enjoyed having some of our visitation events featuring homemade ice cream there.

I was leaving my study in the church office one evening and walked out into our large yard between the church and the parsonage to find the Methodist mayor with some of the Methodist youth rolling our trees with toilet paper. I threatened to report it to the Lowndes Signal and take a picture of their mischievous little prank. They scrambled to clean most of it up.

Ms Bertie with daughters, Mary Sullivan and Sandra DeJong

As stated before, the girls always wanted to go visit Miss Bertie's store. She let them know that they were welcome to anything in the store and as much of it as they wanted. I would try to intervene and tell the girls to not be greedy; just choose one item. She would scold me and say, "Preacher, this is my store, and if I want to spoil these sweet things, that is my privilege!" So, they usually walked out with ice cream, candy, and other snacks. She was a wonderful member of our church and the mother to Sandra DeJong and our organist, Mary (Mrs. Jess) Sullivan. Speaking of the Sullivans, which was a large family made up of several boys, one of the boys, B.I. Sullivan, and his wife, became our good friends by way of their daughter, Jessica. This precocious young lady was Heather's age and best buddy. We were invited to Mary Evelyn's big fiftieth birthday bash in Montgomery to celebrate. They were Methodist, so they did not have church on the Wednesday night they designated to celebrate. We only had a small attendance of 15 to 20 on any Wednesday night service, so I invited my good friend, Lee Greenlee, whose radio name was "Pappy," to come and conduct the Bible study. Jenny and I went to the party. You would have thought that we had committed the unpardonable sin! This dovetailed into criticism of Jenny having exercise classes in the fellowship hall, as well as when she returned early from a scouting retreat because of floodwaters and horse flies. These ten to twelve-year-olds walked into the Sunday morning service with their short pant uniforms on. This started a firestorm of criticism among some. You would have thought they these innocent little girls had committed some heinous crime!

Our troubles were compounded when we hit a deer and smashed the front of our Toyota Cressida wagon. It damaged the radiator, hood, grill, and one fender. We did not have any extra money to repair, so I asked one of my deacon mechanics to take it to his garage and store it until we could raise the money to get it repaired. Wilbur Pettis should not have been ordained a deacon! His constant diatribe was cussing and making derogatory insults toward the Black people in our community. After moving to Texas and I began to recover financially, I called and told him that I was coming back to Alabama to retrieve my car and tow it to Texas. He was so upset and had been planning on repairing my car and selling it "for storage fees."

I had seen my father go through some tough times in business meetings as I grew up in church. Some church members can really be vicious and hateful. Trying to reclaim a preacher in our community who had been thrown out of his church because of his infidelity, I encouraged him to reclaim God's forgiveness and come back into our fellowship. He and his new wife did come back and became active. The nominating committee promoted him to Sunday School superintendent as well as a teacher of the little old ladies' class. He was then activated onto the deacon body. He began to undermine and be critical of everything we were doing. After eight years of a very successful ministry, I resigned, and we contemplated moving back to Tyler. One local businessperson, Tom Mercer, asked what I was going to do. I told him that I was probably going to go back to teaching college. He said, "Oh, no! College kids are not what they used to be! Let me teach you what I do. You can do this work anywhere you live." Tom Mercer invited me to his shop in Montgomery, where he worked on the exam lanes of equipment for optometrists and ophthalmologists. I learned to take many of these instruments apart and repair the chairs, stands, slit lamps, keratometers, projectors, binocular indirect ophthalmoscopes, fundus cameras, non-contact tonometers, and how to clean phoroptors.

Chapter Nineteen:

TYLER, TEXAS 1991 TO PRESENT (2020)

Broke and somewhat demoralized, we moved back to Tyler to live with my sister and her husband, Ed Jackson. We enrolled Summer Joy in the fifth grade at Dixie Elementary and Heather in the third grade. This was a very difficult time as we had lost everything while in Alabama. Our insurance man in Fort Deposit, John Norman, tried to help us prepare for retirement by activating us in the Social Security program. We could not afford to pay the necessary Social Security assessments for the first three years. When we got to Tyler, we owed the IRS more than $3,300.00. Neither Jenny nor I had a job. I was traveling back and forth to Montgomery, Alabama, to spend half of each month with Tom Mercer to learn how to repair eye doctors' equipment, only to return with not much income. Jenny got a summer job at Trane brazing the tubing in air conditioners. It was a hot and grueling job. She still has scars on her arms from that job.

Needing another means of transportation, I noticed that my brother-in-law had an old rusty truck out in the pasture with weeds growing up around it. I asked what would it take to get it running, and he told me, "A battery and some tires." He got a set of tires from Kelly, where he worked, and I found a battery. Not only did the pickup look like it belonged in the junkyard, it also backfired every mile or two and scared the wits out of anyone close by. As I drove it up to the school one afternoon to pick up Summer and Heather from the Dixie grade school, I waited, waited, and waited, but neither of them came out of the school. Finally, after everyone else had left the school, they came out. They both said at the same time, "Daddy, when you come for us tomorrow, we will be down there," pointing to an area over a block from the school.

As I learned to do repairs and cleaning on the eye doctors' equipment, the girls took an interest and helped clean some of the many lenses. Curiosity got to Summer Joy, so she said, "You talk about different kinds of eye doctors using these instruments. You say an ophthalmologist using one and an optometrist uses another. What is the difference between the two doctors?" I told her, "Two things, education and money!"

Her quick answer was, "What do you mean?" So I explained.

"The ophthalmologist has to go to school longer, but he or she makes more money." She was still interested and said, "How much more money?" At about this time, a radial keratotomy surgery was costing about $1500, and the surgery usually took less than thirty minutes to perform, so I told her, "If he or she does ten surgeries a day at $1500 each, how much would they make?" Her eyes got bigger and she said, "Well, that cannot be fifteen thousand dollars!" I said, "Yes, it is! But remember, the doctor went to school longer and his equipment cost more." Nothing else was discussed. A few months later when as she was graduating from grade school into middle school, she walked up onto the stage and said, "My name is Summer Joy Ferguson and I am going to be an ophal...mol...o...gist!" I don't know if many understood what her career goal was. Years later in Baylor University, she called home and emphatically stated, "I am not going to be an ophthalmologist...it requires too many hours of chemistry! Organic chemistry has changed my major...my life! Maybe I'll become an optometrist." Years later, she did!

Those first few months back in Tyler, Texas, we accepted the gracious offer of my sister and her husband to temporarily move in with them. This was an extremely hard time in our lives! Those days were not among my favorite memories. We were so embarrassed to not have jobs or any kind of income. There was only one chair in the living room. It was Uncle Ed's La-Z-Boy recliner. The girls sat on the fireplace hearth, and we pulled up a kitchen chair if we wanted to watch the TV. I guess he did not believe in furniture as my sister had everything neatly organized into boxes. Eventually, they made us an offer to move into their old house across from the Tyler Pounds Field Airport for $750 per month. At least this gave us some privacy. So we moved. The airplanes approaching the runway across the road gave us the feeling that they would land in our kitchen! Their landing lights were so bright, and the roar was scary and deafening as they passed a few feet overhead! We tried to clean the place up and mow the grass burrs in the yard. Our socks and clothes attracted these pesky stickers, and it certainly did not allow the girls to go barefooted! The Texas bluebonnets along the road near the airport were a pleasant sight in the springtime. Packs of coyotes in the fields around us could be heard as they yipped and made a lot of noise at night.

With no jobs yet, I was in Alabama trying to learn how to repair eye doctors' equipment. We got a couple of months behind on the rent. This really placed a lot of stress on both sides of the family. Jenny had a sheriff's deputy call and escort her to a judge. She was compelled to call her mom to wire the $1500 to the sheriff's department to catch us up on the rent. May I repeat, these were very tough times! Shortly after this event, Glenna got a divorce. Years later, she experienced something of God's magic in a chance meeting of a very nice man while waiting in the airport in Hawaii to see her daughter, April. The more they talked, the more they found that they had a lot in common. I guess it would be more appropriate to allow her tell their wonderful story! Jenny and I have both come to admire and appreciate this man, Frank Cravalho, who is a wonderful Christian gentleman!

When I returned from Alabama, we went house searching near the Tyler Junior College area. Driving through the same neighborhood where I had lived 23 years before, we passed a house on Tanglewood with a "For Rent" sign in the yard. We talked with the gentleman who lived in San Antonio but still had his home there in the Tanglewood division. He allowed us to make the move from the airport without a down payment. He was asking the same amount we had been paying, $750.00 per month. Jenny got a job at Trane about this time for the summer, and I started working part-time as a substitute teacher at Robert E. Lee and John Tyler High School. I was not impressed with the lethargy and indolence of the students. They were so unmotivated to do anything! But substitute teaching a couple of days a week helped us to get back on our feet. I tried throwing papers for the Dallas Morning News. This required getting up at 2:00 a.m. to go roll the papers. I had to learn the routes. This entailed learning a map of the Chapel Hill area to leave a paper only in the mailboxes of those who had a subscription. Collecting the subscription dues from customers was also a headache. Some paid annually, some paid monthly. Many left the money in the mailbox or some designated spot. One Christmas night, Summer and Heather wanted to get up in the middle of the night and go help me throw papers. I think they were hopeful of seeing Santa make his deliveries that early Christmas morning! Costs of the gas and the maintenance on the car made paper throwing a break-even situation.

In the fall, Jenny got a job teaching Spanish at Whitehouse High School. I kept trying to get a job that would supply the health coverage to pay for the medicines necessary to treat Summer Joy's cystic fibrosis. These were so expensive!

Thank the Lord, I was hired to work at Trane in January 1992, and that job lasted for eight years. I worked a lot of overtime and, sometimes, double shifts to make ends meet.

We did have to appeal to our church, the Green Acres Baptist Church, to help us pay utilities for a couple of months during this critical time. What a great church! GABC really ministers to not only members like us, but leads the Southern Baptist Convention in mission giving, year after year after year. Pastor David Dykes has been the most talented and best-prepared preacher I have ever known! His sermons are fresh, well prepared, and delivered in a style to keep everyone interested and awake! He has done this week after week for nearly thirty years. Jenny and I enjoyed teaching in the high school youth department, and were especially privileged to work with the pastor's wife, Cindy Dykes. She organized and inspired the young married couples' class. Jenny discovered Cindy teaching this class one Sunday morning in a hallway of the church. Soon, we moved into the bowling alley of the church. Cindy had us wear tennis shoes to the worship service to call attention to the fact that we needed a permanent classroom for the young married couples. As a teacher, she was so gifted with original ideas with our group. I asked where she had learned all of her skills. She replied, "I majored in preschool and adapted what I learned to this age." Note: thirty years later, these couples are among the leaders of our church today.

While in the eighth grade, Summer approached me with a strange request, something she really wanted to do. I listened. She said, "May I enter the Miss Tyler Beauty Pageant?" This blew me away! Here was my little girl with the ponytail. I had not even been able to help her make the ponytail with a hair band. She had braces on her teeth, and now she wanted to enter the Miss Teen division of the beauty pageant? Jenny and I agreed to try to purchase the necessary attire and cosmetics, which included a swimsuit, evening dress, and a bag full of cosmetics that she had yet to learn how to use. Each contestant was required to do their own hairstyles and makeup. After many rehearsals at the city auditorium, I was watching the final rehearsal. I happened to meet the director of the event while waiting for Summer Joy to finish packing her suitcase and her makeup bag. I spoke to him directly, "I am a little upset with you!" He looked quite startled and asked, "Why? What did I do?" So I explained it to him. "A few weeks ago, I had this innocent little girl with pigtails and braces on her teeth who had never applied any makeup to her face! Now, look at her. She is a very poised, independent, and sophisticated lady!" He laughed at my analogy.

Tyler Teen Pageant where Summer wins "Miss Congeniality"

I was trying to be pastor of the Forest Grove Baptist Church around Lake Palestine near Chandler on Sunday mornings. I did this during those eight years of operating various machines at Trane, making parts for the air conditioner compressors, and using a screw gun to assemble side panels and top panels on the AC units as they moved past too rapidly on a conveyor belt. This resulted in carpal tunnel surgery on both hands.

When Forest Grove Baptist interviewed me to become their pastor on Sunday mornings, I expressed my concern that I would not be able to come on Sunday night or Wednesday nights. They assured me that the church had a young man who was working with the youth, and he could use the experience to fill in on those nights. I said, "Okay, where is he? I want to meet him!" Their answer was a bit concerning when they replied, "Oh, he is in jail at the present, but he gets out during the day to work. Then, he has to check back in for offenses that he is serving time for; things he did before he became a Christian!" When he finished his jail term, we gave David Kemp a "Welcome Out" party with a file baked inside the cake.

Even though this small congregation was a part-time ministry, we were privileged to get to know some very special people. My one deacon was Mickey Hargett, and his wonderful wife, Anne. He was also my barber, and these two had a wonderful family that supported us faithfully. Rick was a hardworking painter with two great boys (one of these boys was on the EMS team that came when I was experiencing heart problems, and they loaded me into the ambulance). Another young lady with a boy started coming to church with a mask on. She had gone through a heart transplant, and her body kept trying to reject the new heart. As mentioned above, she married Rick, and she lived another half-dozen years. Her boy was adopted by the Harris family (the family owning the Harris Nursery on Highway 69 near Swan, and he is a very successful young man today).

We began to reach a good number of youth in the Lake Palestine area by running a bus route each Sunday morning. I thought it would be a fun thing for the youth to experience a "Balloon Sunday" like we had done at Hatcher in Richmond, Virginia, and at the United Community in Glendale, California. It was a beautiful day with some wind, and we had smiley-faced balloons that the youth filled with helium gas. A personal message was written on a card with the sending person's name, and my phone number as the pastor, on the bottom of the card. I went on to work that afternoon at the Trane Air Conditioning plant, and when I got a break, I called home. Jenny informed me that we had two calls from receivers of our balloons. One had landed near the Texas border in Waskom, near Shreveport. The recipient was finishing dinner with his visiting pastor. He wanted the preacher to see his garden, so they proceeded to go outside. Hanging on the fence was one of our smiley balloons, so they called and shared the news with Jenny. Then she said, "Guess where the other balloon landed?" Knowing the wind was blowing south and east, I guessed Nacogdoches, Center, Crockett, etc. Her negative response to each suggested that I was not guessing far enough, so I proceeded to guess Houston, Beaumont, Orange, and finally gave up and said, "Where?" She replied, "New Orleans!" I found this astounding! In five hours, that balloon had made that unbelievable flight. The lady calling related the details. "I was walking on De Charles Street in Downtown New Orleans, looking at the merchandise in the windows, and thinking that this is Palm Sunday. If I were in my home country, I would be attending church today, something that I have not done since being in the United States. About that time, something bumped against my head, and I turned to come face to face with a big smiley balloon. It shook me up so badly I went to the nearest bar and had a drink!" Jenny's response: "Well, I'm not sure that the drink was a good idea." The lady replied, "Oh, that's ok, I am not of the same religious persuasion as you, but I can assure you of one thing: I WILL BE IN CHURCH NEXT SUNDAY!"

Jenny was enrolled in a course, ESL, "English as a second language." It required working with an international student to give the student ability to learn and use the English language to communicate and understand the customs and culture of the United States. University of Texas at Tyler supplied her with the name of a student, Simon Suen. He was from Taiwan and married, but attending school here while his wife worked at a radio station in Houston. Jenny took him grocery shopping and taught him how to use our stove and oven. He asked a jillion questions! He became like family, and the girls enjoyed how he taught them about origami, the cutting and folding of small paper animals that move. We were invited to attend his graduation. We invited him to go to South Carolina and take pictures of Heather's wedding. He is still a great part of our family.

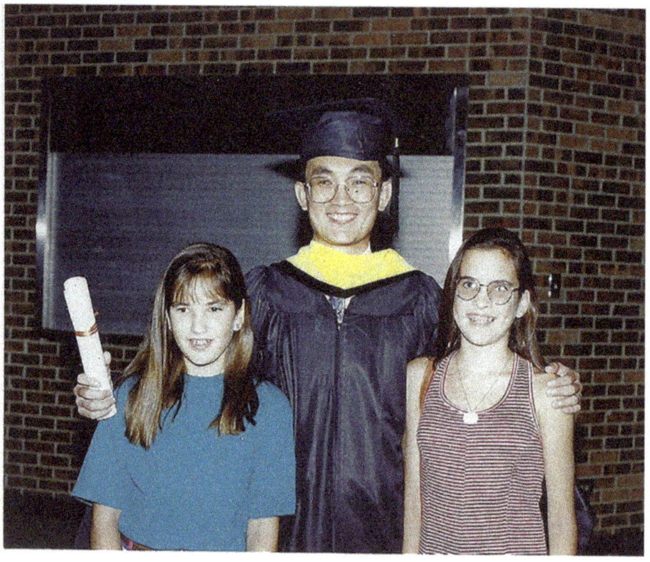

Simon Suen, Jenny's ESL student, receiving graduation hugs from Summer and Heather

While riding with members of our little church, Forest Grove Baptist, to a speaking event in Dallas, the young man, Jay, driving the car, stated, "Pastor, my wife and I have sold a house and feel led by the Lord to share the tithe from that sale with you. Do you have some pressing need for money?" So, I told him that we had been seeking to settle a debt with the IRS that had now accumulated over the past several years. With penalties and interest, the amount had gone up to astronomical figures, but we had just received word that they would settle for only $3,300.00. "We do not have that kind of money." He looked at me with disbelief and said, "That is exactly how much our tithe comes out to!" The couple was so generous and gracious as they followed through with this amazing gift. We paid the IRS, but when applying for a loan to purchase our home later, the lien from the IRS did not show it to be paid. We wrote letters, called, and tried everything to resolve the matter. We had come to the point of a closing on our new house to be scheduled for the next day at 4:00 and the deal would fall through unless we had some kind of assurance that the debt had been settled. I came in at midnight from my shift at Trane. Frustrated and angry, I called the IRS office in Austin at 1:00 a.m., and to my surprise, a timid little lady answered the phone. She assured me that she was working late, and for some reason, decided to answer the phone. When I told her of my need, she said, "I have the record right here and will call the Regions Bank in the morning at 9:00 and fax a copy to them." Hallelujah! Praise the Lord! We closed on our house at 4:00. Truly, God works in mysterious ways...His wonders to perform! We moved into our new home at 3002 Oak Knob in 1998. It is a most comfortable place to call "home!"

Jenny decided to try and organize the girls' preschool and grade school drawings and papers into scrapbooks. I tooled leather binders for each.

Summer and Heather's leather scrapbooks that Norm tooled for a place to keep their preschool and grade school "keepsakes."

A bit later, we decided to visit Mom Mom in Florida for Christmas. While there, I began to experience a good bit of pain in my left arm. When I mentioned this to Jenny, she insisted that we come back to Texas early. I made an appointment with the doctor. He turned the screen that he was looking at toward me and said, "Look, your arteries around the heart have shrunk to pencil-lead size. This negates having stints placed in your heart and will require open-heart surgery. My reply was, "Oh, so I need to go home and prepare to come back for the surgery?" He stated, "No, you are not going home! I am sending you to the hospital immediately for surgery prep so we can operate as soon as possible." My doctor at Trane was Dr. Julia Hwang and her husband, Dr. Gingery, was chosen to do the surgery at the University Hospital located on the 271 Highway. I then went through six weeks of rehab. When I tried to go back to work at Trane, they would not take me with the reason, "We do not have suitable work for you." The eight years that I had paid "disability insurance dues" every week at $8.50 became null and void and was canceled while I was out for the surgery. The union did not help me as it was monopolized and managed by Democrats who used my dues to send delegates to the Democratic Convention every year. With two girls in college by now, I started to view my little ophthalmic business in a different light. As I sent out cards and newsletters, I discovered that the large companies were mostly interested in selling expensive new equipment. I found a niche in servicing and cleaning the older exam lanes of equipment that the larger companies were ignoring. This required long trips to all parts of Texas and Louisiana, but it soon replaced my Trane salary.

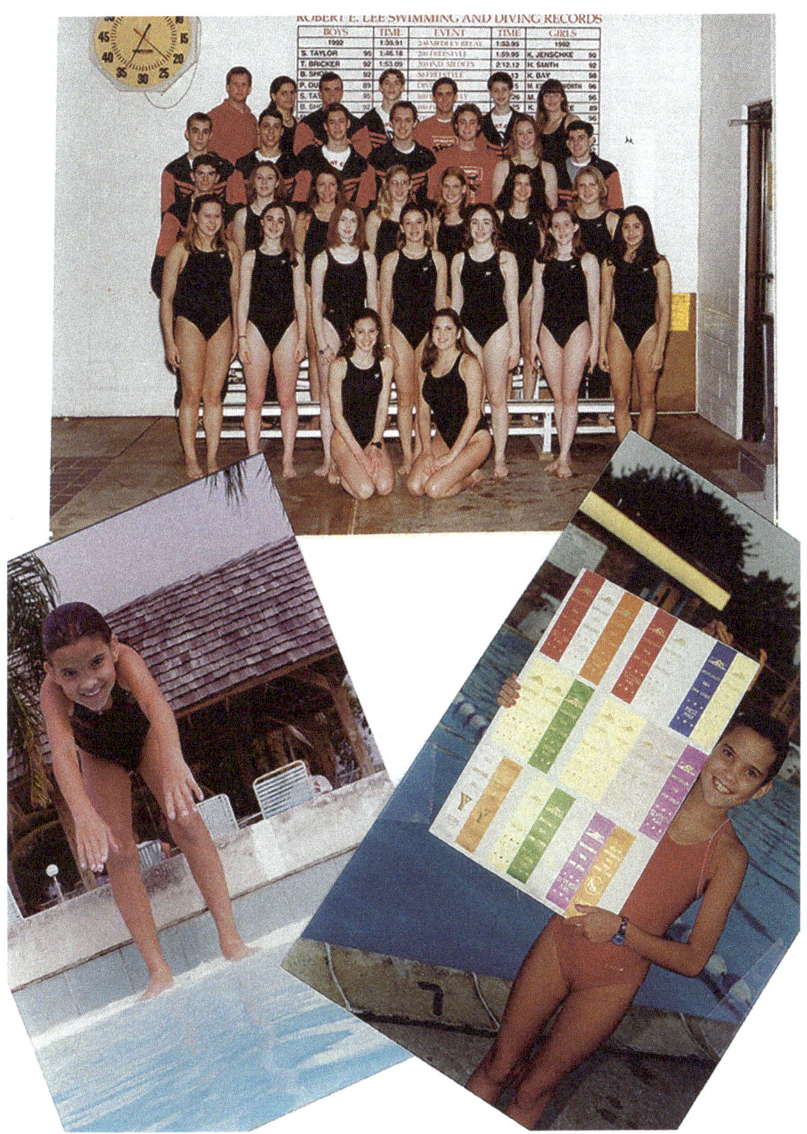

Summer Joy's Robert E. Lee High School swim team

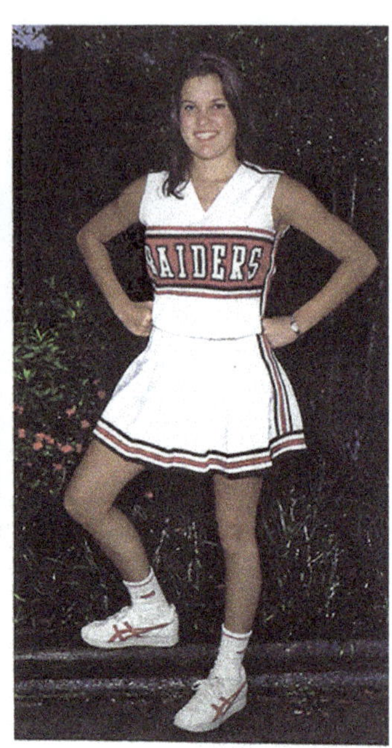

Summer as a Robert E. Lee cheerleader with her squad

Shortly after this event, Summer entered Robert E. Lee High School. I went to Coach Pickle and told him that our daughter had cystic fibrosis and asked if she could enroll in the swimming program since this was such an important part of her health regimen. He readily agreed and said she could swim from 11:00 a.m. until noon. After the first two weeks of school, she came home and informed me that "Coach Pickle wants me at the aquatic center every morning, starting next Monday at 5:30 a.m." My response was, "Whoa, Coach Pickle never asked me about this...and you do not drive yet!" Fortunately, after a few mornings, I discovered a young man on the swim team who agreed to come by our house and chauffer her to the aquatic center. His boombox car radio was so loud the whole neighborhood could hear him coming a block away. He was gracious enough to offer Summer some ear plugs! She was on the swim team all four years and captain of the team during her senior year. These were lasting friendships for her. I was always amazed at her competitive spirit. She would step up on the block to dive in for competition in a swim meet, turn to have a look at her competitors, many of which were a head or more taller than she was, then wink at me with a thumbs up. She was confident that she could win every meet! Note: Oh, did I mention that she was elected to be a cheerleader and made almost all "A's" through high school?!

We prayed for God to provide a means of transportation for Summer Joy when she reached driving age. Skip, a fairly large friend who owned a car repair shop said he had the perfect solution. He owned a red Chevrolet convertible and would let me pay it out as we could afford it. We parked it in the front yard on Tanglewood Street.

When Summer Joy came home, as she came into the house, she asked who was visiting us who owned a red convertible. When we told her that this was her car, she went out, looked it over, inside and out, walked around it several times, and then asked, "Can I drive it?" Well, this little car lasted through high school and went more places than I really want to know about (I have heard about a couple of these from various buddies)! Her senior year, she entered the car in the homecoming parade. By this time, the little car needed a valve job and became embarrassingly obvious as they drove around the football field in a fog of smoke emitting from her exhaust!

This brought up the next hurdle to find a car for her to take to Baylor University. We found a lady who had a gold Mercedes with low mileage. We bought it. It transported Summer Joy to Baylor in two and a half hours (she often made it in about two hours and fifteen minutes). I remember her frantic call when she called home, crying, saying she had hit a fellow student with her car. The girl had not been looking and stepped into the street in front of Summer's approaching car. Fortunately, Summer Joy was not going very fast and the girl was not hurt. She kept on walking, and Summer never knew her name. On another occasion, I got the same kind of call. On her way home, a large dog had run into the road. The impact busted the radiator and air conditioner. I drove to Murchison, rescued a stranded Summer Joy, and brought her home. We left the car, and I later retrieved it to have it repaired. Near where my little church was on Lake Palestine, lived a mechanic that my son Nathan used to repair his vehicles. Lee Castleman was an Army vet and ran a shade tree garage. He had been through some rough times struggling with alcohol, drugs, a bad divorce, etc. I watched him as he worked in the mud, jacking a car up to crawl under and work on it. He was vandalized, and all of his tools were stolen. I asked my son Brad to help with forming up to pour concrete flooring and metal siding for a metal-roofed work area. I ran an article in the paper to help a distressed veteran. Tools were donated, and a few contributed money. I made up the remaining funds needed to pour a concrete floor to help get him back on his feet. I wish we could have done more, but at least he is back in business.

Cheerleader Summer with her red convertible

When Heather came to that wonderful and exciting age of being driver eligible (exciting for the teenager, not so much for the parent). Our good friend, Skip, had another small car, called a Hyundai Elantra, for sale. A seemingly minor problem to me was the gears were not automatic. This was the only kind of car that existed when I grew up: tractor, truck, model A, and '38 Plymouth; all had shifting gears. Heather was about as excited about this car as a calf looking at a new gate. With extreme caution, Heather tried to learn to shift the gears. With both a brake pedal and a clutch, she was often confused and frustrated. One day getting out of school, she tried to get her car out of a cramped space on a hill. Every time she tried to move the car, it would roll backward toward other cars. With little patience, and totally frustrated, she came crying back into All Saints School, appealing to her mom to come and drive that wretched car. She never drove it again because Jenny traded cars with her. From that point on, Heather enjoyed driving her mom's new Ford Explorer. Jenny had a student with a very nice white Jetta Volkswagen. She was selling the car in order to go away to Yale College. Yale would not allow a student to have a car on campus. We bought the car and it lasted a couple of years. Then later, we were able to surprise Heather. On one of her trips home from Clemson, we asked her to go to the garage to get something. Her new red Jetta was hidden away in the garage. She ran back inside and wanted to know where the red car came from and whose was it. When we assured her that it was hers, she welcomed this change with a big smile on her face. On her way back to Clemson with her new puppy, Sassafrass, the car slid across two lanes of icy highway in Shreveport, Louisiana and hit the guardrail. We had to tow the car back. Heather was not hurt, but was badly shaken up! And so was the dog! Sassafrass remained with us and never got over that wreck of being tossed around in the car. When going on a trip or a visit to the vet, the poor dog insisted on sitting. She would never lie down. She just shivered in fear the entire ride. It was a really sad day for all of us when, after about ten years, she became so feeble with an enlarged heart that we had to say goodbye to our dear lovable pet. We have an unbelievable picture of her likeness that Heather painted for us.

Heather often tried to hide behind Summer's take-charge personality. At Moore Middle School, she attracted the attention of the art teacher, who called us to say, "Heather is a very gifted and talented person in art. Please see that she gets some encouragement by an art teacher." When she got to Robert E. Lee, the art teacher reiterated what her previous art teacher had said. She enrolled in the art class. The teacher would write a word on the chalkboard with the instructions, "Do not draw your first impulse, use your imagination, draw something associated with the word and be creative." I still have that notebook of Heather's daily drawings, and each one has an "A-plus" and some very complimentary words. With such great artistic abilities to make a picture look like a photo, we all assumed that Heather would major in art. But, like a true artist, Heather explained that she only wanted to paint when inspired to do so and could not imagine having to go to work required to paint all day!

The swim team, as well as her sister, Summer Joy, enlisted Heather to join the team and become a member of the diving division of the team. She was amazing! In a few short weeks, she learned to do eleven of the dives required in competition. She won district and bi-district competition. But even with that success, no amount of begging or persuasion could get her to compete the second year. She confessed, "Every time that I did those dives, I was mortified and scared to death!" The headmaster where Jenny was teaching at All Saints' Episcopal School encountered Heather on campus one day as she was waiting for her mother to leave. He asked her name and found out that this was the daughter of his Spanish teacher. So he inquired, "Why aren't you attending All Saints?" Heather is few with words and answered, "Money!" He learned of her golf talent and requested that we fill out the forms for a scholarship. She was accepted. We only had to have a few dollars deducted from Jenny's paycheck each month. At this smaller school, Heather came into her own. She was competitive on the golf team, and the soccer team was almost always a winning team! She also played basketball on the JV and varsity teams. She and Paul Adams were nominated to be the fine arts senior representatives for All Saints' homecoming. She and Paul became an "item," and Paul's mother was grateful for Heather's influence on his studies. She also enjoyed visiting Paul's home, where she loved to play the drums. She also relished his dad's good cooking. His mom, Jane Adams, was an art teacher at All Saints, so she appreciated Heather's artistic talents. Heather's art projects were another reason she stood out as a student with "exceptional" talents.

Masterpieces by Heather; she paints when she gets inspired!

More of Heather's artworks

Jenny was encouraged to take a group of about forty students each year to Europe. These trips provided many unusual circumstances and surprises. Megan Jones had her passport stolen while she was on the train. This required Jenny to stay with her as the group proceeded on the trip without them. She and the student had to go to the American Embassy in Madrid, Spain. They waited for another passport to be issued to Megan. Meanwhile, Megan's parents sent money for Jenny and Megan to get new one-way tickets to fly home. On another occasion, one "innocent" young man did not bring any cash with him. He presented his mall credit card and expected to pay for everything with that card. That was a real fiasco! His parents had to wire money ahead to each of the next destinations. When we arrived in Florence, Italy, Jenny, Summer, Heather, and I needed cash. I entered my ATM card into a bank machine. The machine kept my card, so I did not have cash needed for the entire weekend. We had to wait until Monday for the bank to open in order for me to retrieve my card and cash. Another trip included most of our boys' soccer team. The world soccer matches were being played out all over the world while we were in Sorrento, Italy. Our young tour guide noticed how talented our boys were with a soccer ball. He arranged a match in a stadium with a college team. You may find this hard to believe, but our high school team beat those big and talented college guys on their soccer team!

One of my former Baptist Student Union members, named Leo Jones from my 1960s TJC's Bible classes, had a son Summer's age. They were both good students at Moore Middle School and Robert E. Lee High School. Both presented outstanding science projects. Leo kept his eye on Summer Joy and called me the spring of her senior year with the question, "May I come over and talk to Summer about where she is going to college?" "Certainly!" I assured him. Leo had become a very successful businessman in the home insulation business. He asked our daughter to list three of the colleges that she would prefer to attend. She had applied to five and said, "Texas University in Austin, Baylor in Waco..." He stopped her and said, "Which of those two would you like best?" She assured him that Baylor would be her first choice, but the cost was prohibitive. Then he said, "I attended University of Texas and was personally hoping you might choose UT, but I also have a daughter who graduated from Baylor, so here is the deal: I will give you a scholarship that will pay you $400 per semester hour for an "A," $300 per hour for a "B," or $200 per hour for a "C." To qualify, you must write your parents a letter every week! You cannot get pregnant during this time, or the scholarship becomes null and void." Besides this great answer to our prayers, Summer received six other smaller scholarships. What a great privilege...she was going to be a Baylor Bear! She also got very excited when she was accepted into the sorority, Chi Omega!

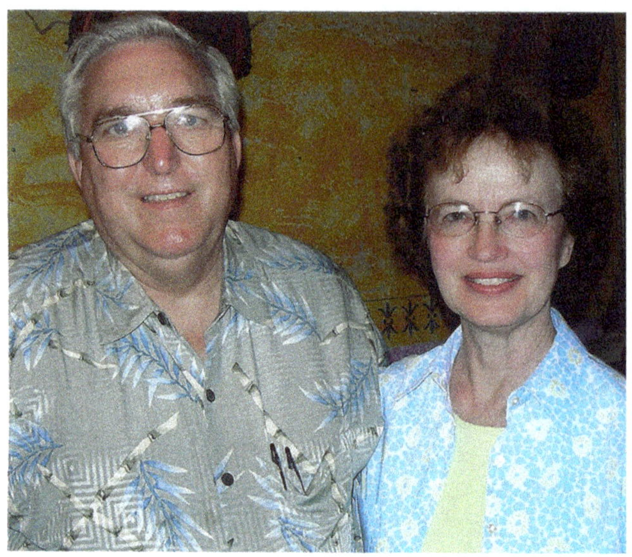

Leo Jones and his wife provided a scholarship enabling Summer Joy to attend Baylor University, Waco, Texas.

It did not seem anytime until we were writing those same five letters of application for Heather to apply for admission into a college. This time around, she wanted to go to the college where her mother had gone, Clemson University in South Carolina. Jenny had been a cheerleader at Clemson. Heather was able to use her good grades and golf expertise, as well as her experience on various golf teams, to become the only girl ever to be accepted into the Clemson Golf Management Program. Preparing for her to enter Clemson, I realized that she was going to need to borrow a lot of money through the student loan program. In a conversation with the registrar, I inquired if there was any way for Heather to cut the out-of-state tuition fees, which amounted to about $8,000 per year. The registrar said that if Heather enrolled in the ROTC program, she would be exempt from these out-of-state fees. I informed Heather that she was going to be in the campus military program. Her immediate response was, "No way!" So, I simply said, "If you cannot find another source for $8,000 a year, then you will be in the ROTC." Reluctantly, she enrolled in the Air Force ROTC chapter on campus. At the end of her freshman year, the colonel called her in and told her. "Heather, your aptitude grades as a freshman have exceeded those of our seniors. We would like for you to enroll in the jet pilot training program. The government is willing to spend over a million dollars to make you a pilot." Heather simply asked, "What is the time required for me to serve if I sign?" He told her the minimum would be about ten years. She promptly rejected the offer.

Shortly after this, as the semester was coming to an end, she called and wanted to know if she had permission to transfer from the Air Force division to the Army division. I expressed my doubts that this was a good idea. I asked why would she want to change. She stated that the personnel in the Air Force were "kinda uppity" and never did anything fun or exciting. On the other hand, those in the Army division went on field trips every weekend. They rappelled down cliffs and steep mountains, rode in tanks, or shot off cannons, etc. She also told me that on occasions where she was required to wear her uniform, she always rode her bicycle. "Why?" "Because a person is not required to salute while riding a bike."

While in the golf program, she had a paying job working for the Clemson Golf Club. This entailed driving the ball, retrieving machines from the driving range, plus washing the golf carts, working in the club pro shop, etc. She served as an intern one summer in Colorado Springs at the prestigious Broadmore Club. She could retrieve two men's golf bags in one trip, one in each hand, and then secure them in the carts. One day, she was a caddy for a group of business men. Her main job was to watch them tee off and spot where their errant golf balls landed. After several holes, one of the men in the foursome told the other three, "I'm going to ask Heather to putt this ball for me, ok?" With their permission, Heather sank a long putt! A couple of holes later, he asked her to putt for him again. Once again, she sank a difficult putt! The other three men in chorus said, "No more Heather putts!" This young lady had a hole in one in high school and two more during her college years. When she drew the assignment of a semester internship in Purchase, NY, she discovered it was a very private, all Jewish, country club. That fall and winter was rainy and cold. She bunked in a dorm full of immature party-type young people. The ladies that she had to teach golf lessons to were not interested in golf. They viewed it as a social outing. About Thanksgiving, she called and told us, "I still love golf, but I do not like the management aspect of it." I told her, "This is a part of your education! When you experience something you do not like, get away from it!" She did, and promptly changed her major.

Heather had to take a year away from her education at Clemson because of my open-heart surgery. She came home and attended the University of Texas at Tyler and was on the golf team. But her heart was still in Clemson. After a year away, she went back. Upon her return, she rented an apartment off campus. She played soccer on a co-ed team and made outstanding grades on sixteen or more hours per semester. She announced a change in her major, again, to "Packaging Science Engineering." I scratched my head, trying to understand what that entailed. She explained, "Well, there are over sixty types of plastics for packaging items, and some are not friendly for food packaging." For experience in this field, she worked for General Electric during the summer. She did not enjoy working in a small cubicle. One of her assignments was to figure the logistics for transporting the blades and tower for a wind turbine, like those erected in West Texas to Africa. She calculated the cost of transporting the body and three blades to the shipyards in Houston, Texas, and, ultimately, to Africa. To prevent the ship from capsizing with the weight, it required the ship to be filled with water first. This was a challenging job and carried with it a large degree of responsibility. Failure to figure the logistics correctly could result in a terrible disaster of an overturned ship or some such fiasco. She graduated with three degrees but did not want to go north, where many of the companies were located. For those seven years of her schooling, she had a grade point average hovering around 3.8. My curiosity asked, "So what do you plan to do now...teach?" She simply stated, "I'm going back to school at TJC to become a dental hygienist... and so she did.

Confiscated college tee shirts from Summer and Heather allowed us to surprise them with special quilts upon their graduation.

Please allow me some time to tell you about our daughters' weddings. Upon graduating from Baylor, Summer Joy kept rejecting the idea of attending optometry school in Houston. "I cannot breathe in Houston." I must admit the heat and humidity gets pretty heavy in South Texas for a person with CF. She received an invitation to interview at University of Southern California College of Optometry. She was so excited to be accepted into that program. One morning, she called and asked for me to guess where she was. I had no idea, so she said, "I'm in Big Bear snow skiing. Do you know where I am going this afternoon?" Again, I answered negatively. She proudly stated, "I'm going to the beach!" What a life!

One summer, she met a young man in California from Boston. She had a job touring prospective honor students to various medical occupational jobs, and Adam was the transportation coordinator for the group. As often happens, the love bug bit, and we started planning a wedding. Jenny's mother had passed away with a stroke. With the money Jenny and Jeff received from Mom Mom's estate, Jenny was able to pay for each of the girls' weddings.

There was to be a wedding shower at Don Juan's restaurant in Downtown Tyler. Guests were coming from Boston, Baylor, California, etc. Jenny and I used this as an excuse to tackle a BIG project that had been one of our dreams. We knocked the window and wall out of the kitchen and closed the existing door to the backyard. We installed double French doors where the window had been before. Jenny, my son Nathan, and I built the most encompassing three-level patio that one could imagine. At first, Jenny objected that it was much too large. It entailed a nice porch-type swing, two exists, solar lights, picnic tables with umbrellas, etc. When Summer walked into the kitchen and saw the double doors going out to the patio, in her shock, she let out a scream, "Well, shut my mouth!" This deck provided the perfect place to entertain the large crowd visiting. It also provided the setting for a surprise party that Jenny arranged to celebrate my 75th birthday. Imagine my surprise while talking with my friends when three ladies walked out, each carrying a cake blazing with 25 candles! With so much fire, I began to yell, "Call the fire department!"

Norm's 75th birthday cakes

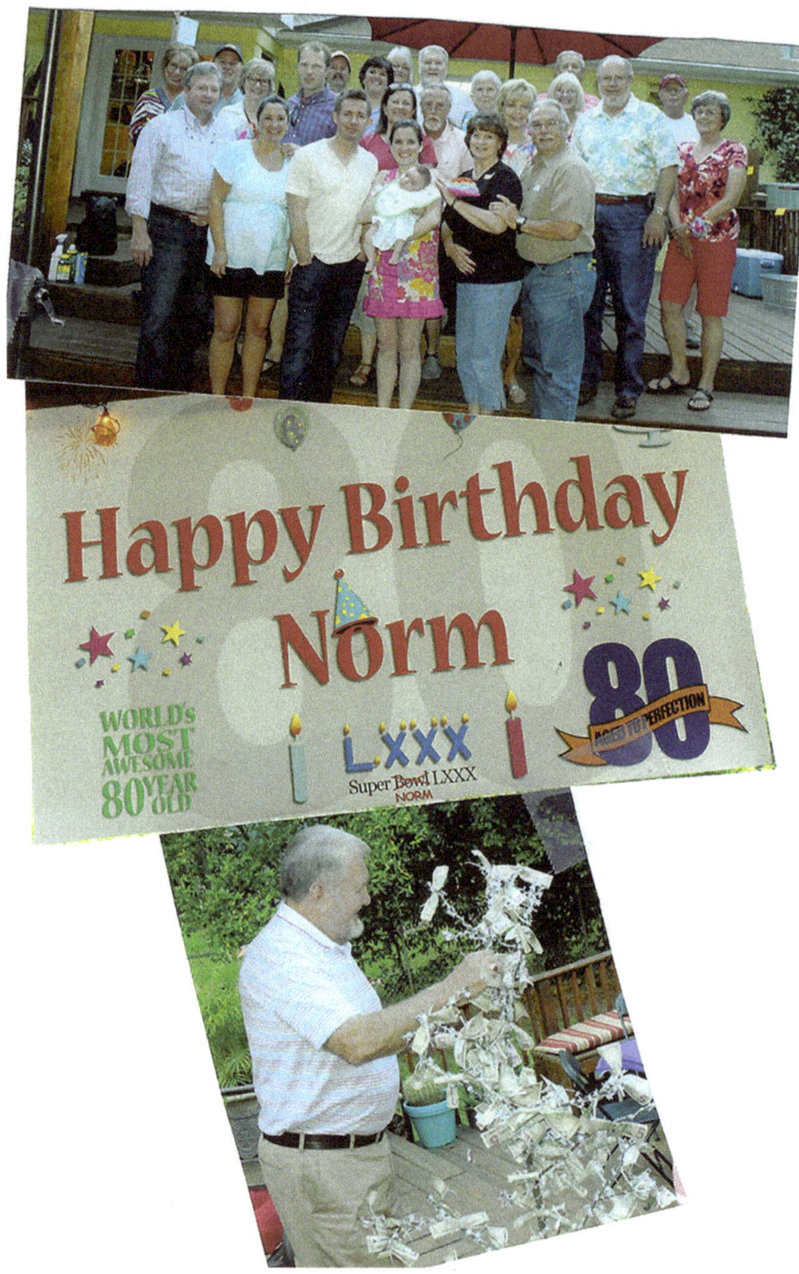

These friends of Norm surprised him on his 75th birthday celebration.
Very special people!

One of the special guests at my 75th was Darell and Wanda Abrahams. I met them while we were visiting Jim Gilliam's Bible study one Sunday morning. We were eating pigs in a blanket and donuts with coffee. Picking up a packet of mustard to spread on my small hot dog delicacy, I tore one edge and squeezed; the mustard squirted across on Wanda's black dress from her bosom to her knees!!! There was no place to hide. How embarrassing! Darell has never let me forget how we met. Since then, I have enjoyed his company, along with his friends, at various restaurants for breakfast and many events at the church. I count them as some of my very best friends! Note: I do not recommend squirting mustard on a lady as a way to make friends!

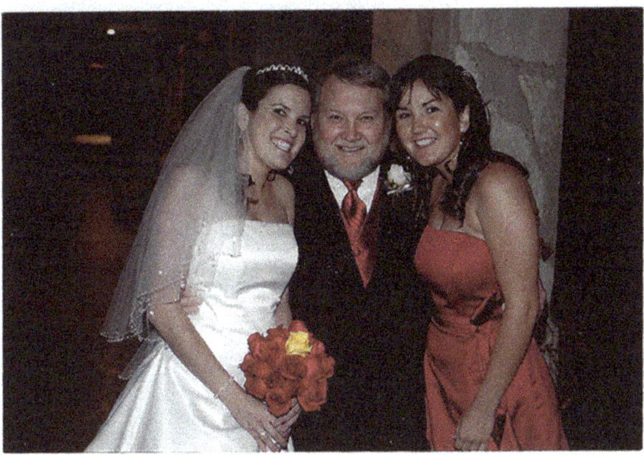

Summer Joy's wedding at the Wayfarer's Chapel at Palos Verdes, California

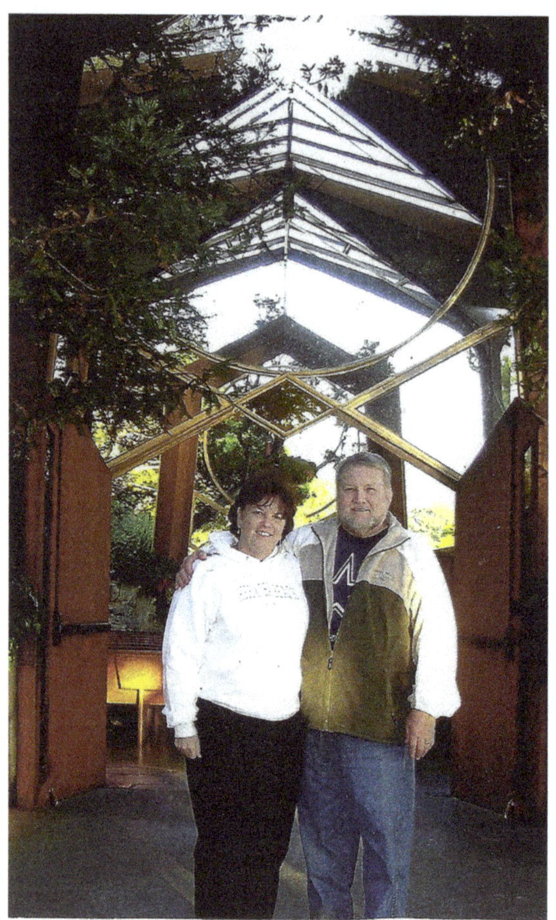

Parents of the bride, Jenny and Norm

Summer and Adam chose one of the most popular locations on the West Coast to have their wedding: the Wedding Chapel, designed by Frank Lloyd Wright. It was made of all glass overlooking the Pacific Ocean. The reception was nearby in The Cheesecake Factory at Marina del Rey. This was a rare time when all of my kids got to fly out and be together: Lori, Brad, Nathan, Heather, and Summer. Jenny's brother and family came, as well as many of our friends from Christ Evangelical Church. Several of Summer Joy's school friends were also there. Summer still had a year of internships to complete in order to finish her doctor's degree. The first internship was in Salt Lake City, Utah. The next was in Amarillo, Texas. Both of these were at veteran's hospitals.

Norm & Jenny, Salt Lake City, Utah in October

Somehow, her last internship lucked out to be in Hawaii at the naval hospital. Jenny insisted that we take a trip to each of these locations. Hawaii looked to be an expensive trip. I dropped notes to the optometry doctors around the naval hospital area to ask if they needed me to clean their equipment while we were there. Four responded favorably. This pretty well paid for our trip. We enjoyed the traditional Luau, whale watching, and I drove the road to Hana, Maui. I even bought a shirt bragging about this strenuous achievement. It was one continuous hairpin curve after another for what seemed like hours as we traveled along the coast.

Heather met Ryan on the Clemson Golf Course as they both worked in the clubhouse and washed the carts. Their wedding was situated on an old pre-Civil War plantation called, The Middleton Plantation. This was located on a beautiful river with ancient and towering trees. The gardens were kept in immaculate condition. Again, Jenny was able to provide a very nice wedding for Heather in Deep South Antebellum, Charleston, South Carolina. Note: not long after this, Jenny's brother had an opportunity to buy a thriving business in the Boston area. He needed to borrow her part of the money that their mom had left to them. She sent that amount plus some of her teacher's retirement money, about $130,000.00, and Jeff was able to make the purchase. It appears that he did not have a capable attorney as the lady owning the business did not place money in an escrow account. It then became apparent that she had not paid any of the suppliers and had outstanding bills of nearly $100,000.00. After a year of trying to stay afloat during a bad turn in the economy, Jeff lost the business and all of Jenny's money. Believe me, these losses are extremely hard to take! This is a time to read Kipling's *Don't Quit* again, and to search God's Word for His assurance and guidance.

Don't Quit
Edgar Albert Guest

When things go wrong, as they sometimes will,
When the road you're trudging seems all uphill,
When the funds are low and the debts are high,
And you want to smile, but you have to sigh,
When care is pressing you down a bit,
Rest, if you must, but don't you quit.

Life is queer with its twists and turns,
As every one of us sometimes learns,
And many a failure turns about,
When he might have won had he stuck it out;
Don't give up though the pace seems slow-
You may succeed with another blow.

Often the goal is nearer than,
It seems to a faint and faltering man,
Often the struggler has given up,
When he might have captured the victor's cup,
And he learned too late when the night slipped down,
How close he was to the golden crown.

Success is failure turned inside out-
The silver tint of the clouds of doubt,
And you never can tell how close you are,
It may be near when it seems so far,
So stick to the fight when you're hardest hit-
It's when things seem worst that you must not quit.

Poem: *Don't Quit* by Roger Guest

In the meantime, Summer and Adam had moved to the Boston, MA area to finish one course that she had not been able to finish because of the difficulties she experienced with her cystic fibrosis during her last year in Hawaii and California. Upon completion, she secured one job with an optometrist and another with an ophthalmologist. Soon, word of her good work and personality spread, and she received a call from Lens Crafters. They wanted to send her to Maine for three days of interviews and training. I encouraged her to go. She did, and this became perhaps her best sources of income to date. One of her contacts was a national officer for Chi Omega, her college sorority at Baylor. She was impressed with Summer Joy and wanted to know what office she held at Baylor. Summer explained, "I was almost a nobody on campus, because there were so many talented and personable girls there." The lady insisted that Summer should apply for a national position in Chi Omega. Soon, she was installed as the secretary/treasurer of the national organization of Chi Omega. Quite an honor!

Speaking of honors. I was pleasantly surprised recently. Some of my doctor friends had nominated me to receive a "Top Doctors of America" award.

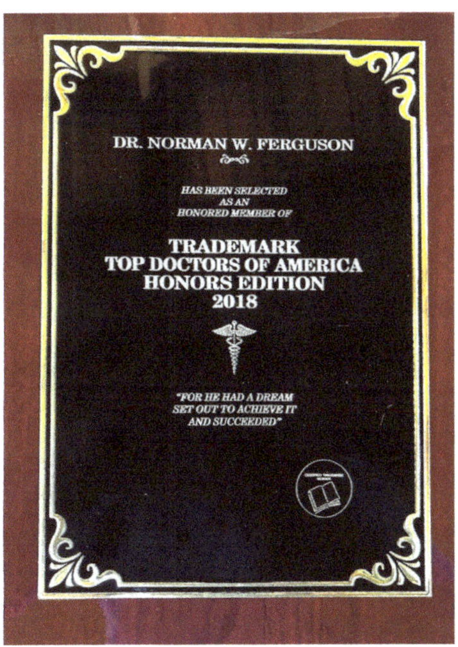

"Top Doctors of America" award

We visited Summer and Adam one Christmas. The day before Christmas came a snowstorm and dumped seventeen inches of snow on the city of Boston. Everything was buried! Their poor dog could not find a place to go potty! As if the snow had not buried the cars enough, the snowplows threw a couple more feet of snow atop the cars. This was enough snow to last me a lifetime. They had enjoyed living in Adam's mother's two-story house with a basement because she was in Florida most of the time in her other townhouse.

Summer and Adam wanted a family and decided to go through the difficult process of in vitro fertilization because this would allow a pregnancy without the risk of the baby having cystic fibrosis. They were successful. At six months, the doctors became very concerned with Summer Joy's health. They agreed to go ahead and take the baby via caesarean surgery. At birth, Bridget only weighed a pound and four ounces! Her arm would slip into Summer's wedding ring. She remained in the perinatal unit of the hospital from October first until January fourth, three long months. Bridget became our miracle baby, and the Lord be blessed and praised for answering our prayers.

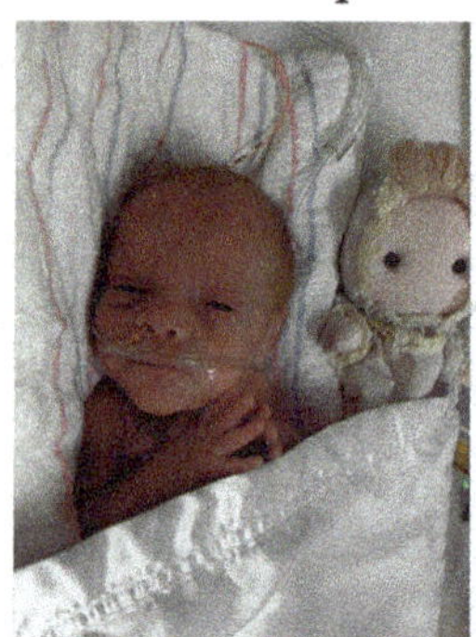

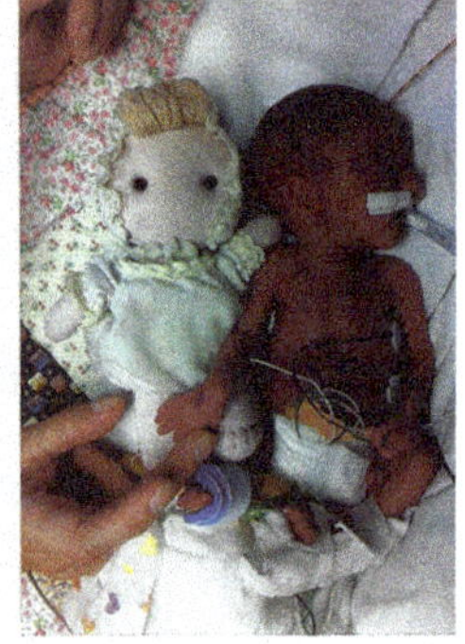

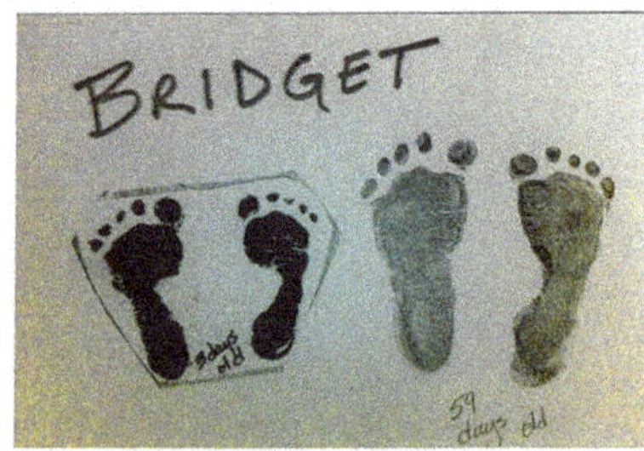

Our miracle grandbaby named Bridget (one pound, four ounces)

The cold weather and snow began to weigh on Summer, and they decided to move to Tyler, TX. She started to work for one of my long-time doctor clients, Dr. Gene Bennett. He also signed the note to allow them to qualify to buy their first home. What a blessing to have them living close. Bridget was enrolled in our church daycare and, eventually, kindergarten. The school provided gymnastics and dance recitals too.

One morning, when I woke up with my chest hurting, I called Jenny at All Saints and told her of my problem. She screamed for me to call 911. I did, and by the time she got home, an ambulance and a fire truck were both here. I asked if I could go to the restroom, and they said, "No, lie still." They loaded me into the ambulance, and before I knew it, I was under the lights in surgery. I had experienced a heart attack, but they were able to prevent much damage and insert two stints into the arteries of my heart by inserting them through my groin up to the heart; amazing time to be alive!

Heather and Ryan moved to Houston. The last year of her schooling in dental hygiene school, she stayed here in Tyler.

Eventually, Ryan got an offer to transfer to Dallas with his expertise in graphic design, and they were able to buy their first home in Fate, Texas. While going through Tyler Junior College for her dental hygiene degree, she was very conscientious about each day's assignments. Upon her graduation, I was surprised to see that her name was not listed with the honor students. Over the past years, she was calling me almost daily in panic, "Daddy, my patient did not show up today! Can you find someone to come and fill the gap?" On short notice, I would go and pick up Nathan's kids, the neighbor's kids, etc., and raced against time to get them to Heather's chair in order for her to have a patient to work on. She was always saying, "I may not graduate if my people keep failing to show up!" The TJC president recognized the dean of the dental school and announced, "We have a special award to present. Heather Ferguson Denman, will you please come up?" Heather was about seven months pregnant with Austin and was somewhat glad the graduation robe gave her a little coverage. When she arrived on stage, the dean asked, "Heather, do you know what your grade point average is?" She did not answer, so he said, "Well, since you won't tell, I'm going to. You have the highest grade point average of any student to ever go through the dental hygiene program, a 3.9.

Heather graduating from dental hygiene school, TJC, Tyler, Texas

When we got outside, I cornered Heather and chided her. "I am never going to believe your panic cries again. You kept telling me that you may not even graduate if I did not get someone to fill the vacancies of your no-shows!"

It is a bit ironic that on her way to Boston to see baby Bridget, Heather discovered that she was pregnant. On August 11, 2013, grandson Austin was born in Baylor Medical, Dallas, Texas.

Family pictures:

Norm's grandchildren, Bridget and Austin,
admiring Ms. Lee's daffodils, Gladewater, Texas

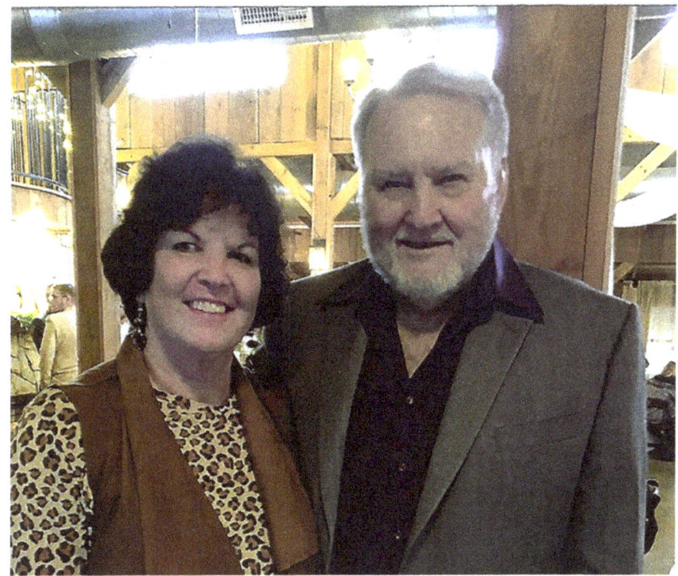

Norm & Jenny

Norm's parents, "MeMe" and "PaPa"

four generation of the Ferguson clan:
Norm's dad, Norm, Nathan, and River

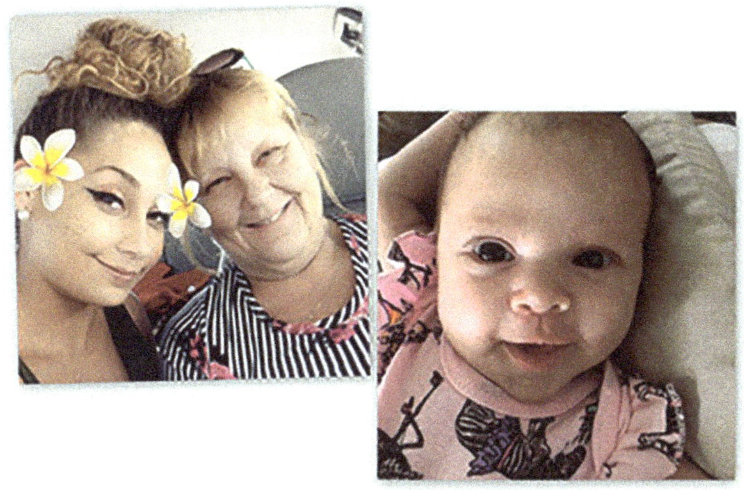

Three generations: daughter Lori, granddaughter Darci, and great-granddaughter Harley Sky

Son Bradley with Jenny and the girls

Son Nathan with his family

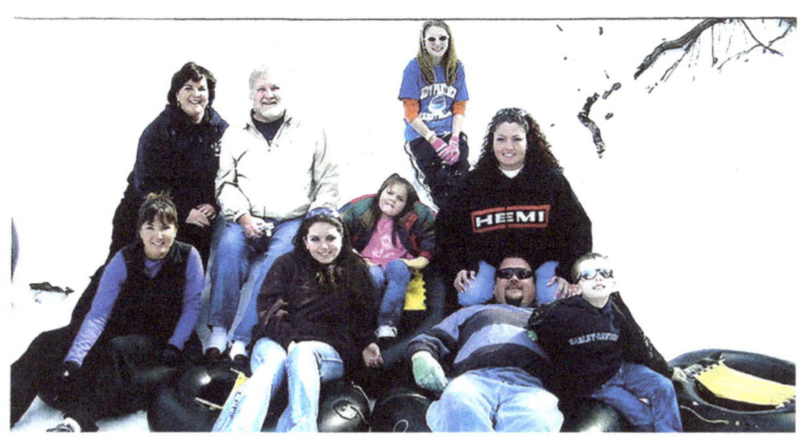

Tubing on the snow in California after Summer's wedding

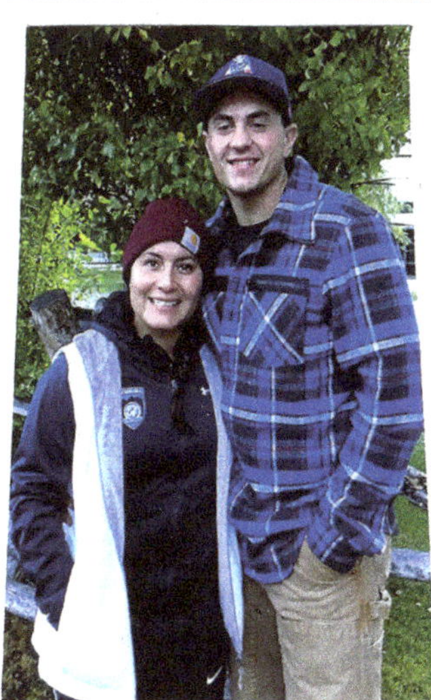

Jenny's brother, Jeff with wife, Peggy; Jeff's son, Richard with his wife, Andrea

Jenny's older brother Rick, at age 24 died in a crash when his Phatom IV Jet airplane malfunctioned in California; and Jill, at age 27, died when her car overturned on a curve on Singer Island, FL.

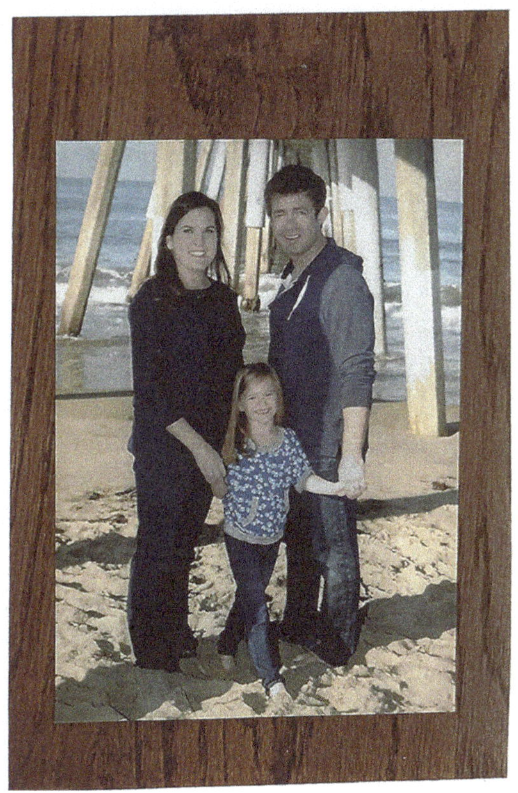

Summer Joy with husband Adam and Bridget; Heather with Austin

father, Jack Largey and mother, Jeanne "Mom Mom" Largey

Norm's family helping Brad move a house

Son Bradley Wayne riding his horse

We love Ryan and his parents, Eddie and Lyn Byrd. They are affectionately called "Lolly" and "Pop" by Austin. They reside in Orangeburg, South Carolina, and have graciously hosted some memorable vacations on Edisto Beach. Those times on Edisto Beach stand out among our "Indelible moments!" Ryan and Heather's seven-year-old son, Austin, is such a delightful young man, and it is my honor to be his "PaPa." I have just finished a desk for him that should provide a great study tool through his school years.

The Bridge Builder

by Will Allen Dromgoole (1860-1934)

An old man, going a lone highway,
Came at the evening cold and gray
To a chasm vast and deep and wide
Through which was flowing a swollen tide.
The old man crossed in the twilight dim;
The rapids held no fears for him.
But he turned when safe on the other side
And built a bridge to span the tide.

"Old man," cried a fellow pilgrim near,
"You're wasting your time in building here.
Your journey will end with the closing day;
You never again will pass this way.
You have crossed the chasm deep and wide;
Why build you this bridge at even-tide?"

The builder lifted his old gray head.
"Good friend, in the path I have come," he said,
"There follows after me today
A youth whose feet must pass this way.
This stream, which has been as naught to me,
To that fair youth may a pitfall be.
He too must cross in the twilight dim —
Good friend, I am building this bridge for him."

"The Bridge Builder"

The Bridge Builder's inspirational words expresses my hope that in some way I will be able to leave bridges for not only my kids to use, but my grandchildren and now my new great grandchild, Harley Sky. Harley was born to granddaughter, Darci, daughter of my Lori Lynette this year. Heather and Ryan have recently divorced, but each seems to be content with that decision. I hope that they will individually find the new road they have chosen to be fulfilling and lead each to happier days. Both must undergird Austin with assuring love.

In Summer's search for an opportunity to buy a business in California, they finally secured a contract on one and were excited about the future. At the last minute, the deal fell through. The problem: they had already leased their Tyler home for a year! Since we had plenty of room in our house that God had so miraculously provided for us back in 1998, we invited them to use our empty rooms. It was really a fun year! We enjoyed having Bridget and the family close. Heather was not far away in Fate (about two hours), so we could have time to gather for birthdays, holidays, etc. After a little over a year, they moved to Hermosa Beach, CA, which is only about two blocks from the beach. Dr. Summer has observed improvements in her lung capacity in this new environment, along with new advanced medications. This, again, is a direct answer to our thirty-nine years of prayers. God is faithful.

Summer Joy fell in love with California while in optometry school and dreamed of going back someday. Not only the beauty, beach, and entertainment venues, but also the weather is a much more friendly climate for Summer's health. The opportunities appear to be better in spite of the housing shortage. The liberal policies of an amoral leadership statewide cause me great concern. The detrimental control by liberals in government consume my prayers for God to intervene soon. Before we could go to press, the COVID-19 China flu has paralyzed our country, and Dr. Summer Joy and family have been out of work for five months. After two years in California, they have moved back to Boston to find work and health benefits. Please continue to keep them in your prayers.

Jenny retired from teaching her five preparations per day for different levels of Spanish classes. After twenty years of teaching some of the brightest, most intelligent, and gifted students at All Saints Episcopal High School, the heavy preparation load, and the discipline challenges in handling some of the more incorrigible students, Jenny was driven to the breaking point. She came home crying and said she did not think she was up to the challenge for another year. This precipitated her surprising and unplanned resignation. Many of her teacher friends developed through the years of camaraderie and friendship had also preceded her in retirement. These friends are like family. They have gone through life's gamut of adventures and similar emotions together: victory, defeat, sickness, health, heartaches, etc. These retired warriors have become each other's family of supporters. They are there at your side when you need them most! We still get together and remain close to several of these:

Vickie Perry and husband, Randy
Lisa Flowers and husband, Tom
Patricia Jacks and husband, Jim
Rhonda Ferguson and husband, Stanley
Pat Brown and husband, Tom

Others with whom Jenny endeavors to stay in touch include: Pat Martin, Kyle Edgemon, Tom Marsh, Kimberly Reed, Marsha Phillips, Jane Adams, Debra Parham, Debra Robbins, Gerald Roulette, and Coach Francis, along with his lovely wife, Misty.

Jenny still gets together monthly with some of the All Saints group. There is another group of comrades who were teaching companions at Whitehouse High School. She tries to get together with this group at various restaurants in the area on a monthly basis.

Her decision to retire was a bit unnerving for both of us. It has always required both of our incomes to pay bills and get our daughters educated and out on their own. I encouraged her in the decision to resign and retire. I had already "retired" almost 30 years before and my part-time business had now become a full-fledged, full-time and all-consuming job. What a blessing to now be able to travel together. Jenny is a better lens cleaner on a phoroptor than I am, plus she has learned to diagnose many of the repairs needed on the equipment. Here, again, when we had nowhere to turn and needed financial income, God provided a way.

My Norm's Ophthalmic Business has not only sustained us these many years, but has provided us with scores and scores of wonderful friends. Eye doctors are special! They are among the most noble of humanity, and most live by a code of Christian ethics. These optometrists and ophthalmologists are the leaders in their communities. Most are honest, generous, compassionate, and fair. Many of them have been my customers for two dozen years or more, and we now consider them to be family. Many of them sacrifice their vacation time to go as missionaries to minister to the poor in other countries.

Jenny and I had the privilege of making a trip to The Lighthouse for Christ Eye Clinic in Kenya, Africa. A big thanks to Linda Ellis, secretary to the Lighthouse for Christ ministry, and my former association with Dr. Charles DeHaven here in Tyler for making the trip possible.

I aided Dr. DeHaven in packing and shipping much of the donated equipment to Africa through Mercy Ships.

On arriving in Africa, we taught two young men how to set up, repair, and clean the equipment in the exam lanes. The monkeys in the compound seemed to enjoy throwing mangos at us, and they would steal anything left on the picnic tables. This trip included a once in a lifetime African Safari! Sleeping in large elevated tents, we heard the angry, stomping elephants outside of our tent at 4:00 in the morning. We did not learn what had spooked the elephants until we went to breakfast and met with our guide. He informed us that the lions we were hoping to see had come to us and had spooked the elephants. Then the lions bedded down and slept right in the back of our tents! We had walked within a few feet of these sleeping beauties on our way to breakfast! Another hair-raising moment came when we first arrived; Jenny spotted a beautiful green snake on the porch of our apartment in the mission compound. Notifying the missionary doctor, he came and took a look, hurried out and came back with a hollow pole and rope going down the center of the pole with a loop on the end. He looped the rope around the head of the snake and captured it. Then he killed it and informed us that it was Africa's most poisonous, the "Green Mamba."

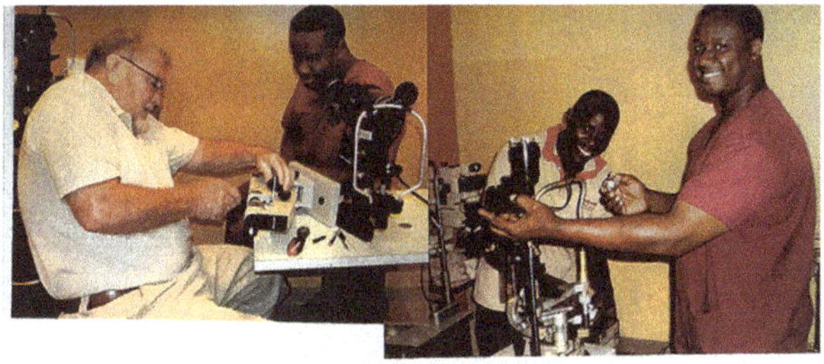

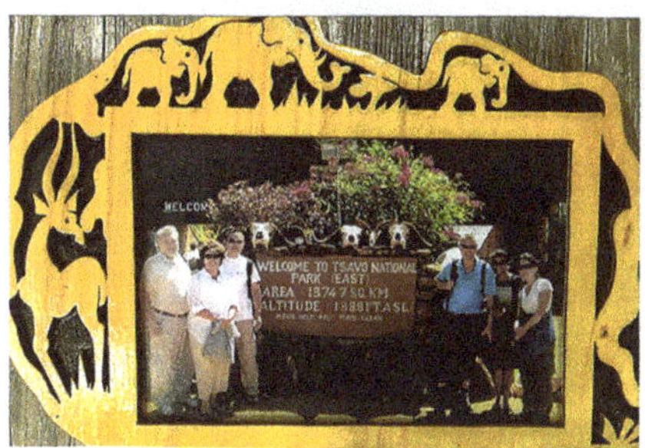

Our trip to Lighthouse for Christ mission in Mombasa, Kenya, Africa.

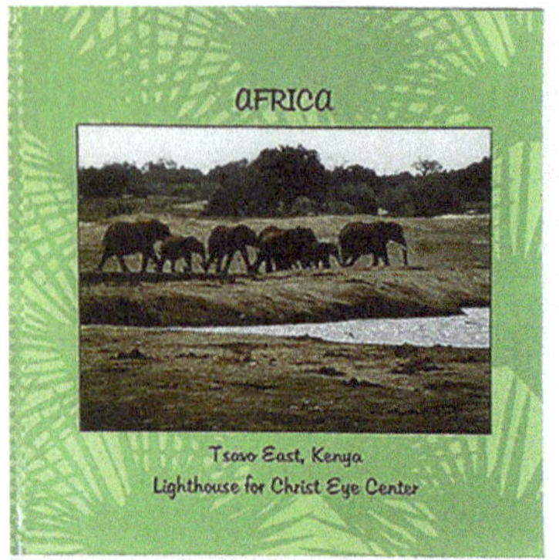

AFRICA
Tsavo East, Kenya
Lighthouse for Christ Eye Center

Our Unbelievable African Safari

Traveling the world has been such a great privilege. Jenny was allowed to take a group of forty students every other year to Europe. Sometimes it was to Spain, France, Germany, or Italy.

We took several very nice trips via cruise ships. Taking forty students to other foreign countries does not really qualify as a vacation, but it certainly adds zest to life's experiences. It would require another long manuscript to review all of these trips with you, and since I have been trapped a few times to watch boring pictures of my friends' endless vacation pictures and stories, I will spare you with only a few "indelible moments." Hopefully, taking your time to read these will be entertaining, although embarrassing for me. I wish we could return to the time when people could laugh at themselves and their foolish actions.

We were in London. Jenny, Summer, Heather, and other students were leaving an ice cream store without getting even a taste of their mouthwatering ice cream concoctions. I wanted to stay and enjoy one, so I assured them that I knew the name of our hotel, the street, and the streetcar needed to get there. About 6:00 in the evening, I caught the trolley car and got off at the appropriate street when that stop was announced. I walked about six blocks and came to the end of the street, but never came to our hotel. I walked back on the other side of the street and made the six-block trek again; still, no hotel. I made this six-block trip for hours and stopped at each little restaurant and asked for directions to our hotel. No one could tell me. They had never heard of such a place. I am not one to give up easily, and as 11:00 p.m. approached, I knew Jenny and my girls would be getting concerned about me. On one of the corners was a public phone booth. I entered and could not find the hotel listed. Next, I tried the operator...no luck. As a last resort, I dialed one of the police precinct numbers. Each of these calls required cash, which I had run out of and found it difficult to use my credit cards. I finally dialed the first police station, and they were closed but gave an auto message of the number of an available police station. I went through the process again, and success; a real live person answered! I started by saying, "I think I may be a missing person on your alert list." The officer asked my name, and when I told him, he exclaimed, "Yes, you are the person we have been looking for!" I explained how I had walked the correct street for hours but could not find my hotel. He said, "That is because that particular street does have a dead end, but the street picks up again three blocks away." I said, "Wow, I can find it now, thanks!" and I started to hang up. He cautioned, "No, stay where you are! I am sending a squad car over to pick you up." When the squad car came, I started talking with the two young officers. One asked, "Where are you from?" "Texas," I told him. Their exclamation together was "Dallas! J.R." Evidently, they like American TV. During the six hours of my having gone missing, the forty students had formed search parties and had gone looking for me. At midnight, I received quite an embarrassing but welcomed homecoming reception!

The two London policemen "Bobbies" who escorted Norm back to the motel.

On another trip, I was having a lot of sinus congestion. One of the parent chaperones, my friend, Linda Rowe, looked into her purse and gave me a couple of tablets to alleviate my congestion. I went to bed and slept well, but the next morning, I was worse. I could hardly hold my head up. I tried to eat breakfast but could not, so I told them to go ahead and enjoy the sightseeing for the day. I went back to bed! The next morning, I was still in the same semiconscious condition. Finally, the third day, I perked up and was able to finish the trip. Upon our return to the United States, the friend who had given me the allergy pills called to confess that she had just discovered her extra super powerful Dramamine were missing. She concluded that my two days of sickness was due to an overdose of her medication. Mystery solved!

I have had half a dozen trips to nearly every country in Europe, and one experience stands out as if I viewed and visited one of the greatest wonders on earth, built by Catholic monks on pinnacles so steep it defied my imagination.

Initiated by 9th century hermits and a refuge from Turkish pirates, the monasteries of the monks who farmed the land in the valleys below began to climb and build atop the sheer cliff walls for safety. They devised a net hitched over a hook and hoisted up by rope. This process was engineered by a hand-cranked windlass to winch towers overhanging the chasm. At the height of the development, Meteora's cliff rock monastery community consisted of 24 monasteries. Today, only six survive as museums. This is one of the most awesome feats that I have witnessed!

Briefly, on one of these trips, our tour director had observed what talented young soccer students we had in our group. He, too, loved soccer and scheduled a game in the Sorrento City college stadium for their college soccer team to play our high school boys, along with our director. Imagine their shock and our elation when our team defeated the home college soccer team!

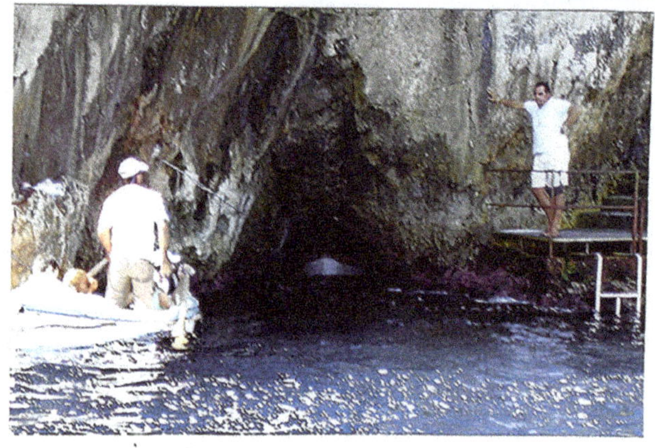

"The Blue Grotto," Capri, Italy

We took boats to the "Blue Grotto." The entrance was a small sea cave opening. This required the skill of the man directing the boat oarsmen rowing to time our entry with the ebb and flow of the waves. Inside were the most beautiful and ethereal sensations of another world. The water, although about twenty feet deep, was so clear every detail of the bottom was visible. Several of the students, including my adventurous wife, jumped into the waters and had a nice refreshing swim.

Another trip included a cruise of the Greek Islands. Each was impressive. We traveled by night to arrive each morning to a new island and tour the island during the day. Most of the buildings are painted a pure whitewash and trimmed in sky blue. Our next stop was the Isle of Patmos, where John, the beloved of Jesus, was banished and received the amazing revelation of the last times in the final book of the Bible, Revelation. We arrived on a Sunday and had to wait until a Greek Orthodox church service in progress was dismissed. This was an enormous cave. It was quite a privilege for me to visit this wonderful and historical biblical site.

Another impressive cruise was to Alaska. We viewed the calving of the enormous glaciers as they broke off into the bay.

We flew over the glaciers in a bi-plane and landed on the water of a river, where we were treated with fresh-caught salmon cooked on the grill just outside the log cabin. A number of the workers had to prevent two bears from stealing the dinner off of the grill by wielding long poles to fend them off.

After the fish was removed from the grill, the big papa bear climbed up and licked the grill, all the while dancing because it was so hot. The papa bear did not want the mama bear to share in the delicacy. Two darling cubs in a nearby tree observed all of this from their perch.

We also experienced two adventures into the art of gold mining. Each of us was able to show a bit of gold. These were placed into small vials for us to keep. A couple of months later, I combined these to make baby Bridget a small baby heart-shaped necklace. Note: I would not hesitate to make this fascinating trip again.

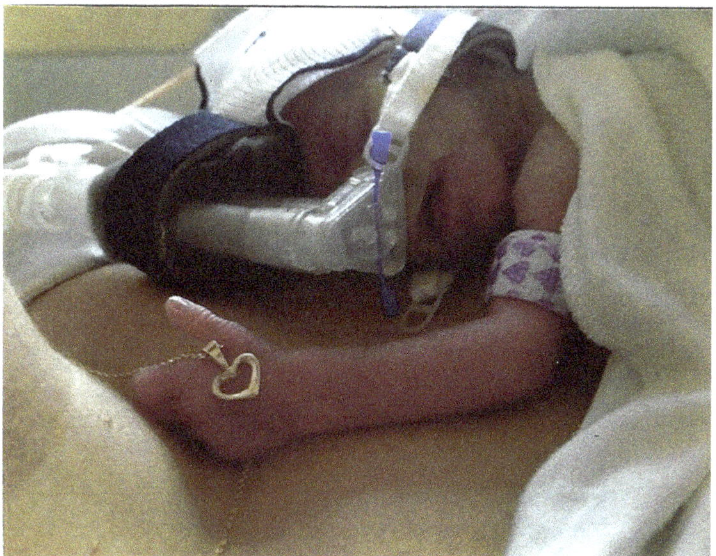

Bridget with her gold heart necklace made from our panned gold while in Alaska.

One of our last big trips was here in the good old USA! We went to Yellowstone, saw Old Faithful blow steam out of the ground, enjoyed the patriotic program at the base of Mount Rushmore, Crazy Horse mountain sculpture, lots of buffalo, the awesome Devil's Tower, and Jackson Hole, Wyoming.

Buffalo grazing, Crazy Horse Mountain monument

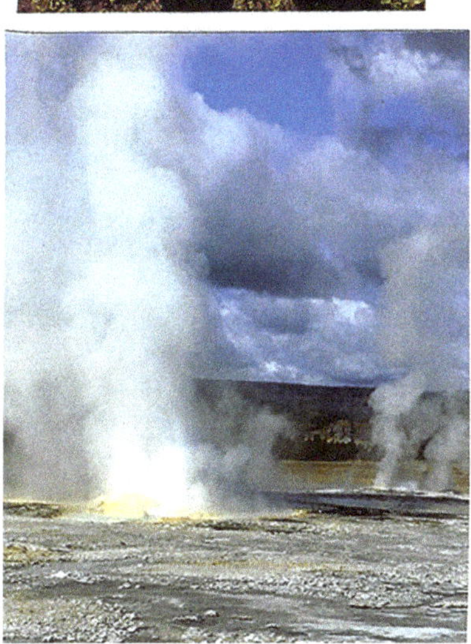

Mt. Rushmore, Devil's Tower, Old Faithful geyser, Yellowstone Park

People sometimes wonder how I choose my friends. I have a small list of traits that I admire. These qualities catch my attention and encourage me to get acquainted and call them friends:

1. <u>A beautiful person</u>, in various ways of beauty. This does not equate with physical attributes. It may be a beautiful smile, a twinkle in the eye, a calm answer to an angry charge, a quiet

spirit, a "thank you" (see the beatitudes in the Sermon on the Mount).

2. A visibly happy person. A person with zest for life!
3. A content person who is secure with who they are...not a person who tries to change and please the whims of everyone. The ability to let go and let God.
   Both my mother and her mother, Granny London, had this trait. Neither ever had much of this world's goods or riches but they learned to trust God in difficult circumstances.
4. An optimistic person. I have had my share of church members who were born in the "negative mode." They never believed it was possible for things to get better.
5. An organized person. "A place for everything and everything in its place." When I get up, I want to know exactly where the coffee is, plus where my cup is stored.
   I do not want to have to search for socks and underwear. I get upset if someone has borrowed one of my tools and did not return it to the spot from where it was taken. I spend time keeping a good filing system.
6. A humble person. I am not drawn to a person who knows it all, has been everywhere, brags about all of the important people they know, or extols all of their virtues.
   Jesus' harshest criticism was laid onto this group called Pharisees. Pseudo intellectualism and superiority does not impress me. Jesus lived a very simple life. During His ministry, He did not have a house, an income, or any kind of security.
   "The birds have nests, the foxes have holes...
   but the Son of Man has no place to lay His head."
7. A frugal person. I do not mean a "penny pincher" or some greedy person, like Judas, who betrayed Jesus. I grew up under the influence of Ben Franklin's advice:

"A penny saved is a penny earned!" I still stoop to pick up a lost penny in the parking lot! Yes, I was yelled at if I left a room without turning off the lights. Insert story:

A man walked into a bar and did not close the door. The bartender yelled, "Shut the door! Were you born in a barn?" The man shut the door and began to sob and cry. The bartender began to apologize.

Between sobs, the man said, "That's ok, you see, I was born in a barn and every time I hear a jackass bray, I get homesick!"

Government assumes our tax money is for the bureaucrats to spend on their every whim and vote themselves raises.

Today, I pay taxes and see the government squandering billions of dollars and bankrupting our country. I abhor people who flaunt their name brand clothes, insist on expensive personal care for their hair, fingernails, etc. And in my view, tattoos are a desecration of the holy body that God created for us!

8. A "never give up" person! Someone who does not give up easily. One who fights for what's right. Don't Quit!
9. Last but not least is a person with humor! I like people who can laugh at themselves. The first thing I do in the morning is get the newspaper, scan the headlines on the front page, the sports page, and then read the comic strips. I love satire and the humorous situations that the comics capture in everyday life. Growing up, people were not so sensitive and politically correct! The visiting preachers that came to stay in our home, shared jokes about fishermen, people who were Black, Jewish, Italian, Pollock, Baptist, Methodist, Presbyterian, Seventh Day Adventist, etc., and no one took offense. Each accepted certain traits that have fit the narrative of individual classes of people. It was acceptable for generations. When did we come to be so sensitive that we cannot laugh at ourselves? Lighten up! Relax! Forgive a little; have some fun laughing your way out of an embarrassing situation.

I hope to come to the end of this life with some kinship to what the apostle Paul said, "I have fought a good fight; I have finished the course." I do not deserve to go to heaven, but by His grace, He has promised to forgive my sins and has provided for my salvation. I stand amazed to look back and see where He has led me through these 87 years. Maybe there will be an opportunity in the unknown future to apologize to my guardian angel(s). They have not had an easy job and have had to work overtime to keep me safe! I am happy to know that He (the Lord) has led me all this way, but more elated and eager to see where He will lead me in the future.

Thankfully, at this writing, I am still alive and in relatively good health. I am recovering from my third heart procedure, where I received a pig's valve and a pacemaker. This adds to my five bypass open-heart surgeries seventeen years ago, and my two stints inserted five years ago. While recuperating, I can sit here and ponder what kind of influence that pig valve may have on me. Will I have a tendency to wallow in the mud? Will Jenny approve? But on a more serious note, will Jesus approve of the way I spend these extra days, and hopefully years, that He is allowing me to spend here on earth with my friends?

At each juncture of my life and in each geographical location, I have tried to honor the myriads of people who have contributed to my life during each phase, most of them in a very positive way. I cannot walk away or close this narrative without acknowledging those, who in these last thirty years, have been such positive supporters to the success and stability of our family through their support of our small company: "See Norm, The Eye Doctor's Friend," dba "Norm's Ophthalmic Company." I want to recognize the many wonderful optometrists and ophthalmologists who have trusted our company to maintain their equipment. Several of these doctors have been with us almost from our insignificant beginnings in 1991. "Our family" has become enlarged to include so many of these on a friendly first-name basis! First, I must acknowledge that without Tom Mercer and his wife, Mary, in Montgomery, Alabama, I would never have been able to have this wonderful business. He is the most knowledgeable of the many complicated instruments that eye doctors use, and has helped us many, many times. Bert Brush in Gulf Shores, Alabama, was also my "professor" through the years as he coached me through many difficult repair jobs via the phone. His early death has left a great void in my heart.

Trying to get help from some of the techs in the big companies was met with some resistance and comments like, "You're not one of us or trained by us; no, we cannot sell you a part." Slowly, I found great tech helpers at Reliance, Reichert, Marco, and Top Con. Mike Sonandres with Cal Coast, Torrance, CA, has always been helpful, but overwhelmed with work, so we depend on Noah Deese at Mid Gulf Instruments in Slidell, LA, to aid in many of our repairs and purchases. Other good dealers along the way have been David Bishop, Alabama;

Dale Streib, Georgia; Brad Chasnoff, Florida; and the Henley Optical in Grand Prairie, Texas.

After being away from Tyler for 23 years, when I called on Dr. Ron Smith, he said, "I know you! You were my chaplain when I played football at Tyler Junior College. His beautiful wife was an Apache Belle. Dr. Gene Bennett and his wife, Donna, were among my first and best customers, partly due to their manager, Becky Tate. She is also a wonderful neighbor! Rhonda Robinson, manager of East Texas Eye Care, is another great supporter of our ministry to eye doctors (she has earned her retirement during my penning of these words, but is succeeded by our friend, Stephanie Wellman). Also among those in-town Tyler faithful, would include Dr. Larry Chism, Dr. John McGough, and wife, "Dinky," along with his partners Dr. Drew and Dr. Mona Douglas. Mary Sue Jacka and her husband, Ford, have provided us with a level of security by calling on us consistently for over 25 years. Their business is located in West Monroe, Louisiana, and is the Haik Humble Ophthalmic Company. Shortly after my open-heart surgery, which brought a halt to my job at Trane, I bugged Mary Gary, head supervisor for equipment management in San Antonio for Eye Masters, to give me an opportunity to prove my worth to her. She finally agreed. One of the first assignments came by way of Shawn Dafforn, supervisor for the Houston area. A fire had occurred next to the Eye Master's office across from Willow Brook Mall. She wanted me to quote a price for cleaning two lanes of equipment with smoke damage. I had never done this before and told her so. Shawn replied that she could not allow me to proceed without a firm quote. I asked if any other company had given her a quote and she said, "Yes, Universal did." A light dawned, so I said, "I will do it for half of what Universal quoted." She agreed, and after Jenny and I did the job, we received a check for $2,650.00! I would never have dreamed of charging that much. If only I could follow that guy from Universal around and offer to do it for half, I would really be well off today! Shawn and Mary Gary combined to send me about 40% of our work over the next ten years. Mary is retired now, and Shawn is with Vision Source, along with another great friend, Dr. Claudio Lagunas. Also in Houston is Dr. Megan Stubinski, a steady customer with three offices, one with some much older equipment that requires constant upkeep. In the Dallas area, several doctors jump to my memory. Dr. Michael Grace, with whom we have compared the progress of our two girls each through the years. Dr. Jacobs, who has offices in the Renaissance Building and another on Zang Boulevard. Dr. Mark Zebrowski, one of the many Eye Master, now Vision Works, offices, where we set up the original lanes of equipment and have serviced annually. Dr. Rebecca Ponder, whose office is located in one of the most beautiful buildings in the Highland Park, Dallas area. She and her husband, Richard, are dear Christian friends of the family as well. Dr. Charles DeHaven brought equipment home from Africa for us to repair. I also helped him pack cargo boxes of equipment for Mercy Ships to transport to Kenya to the Lighthouse for Christ mission. After he retired, a young lady, Linda Ellis, headed up the efforts of their support. She persuaded and provided the finances for Jenny and me to make the trip of a lifetime to their work in Kenya to teach two young men how to set up, repair, and clean the lanes of equipment. We were allowed to take an overnight African safari!

May I transfer you from your visual image in your mind of our world travels to the blessings we take for granted here at home every day:

I just went to our local UPS store, where Jeff, Bette, Jasmine, and Bill all help me ship items every day.

On the way back, I met our garbage truck and stopped the car where the men were emptying the garbage cans. I rolled the window down and thanked them for being so dependable in keeping us clean and safe from garbage.

Our mail carrier is so punctual you could almost set your watch by her timed delivery of the mail. The lady who throws our paper every morning before 5:00 a.m. has been faithfully delivering the news for at least twenty-five years! I am thankful to live in a country where extraordinary people do such a consistent job of serving the community. Then add to these the everyday heroes of firemen, policemen, sheriffs, doctors, and nurses, and I run out of fingers and toes counting my blessings!

A real Godsend has been the work through the years that we have received from the assignments of the Wal-Mart and Sam's Optical tech crew in Crawfordsville, Indiana. With my years of teasing these wonderful ladies, they have become our very dear friends. They go beyond business relationships and give us so much warmth and friendship. This puts each of them in a very special category of friends.

Walmart Optical Tech Crew located in Crawfordsville, Indiana.

Picture: Back Row left to right – Jennifer, Bobbie, Mindy, Susan, Jillian, Jill, Leanne, Brenda
Front row left to right – Michelle, Kiley, Kasie

Before I forget, even though our work with Wal-Mart and Sam's eye doctors' offices often request that we work on the weekend so as to not interfere with their schedule of seeing patients, our Sunday morning Bible study group has been so supportive!

I have confided with our wonderful attorney teacher, Jim Gillen, and wife, Carye, that he is a better teacher than any of my teachers at Bob Jones University, Greenville, SC, or Southwestern Baptist Theological Seminary in Fort Worth. We share his lesson outlines and notes with my son, Brad, who is in prison at this time. He, in turn, shares with some of the inmates in the prison. For caring and prayer support and keeping us informed via the internet, none come close to Barney Rubin, our class president, and his wife, Carolyn. She responds on a moment's notice when there is a prayer request that needs everyone's attention. Of course, Darell and Wanda Abrahams are close to the top of our friends list in this wonderful class. Other special friends in our class: Smith County Sheriff Larry Smith, and his wife, Leslie, Mark and Tracey Bedgood, Mark and Leisa Bickerstaff, Rick and Janie Featherston, Dr. Richard and Suzanne Handley, Mike and Sherry Hilliard, Mark and Becky Jones, Dave and Cindy Robinson, Don and Pam Thedford, and former members Brad and Kendra Graham. Please forgive me if I have inadvertently omitted some names. My memory is not what it used to be. Was it our pastor, David Dykes, who told one of his many funny stories?

The preacher was talking to an older man who had not yet made an open decision to accept Christ, so he tactfully suggested, "John, don't you think it is time for you to start thinking of the hereafter?" To which the elderly man replied, "Oh, preacher, I do! Every day I walk into a room and say to myself, 'Now what am I here after?'"

My notebook of business cards of doctors that we have serviced over the last thirty years, number over seven hundred! Please forgive me if we have inadvertently omitted your name here. We value and appreciate each one who uses our services.

Dr. Mike Nell, with Texas State Optical in Conroe, Texas, goes on mission trips every year to various countries in need. Dr. David Spivey, Fort Worth, is another one who is an annual missionary taking healing to all parts of the world. One of the very first two faithful customers was in nearby Longview: Dr. Mark Little and Dr. Jeffrey Jones. In

Fort Worth, Dr. Matt Barber has been faithful to reach out to us when his equipment needs servicing. While Heather was in Clemson, we enlisted about twenty-five doctors in Greenville, Spartanburg, Seneca, Anderson, and Clemson itself. We continue to make that trip once a year. When Summer Joy was doing an internship at the naval hospital in Hawaii, I sent cards to a few doctors in the area that we were coming. Four doctors invited us to service their lanes of equipment, which helped pay for the trip!

I like to think that my "See Norm, the Eye Doctor's Friend," dba "Norm's Ophthalmic Company" business has provided support in some small way that Jesus gave to blind people or those with vision needs. My business will not be needed in heaven. Everyone will have perfect vision. "The blind will see, the lame will walk, neither will there be any more death." I am so glad that His Word gives us glimpses into heaven. We have assurance that those who have gone on before us, God's chosen people who have accepted Jesus as their Lord and Savior, are there and are capable of seeing those of us still struggling here below. Paul declares, "seeing that we are surrounded by such a great cloud of witnesses, let us run the race..." This gives credence to the fact that your parents, friends, and neighbors who made it to heaven before you are cheering you and their many friends on to victory. If I get there first, I promise to be your cheerleader!

I have conducted many funerals. This is the most difficult of all the services that a minister provides.

An undertaker was preparing the body of an elderly woman for burial. She had requested that the undertaker place a fork in her hand so that those who passed her casket to view her for the last time would be curious. She wanted them to think this was a bit strange. This would undoubtedly cause friends to ask, "Why the fork in her hand?" The officiating minister provided the answer. The minister related her request to be buried with a fork in her hand. She had told the minister, "Often, when I eat at a restaurant, the waiter will come to take up my plate at the end of the meal and suggest, 'you may want to keep your fork; there is more to come.' This always alerted me to the fact that there is something more delicious to come! I would then anticipate the offer of 'yummy' deserts coming my way."

It matters not whether the main course of your life has been thick sirloin steak dinners or a life of plain hot dogs or rice and beans; Jesus came to remind you to keep the fork of faith.

His promise to you: "I go to prepare a place for you, that where I am, there you may be also!"

There Is More to Come!

EPILOGUE

What about the roads you have chosen at each crossing of your life? I would never suggest that the ones that I have chosen have been wise or profitable for me or anyone else. What I am saying in this book is no matter which roads you have chosen in life, and you may have chosen one that is a "dead end," and your hope for the future is not good, God has the power to make even your worst decisions turn out good!

It requires us to confess our mistakes (sins) and turn to Him and allow His Holy Spirit to take control of your life because He knows the future. He can be of immense help when you need wisdom in choosing the right road!

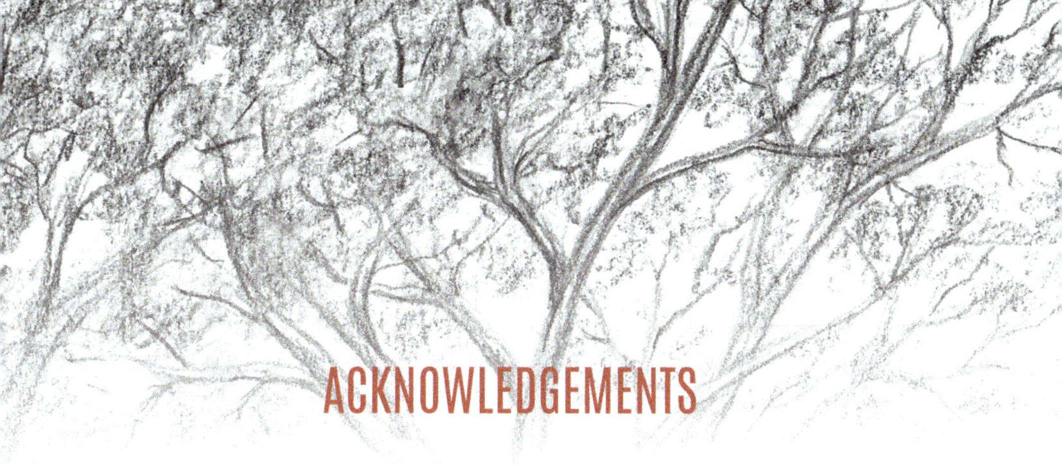

ACKNOWLEDGEMENTS

Obviously, Jenny has been at her best in assisting with this book endeavor. She, along with the girls, encouraged me to take the time to write all of this down for posterity. She researched the tons of pictures that we have taken over the past forty-four years, and suggested the insertion of many of the pictures you have seen in this book.

It will come as a surprise to those who know me and have experienced my virtual lack of computer skills that this book has progressed this far. When the girls were growing up, they kept insisting that I get a cellphone and a GPS. I would argue that I could use a payphone, and I possessed good maps of wherever I needed to go. When computers came into existence, all of my tragic mistakes caused both my wife and daughters to declare, "Dad, do not touch the computer!" Fortunately, my sister married a brilliant man named Frank Cravalho. He is the mastermind that we prevailed upon daily to guide us in navigating through the computer steps needed to scan, copy, download, transfer, create collages, etc. I am so glad he joined our family! He is also a great chef!

Frank Cravalho and wife (my sister), Glenna

Acknowledgements would fall woefully short if I failed to show gratitude for the great freedom and liberties I have enjoyed in this wonderful "land of the free, and home of the brave."

It alarms me that in the last sixty years, our country has drifted away from God. Our universities hire liberal professors to teach our youth to hate capitalism and the conservative principles that our forefathers, in great wisdom, incorporated into our revered Constitution. <u>We are the only nation ever to have such freedoms.</u> The NEA and our boards of education have deleted basic studies of history, civics, government, foundational math, English parts of speech, and cursive writing to teach social justice and rewrite history. The Ten Commandments are forbidden to be posted in any public places. Sharia law has been allowed to supplant our own laws and justice systems. Abortion has snuffed out the lives of millions of our kids in the name of a woman's rights. Where is the constitutional right of every individual's God-given right to "life, liberty and the pursuit of happiness" being taught? Liberal professors have brainwashed our young people into thinking that, somehow, capitalism is wrong and hurtful. When, in reality, it has built the greatest civilization with the most lavish lifestyles anyone has ever enjoyed. Supply and demand produces entrepreneurs. I have never inherited anything. I grew up without running water (we ran to the well to draw a bucket), no electricity (kerosene lamps), no indoor plumbing (a path to the toilet), no gas heaters (woodstoves and wood fireplaces that required cutting logs and kindling, plus taking the ashes out every morning), no air conditioning (Texas summers with funeral home paper fans to fan your face during church), no refrigerators (an icebox that the iceman delivered a block of ice for every other day), no automatic washing machine and dryer (a washing machine with dangerous wringers to run the clothes through to squeeze the water out before hanging them outside on a clothes line to dry), no TV until I was a senior in high school, no computers, no tapes, CDs or DVDs, no cellphones, or GPS. We still used a lot of horses and animals to prepare the soil and grow our food. I am very thankful that I endured, and, for the most part, enjoyed growing up with those challenges! We have raised a generation of "soft" people! Young people are enticed by the promises of a socialistic gospel that proposes that the world owes them something just for being born! Then the politicians urge you to allow the government to guarantee you all of the free things you can imagine: guaranteed jobs, free health care (even for those here illegally), free education, reparations, free social security, etc.

I thank God, every day, for a president who has openly stood for freedom of religion (especially Evangelical Christians and conservatives) and school choice. He stands up for our First and Second Amendment rights, protects our borders, supports law and order, fights deep-state corruption, negotiates better trade deals, repeals business-killing regulations, passed prison reforms, enacted legislation for Black schools, produced the most jobs for Blacks, Hispanics, and women in the work force, ever! He has appointed three Supreme Court conservative justices and 200 lower court justices. He continues to lower taxes, fight terrorism, and the drug traffic. He has raised and trained very successful children. He serves voluntarily after becoming a successful businessman. He donates his salary to non-profit organizations that promote worthy causes. He does not have the backing or compromised support of corporations or donors. He is beholden to no one. His stately and successful wife is a beautiful mother, speaks five languages, dresses in fashionably appropriate attire, initiates helpful programs for children, and stands faithfully by our president's side in the midst of overwhelming criticism and opposition from radicals and "rabble rousers." God bless him as he continues to serve as the greatest president our country has ever had! Thank God enough people with common sense still support and elect him to govern with his great wisdom. It is our prayer that people will give him more time to continue to "Make America Great Again!"

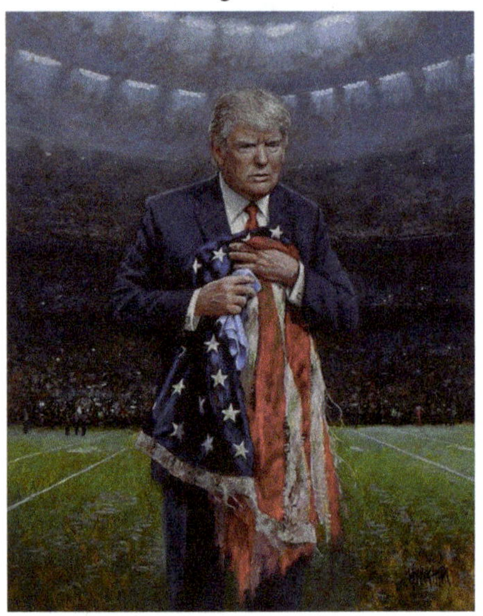

Forty-fifth president of the United States of America,
President Donald J. Trump

"Life's Indelible Moments"

Heather Jill Ferguson

Front cover artwork by Norm's daughter. Heather is a graduate of Clemson University and a dental hygienist in Rockwall, Texas. As a single mother, she resides in Fate, Texas, with her seven-year-old son, Austin Denman. More of her artwork is pictured inside.

CPSIA information can be obtained
at www.ICGtesting.com
Printed in the USA
LVHW072219220221
679662LV00037B/1407

9 781662 807855